PIMLICO

734

THOUGH THE HEAVENS MAY FALL

Steven M. Wise, J.D., has taught at the Harvard, Vermont, and John Marshall law schools. He is president of the Center for the Expansion of Fundamental Rights, which he founded in 1995. Wise's articles and books probe the roots of Western law. His books, which include *Rattling the Cage* and *Drawing the Line*, have been critically acclaimed worldwide.

THOUGH THE HEAVENS MAY FALL

The Landmark Trial that Led to
the End of Human Slavery

——

STEVEN M. WISE

PIMLICO

Published by Pimlico 2006

2 4 6 8 10 9 7 5 3 1

Copyright © Steven M. Wise 2005

Steven M. Wise has asserted his right under the Copyright,
Designs and Patents Act 1988 to be identified as the author of this work

First published in the United States by
Da Capo Press in 2005

Pimlico edition 2006

Pimlico
Random House, 20 Vauxhall Bridge Road,
London SW1V 2SA

Random House Australia (Pty) Limited
20 Alfred Street, Milsons Point, Sydney,
New South Wales 2061, Australia

Random House New Zealand Limited
18 Poland Road, Glenfield,
Auckland 10, New Zealand

Random House South Africa (Pty) Limited
Isle of Houghton, Corner of Boundary Road & Carse O'Gowrie,
Houghton 2198, South Africa

Random House UK Limited Reg. No. 954009

A CIP catalogue record for this book
is available from the British Library

Designed by C. Cairl Design

ISBN 1-8441-3430-X

Papers used by Random House UK Ltd are natural, recyclable products
made from wood grown in sustainable forests. The manufacturing processes
conform to the environmental regulations of the country of origin

Printed and bound in Great Britain by William Clowes Ltd, Beccles, Suffolk

For my wife, Gail, for whom the heavens fell.

And for my parents, Selma and Sidney Wise.
How lucky was I to get to know you all over again.

CONTENTS

PREFACE

THIS BOOK TELLS HOW an invisible man became visible and how that changed the world. Like Ralph Ellison's invisible man, an eighteenth century English slave was not a "spook." He was a bearer of "flesh and bone, fiber and liquids," and he possessed "a mind." But he was legally invisible. Slaves were property, bought, sold, leased, mortgaged, and inherited like any other property, and so judges could not perceive them, because they were not persons, and persons were all judicial eyes could see.

Then, as today, only legal persons counted in courtrooms, for only they existed for their own benefits, while legal things existed for the benefit of persons. In was in 1772 that this one invisible man, James Somerset, managed to achieve judicial perceptibility through a lawsuit in London's Court of King's Bench, presided over by Lord Mansfield, perhaps the greatest judge the English-speaking world has produced. As a result of Mansfield's judgment, James Somerset shed his legal thinghood and became legally visible, and that was the beginning of the end of slavery.

This book's cover reproduces one of the most powerful and, in its time, familiar symbols the world has seen. It was the creation of Charles Darwin's father-in-law, Josiah Wedgewood, and is his engraving of a chained slave, on one knee, imploring, "Am I not a man and a brother?" That the slave was "a man" appeals to our sense of liberty, for a grown man is presumed to possess what is needed to count as a legal person.

That he is "a brother" appeals to our sense of equality, for our brothers are like us and should be treated as we are treated. Those eight words captured the gist of the legal arguments that carried James Somerset to personhood, and they serve today as a model for how things, wrongly designated, can attain the personhood to which justice entitles them.

The American frontiersman Daniel Boone claimed never once to have been lost in the vast American wilderness, though he admitted having been, on occasion, bewildered for some time. I claim never to have been completely lost in the wilderness that is eighteenth century British law, procedure, and history. But I owe a great debt to those, on both sides of the Atlantic, who so generously pointed the way when, on occasion, I found myself wandering.

Above all I thank Ruth Paley, an historian of the British Parliament, who showed nothing but endless patience with me. Also, the Eighth Earl of Mansfield, with a special thanks to Lorna Wort at Scone Palace, the crew of the Freedom Schooner *Amistad*, Professor Mary Bildner, Henry Cohen, Esq., Professor David Brion Davis, Professor Daniel Coquillette, Professor Sally Hadden, for informing me about the Diary of Henry Marchant at the Rhode Island Historical Society, Professor John Langbein, Professor Sharon O'Connor, Professor John Oldham, Professor Randy Sparks, Jennifer Sperling, who earned my undying gratitude for agreeing to transcribe the ancient faded diary of Henry Marchant, whose penmanship left much to be desired, from microfilm, then did it, Dr. Bernie Unti, Professor Jenny Wahl, Professor Mark Weinberg, Lord Wilberforce, and the Rt. Hon. Lord Woolf, Lord Chief Justice of England and Wales, as well as the Boston Athenaeum, with a special thanks to Stephen Z. Zonack, Boston College Law School library, the Boston University Law School Library, the British Library, the British Museum, the Colonial Williamsburg Foundation, the Columbia Law School library, with a special thanks to Whitney S. Bagnall, the Corporation of London's Record Office, Harvard University's Lamont Library, Harvard University Law School Library, with a special thanks to David Warrington, Harvard University's Widener Library, the Library of Congress, with a special thanks to Claire Feikert, the City of Medford, Massachusetts' library, the New York Historical

Society, the New York Public Library, the Schomburg Center for Research in Black Culture of the New York Public Library, the New York University Law School Library, the Nova Southeastern Law School Library, the Rhode Island Historical Society, the University of Chicago library, Westminster Hall and Westminster Abbey.

Over years, Merloyd Lawrence has become more than my editor, though she is a wonderful editor; she has become a friend, and the object of my greatest esteem and affection. A thank you to my fine agent, Elaine Markson, and another to my publicist, Lissa Warren, of Da Capo Press; you are probably reading this because of her.

Finally, I thank my wife, Gail Price-Wise, for her love and support and Roma, Siena, Christopher, and Mariana for being my children. I am immensely proud of each of you and love you to the end of the universe. And back.

Coral Springs, Florida
October 12, 2004

PROLOGUE

JUST PAST TEN O'CLOCK on Monday morning, June 22, 1772, a black man's lawyers shouted into his ear over the din of a celebration in Westminster Hall. What he heard set him racing through central London's dirty narrow streets to Old Jewry, Granville Sharp's home. It must have been a joyful run as, for the first time since he was eight years old, thirty-one-year-old James Somerset was no man's property but his own. Thirty-three months before he had sailed from Boston with his American master, Charles Steuart.[1] Forty-one days on the open sea later he had taken his first breath of English air. For the past seven months, the African had languished on bail, waiting for the most powerful judge in England, the Right Honorable William, Lord Mansfield, to decide whether that breath had made him a free man or whether he would spend the rest of his short life harvesting sugar cane on a roasting West Indian plantation.

On Friday, July 14, 1972, the Corporation of London gave a lavish dinner at the Mansion House "to celebrate the Bicentenary of the Prohibition of Slavery in Great Britain" by commemorating what, in two hundred years, had become known simply as the "Mansfield Judgment."[2] The program noted that "(a)s a result [of the *Somerset* decision] over 15,000 slaves in England were liberated." The evening's luminaries included Britain's highest judicial officers, Mansfield's latest successor, the current Lord Chief Justice, the Lord High Chancellor, the Lord Mayor of London, the ambassadors for Brazil and Denmark, the High

Commissioners for Gambia and Ghana, and private citizens descended from major participants in the case and from prominent English abolitionists: the Eighth Earl of Mansfield and Miss Olive Lloyd-Baker, C.B.E., J.P., the sole living relative of Granville Sharp, and Lord Wilberforce, C.M.G., O.B.E. Present also were representatives of the *Times* (London), *Press Association, City Press, Daily Telegraph,* and the journalist Martha Gellhorn.[3]

After toasts to the Queen, each of the represented heads of state, the Anti-Slavery Society, and the Corporation of London, the Lord Mayor observed that some countries had abolished slavery through politics, the United States through civil war. But the British had "abolished slavery by legal precedent." In turn, the Lord High Chancellor warned against underrating the Mansfield Judgment's significance.[4] The *City Press* would declare that the decision had "established for all time the axiom: 'As soon as any slave sets foot on English ground, he becomes free.'"[5]

The Mansfield Judgment had been forged in the struggle between two radically different men. Possessed of "the most inflexible of human wills united to the gentlest of human hearts," Granville Sharp at thirty-six was an obscure self-educated Anglican fundamentalist, fiercely anti-Catholic, who labored in London's shadows as an ordnance clerk at the Tower of London. He had come to loathe every abuse of power, not just black chattel slavery and the African slave trade, but the impressment of men into the Royal Navy, which he thought a form of slavery, and "that *unsuspected test of moral character,* by which he might safely ascertain the worth of every man's heart," the maltreatment of animals.[6]

Sharp's Poets' Corner plaque in Westminster Abbey records that "he aimed to rescue his native country from the guilt and inconsistency of employing the arm of freedom to rivet the fetters of mankind, and established for the negro race, in the person of Somerset, the long disputed rights of human nature." At his death, the London Council resolved to place his bust in Guildhall, citing "his having ardently persevered and finally obtained the judgment of Lord Mansfield, which established the great principle, that every man, of whatever colour or clime, is a free man as soon as he lands upon the British shore."

The man from whom Sharp wrested the Judgment was sixty-seven years old, a product of the Westminster School in London and Christ Church at Oxford, religiously tolerant, a man who lived in London's footlights. One epitaph declared him "the brightest ornament of human nature that any age or country has hitherto been able to boast of." Mansfield, when still young William Murray, had been the subject of flattering verse by Alexander Pope ("long enough his country's pride"); of lesser poetry by his friend the great Elizabethan actor David Garrick ("'Upon Lord Mansfield's desiring my picture' . . . / Till He, who asking grants a favour, Mansfield has fix'd me vain for Ever!"); and of terrible verse by an over-awed student named Jeremy Bentham ("Hail, noble Mansfield! chief among the just, / The bad man's terror and the good man's trust").

A former and future Speaker of the House of Lords, former Solicitor General, former Attorney General, former Chancellor of the Exchequer, a long-time cabinet member, Whig party leader first in the House of Commons, then in the House of Lords, Murray became so powerful and effective in the Commons that the Prime Minister thought him more valuable there than on the bench. When Dudley Ryder, the Chief Justice of the Court of King's Bench, died, the Duke of Newcastle tried to avoid appointing Murray to replace him. Then Attorney General and so, by custom, next in line for the Chief Justiceship, Murray would have none of it. Newcastle tried bribery, an offer of the Duchy of Lancaster for life, and a pension. When Murray stood fast, he sweetened the offer. Murray still refused. Newcastle reluctantly gave in on the Chief Justiceship, but declined to make Murray a peer. Unless he was made a peer, Murray threatened, he would not only refuse the Chief Justiceship, but resign as Attorney General; in other words, he would go in opposition.[7] Now Newcastle capitulated. On November 8, 1756, Murray was given the title Baron Mansfield of the County of Nottingham and appointed Chief Justice of the Court of King's Bench, where he would remain until just before his death more than three decades later. Three times he would decline appointment as Lord High Chancellor of England. At the time he presided over the 1772 *Somerset* trial, Mansfield was the most powerful judge in England, respected to the point that his Court of King's Bench had nearly usurped the entire caseload of its chief rival, the Court of Common Pleas, as litigant after litigant chose to place his case before "noble Mansfield."

The *Somerset* case was exceptional, not just because it was chiseled into marble, not just because it pitted a lowly ordnance clerk against a mighty Lord Chief Justice, not just because it provided a platform for airing the stirring issue of the legality of English slavery, but because it catalyzed what was, for late eighteenth-century London, an unusually prolonged and public struggle, one that echoed not just through cavernous Westminster Hall, but in the pages of monographs, newspapers, and magazines, in extraordinary letters to the editor, and in pubs and drawing rooms throughout England and the Americas. Everyone began talking about black slavery and the African slave trade, and they didn't stop until both had been abolished.

Sharp, not wishing to antagonize the Lord Chief Justice by appearing in court, learned of the Mansfield Judgement from James Somerset at his home near the Bank of England. With accustomed brevity, he recorded what he was told in his diary:

> This day, James Somerset came to tell me that judgment was to-day given in his favour. Somerset was the last Negro whom G.S. brought before Lord Mansfield by writ of Habeus Corpus; when his Lordship declared, as the opinion of all the Judges present, that the power claimed by the master "never was in use here, nor acknowledged by the law: and therefore, the man, James Somerset, must be discharged." Thus ended G. Sharp's long contest with Lord Mansfield, on the 22d of June, 1772.

This is the story of that contest.

CHAPTER I

From Africa to Westminster Hall

A Singular Instance of Ingratitude.

Obituary of Charles Steuart
Gentleman's Magazine 68 [January–June, 1798]:442

T HE STORY HAD BEGUN twenty-three years before. On March 10, 1749, eight-year-old James Somerset, then with a different name, was thrust below the decks of a Guineaman, or British slave ship, bobbing at anchor off the West Coast of Africa, whether present-day Nigeria, Angola, or Sierra Leone, we don't know.[1] The ship may have been the *William,* captained by Robert Simmons, or Captain William Freyer's *Susanna,* both of Liverpool. We don't know his African name, his mother's name, or his father's, or whether he had siblings. We don't know where he was kidnapped or how. If he was like many of the 10 or 11 million Africans who would be forced across the Atlantic, he spoke Bantu, and he was small. We have no likeness of him, as we do of Sharp, Mansfield, and Steuart. But he survived a Middle Passage so harrowing that sharks, waiting for bodies to be pitched over the sides, often trailed Guineamen across the Atlantic, and were rarely disappointed.

We have hints about how the boy came to be owned by Charles Steuart. Olaudah Equiano, who would write a famous autobiography, was born in Guinea in 1745, four years after Somerset. He and six siblings survived infancy. One day, two men and a woman seized him and a sister, stopped their mouths, tied their hands, and carried them into the woods. After the siblings were separated, Olaudah was so grief-stricken that he refused to eat for days. Over the next seven months, the boy was shunted from one master to another. Because he almost always found someone with whom he could converse, he picked up two or three languages in his long journey from the African interior to the Atlantic Ocean. Along the shore, he encountered long-haired, red-faced whites chattering in a foreign tongue. Because Olaudah decided they were going to eat him, when he was carried aboard and poked to determine his soundness, he promptly fainted. The airless, stinking, pestilential ship's hold roasted and suffocated him. Olaudah was flogged when he refused to eat and would have thrown himself over the rail had he been able to surmount the netting installed to prevent just that method of suicide. Africans died daily around him and their remains were flung overboard. At the island of Barbados, planters and merchants came aboard to inspect the cargo; when they had finished, the Africans were unloaded and taken to a merchant's yard, where they "were all pent up together like so many sheep in a fold." At a drum beat, the prospective buyers rushed into the yard and staked their claims. Equiano emphasized that he suffered little that was uncommon, and so James Somerset probably suffered more or less a similar fate.[2]

On August 1, the boy was sold to Steuart, then a twenty-four-year old Scottish merchant living in Virginia, who made a living trading in rum, sugar, tobacco, molasses, corn, pork, wine, and slaves, while collecting local debts for faraway English creditors. There Somerset was absorbed into the sea of African slaves, four of every ten humans he saw, that swirled through mid-century Virginia.[3] Steuart named the boy Somerset, Sommersett, Sommerset, Somersett, Summersett, or Summerset.[4] Or the name may have been given him by slave traders in Africa, or in Jamaica, if that was where he first landed, just as Equiano would be named there, perhaps even "seasoned," on that West Indies island, before being taken to Virginia. Somewhere, sometime, he acquired the Christian name of James. This probably occurred after Steuart took him to London in 1769, for a letter exists from Nathaniel

Coffin, Steuart's Boston customs deputy, written two months before they sailed to England, saying that two slaves, Sapho and Tombo, wished to be remembered to "Sommerset Steuart."[5] He may have been named as late as February 12, 1771, when he was baptized at St. Andrews, a small stone church near Holborn Circus designed by Christopher Wren to replace the church that had been destroyed in the Great Fire. Somerset was described in the church's records as "an adult black male about thirty years old."

On the day Steuart purchased Somerset, the Scotsman had been living in America for eight years, having arrived as a lad of sixteen to apprentice in the store of a fellow Scottish tobacco trader. At the age of nineteen, Steuart left for Massachusetts, where he entered his uncle's counting house, but soon returned and joined a Virginia mercantile trading firm. A few years after he purchased Somerset, Steuart began his own successful trading company in Norfolk, where he also served as quartermaster to the county militia. Eventually, he moved to Portsmouth.

By every account, this Scottish slaveholder was a mild, kindly, and generous man who supported his nephews when their father died, dispatched them to school, and helped them establish their business lives. He financially assisted many others, especially Loyalists who had been displaced by the Revolution, after he moved to England. But Steuart cared nothing about the cruelties of the slave trade, either domestic or international, and never would. In 1790, then sixty-five, Steuart would still be corresponding with a nephew about that man's slave-trading business, which Steuart had helped him establish.

On July 5, 1751, Steuart wrote to a client for whom he had traded forty-eight slaves: "One of the women came ashore very sick and is since dead; four of the rest complained a little and two of them had the same symptoms with which the woman was taken." He had been forced to make "an immediate sale of them at 26 pounds." In another letter to a client, for whom he had sold two slaves, written ten days later, Steuart wrote that the buyer wanted to return his purchases because the intestines of one were dangling from his anus, and the other had barely the use of one arm. He insisted, for the sake of recouping expenses, that the pair be resold, but at a lower price.[6]

In the fall of 1762, Steuart's life dramatically turned when a ship carrying surrendered Spanish sailors and a titled lady from Havana to Cadiz made an emergency call in a river near Norfolk and was savagely attacked by the colonists. Virginia's Governor Francis Fauquier had contracted with Steuart to outfit the passengers with everything they needed. In word and deed, Steuart supplied them with a stout defense when they were attacked and saved many lives. When he arrived the next year in London, he learned that news of his backwoods heroism and diplomacy had preceded him. Attired in magnificent clothing that would be memorialized in a portrait, he was presented to King George III. The future prime minister, George Grenville, then Chancellor of the Exchequer, made Steuart surveyor general of customs for the Middle Eastern District of America, a huge swathe of territory running from Virginia to Quebec. Two years later, Steuart was promoted to receiver general of customs, the highest-ranking British customs post in North America. At his death, Steuart was said to have "discharged [his customs duties] during the difficult times of the Stamp Act with the approbation of his superiors and the applause of the people."[7] When Steuart came to Boston, few Bostonians applauded.

Somerset was not Steuart's only slave. He owned Old George, Lawson, Nanney, Quashabo, Ananake and her children, and others, but Somerset was probably the only slave Steuart took to Massachusetts. The pair traveled frequently through the northern colonies and as far south as Williamsburg and Norfolk. We can only speculate how often Steuart brought Somerset on local Boston visits, but we know they often visited the home of a friend, James Murray, who lived just to the south, in Milton.[8] By now, Somerset had become Steuart's intimate, a trusted manservant, and, at times nearly his master's alter-ego; here was a man who enjoyed his master's affection and that of others, black and white. "Don't forget," Nathaniel Coffin would write to Steuart in London, "to mention [his wife and children] to our friend Somersett."[9] In turn, Steuart was generous to Somerset: The accounts show that Steuart purchased silk, stockings, and ribbon for his slave, and gave him a little money, too.

As he moved about Boston and traveled with Steuart to New York, Philadelphia, and Williamsburg, Somerset must have marinated in the arguments about natural law, natural rights, and entitlement to liberty and equality that were engulfing the colonies. Invoking universal unchanging natural law in the winter of 1761, the Boston lawyer James Otis had railed against the writs of assistance, which allowed customs officials to enter and search just about anywhere they wished. The 1765 Stamp Act infuriated the colonists, and none more than those of Massachusetts and Virginia. On the floor of the Virginia House of Burgesses that May, Patrick Henry ignited cries of "Treason! Treason!" with a fiery speech in which he linked George III to Caesar and the detested Charles I, not forgetting to mention Brutus and Oliver Cromwell.

Though the Stamp Act was repealed the following year, new and equally unpopular taxes, especially the Townshend Duties, were levied against such items as tea and glass. In 1768, the Massachusetts legislature circulated a letter to its sister colonies urging a united opposition to these taxes. When the British Parliament ordered the colonial governors to dissolve legislatures that sided with Massachusetts, Virginia's Governor Botetourt dissolved the Burgesses. This only spurred them to continue in office informally and to draw up a paper, which many signed, in which they promised neither to import nor to purchase goods that were the subject of these taxes. The landing of British troops in Boston that year to enforce the Townshend Acts and keep order sparked a series of violent run-ins between the Lobsterbacks and the colonists.

In Boston, Somerset would have encountered John Adams, who lived and worked in that small New England city, his cousin Samuel Adams, John Hancock, and Robert Treat Paine. In Virginia, he would have seen Patrick Henry, Richard Henry Lee, George Washington, one of Steuart's former clients, and Thomas Jefferson, who took his seat in the Burgesses in the spring of the year Somerset and Steuart sailed for London. To a certainty, Somerset heard of them from Steuart, a staunch Loyalist who had nothing but contempt for Patriots, or from Steuart's cadre of Loyalist customs officials.

In the summer of 1768, Steuart sought permission from his London superiors to recuperate from the toll the arduous colonial traveling had taken on his health. When this request was granted, Steuart sailed from Boston for London on the *Earl of Halifax,* with Somerset, on October

1, 1769. They landed on November 10, and settled into Holborn's Baldwin's Gardens, in the parish of St. Mary-Le-Bow, in the ward of Cheap (named because of the behavior of its merchants) near the heart of the City, perhaps 800 meters southeast of St. Andrews, where Somerset would be baptized, and a bit closer to the northwest of Old Jewry, where Granville Sharp had awakened to the injustice of African slavery and was then plotting its abolition.[10] Their lives continued very much as they had for two decades. In America, Somerset had run errands for Steuart, taking and returning letters, messages, and packages, and he continued to do so in England, within London, even when Steuart was out of town, and between such cities as London and Bristol or Edinburgh.[11] He had many opportunities to learn the city and make key friends, white and black, free and slave, upon whom he could call for assistance when, and if, he decided to strike out on his own.

Two years after they left Boston, Somerset left Steuart. On Steuart's death in 1797, *Gentleman's Magazine* would characterize the African's bid for freedom as "a singular instance of ingratitude," for James Somerset, "idle from indulgence, and base from idleness, deserted [Steuart's] service, and insulted his person."[12] Now Somerset needed all the help he could muster, for Steuart, outraged by the insult to his person, enraged by the betrayal of his most loyal servant, perhaps even anxious to recoup his investment, set slave-catchers on Somerset. Either he hired them for the specific purpose or he advertised the escape in a newspaper, perhaps giving Somerset's age, description, identifying marks, and clothing worn, and offering a typical reward, a guinea, or half guinea, and expenses.[13] Somerset must have known he would be pursued. On the day before Christmas, 1751, two years after he purchased Somerset, Steuart put a notice in the *Virginia Gazette* seeking the return of a young mulatto sailor named Joe, who had left wearing "a blue Fear-nothing Jacket, Trousers, and old Hat and Wig, Yarn Stockings, and Shoes." Whoever apprehended and returned Joe to Steuart or secured him—"so that I may have him again"—would receive a pistol and whatever else the law allowed.[14]

How would the slave-catchers find him? Mid-century, the novelist and London magistrate, Henry Fielding, noted "the great irregularity of

[Greater London's] buildings, the immense number of lanes, alleys, courts, and by-places . . . had they been intended for the very purpose of concealment they could scarcely have been better contrived."[15] The London into which Somerset vanished was the largest city in the world—800,000 souls, chaotic, compact, crowded, cruel, dangerous, dark, dirty, diseased, squalid, stinking, and violent, a twisting maze of alleyways and courtyards.

The population was transient and terribly poor. Journeymen workers might labor twelve hours a day, six days a week; time off might amount to three annual holidays and an additional eight days a year during which they could flock to Tyburn to gawk at public hangings. Debtors unable to repay even small sums were thrown into hideous prisons and forgotten. Men walking down the street were routinely impressed by gangs into lengthy service in the Royal Navy. Unemployed women starved to death and 60 percent of christened children were in the ground by age five.[16] In 1767, Jonas Hanway, protesting the apprenticeship of the very young, sometimes seven-year-olds, to chimney sweeps who nearly owned them, wrote in complaint: "These poor black urchins . . . are treated worse than a humane person would treat a dog."[17] Alcohol so thoroughly soaked most lives that, in 1750, one Westminster house in eight was a gin shop, one Holborn house in five, and one St. Giles house in four.[18]

Cruelty was endemic. In 1751, one of Hogarth's famous "Four Stages of Cruelty" depicted a dog being shot with an arrow, animals being encouraged to attack one other, a cat being tossed from a window, a fallen horse being whipped, and a donkey being overloaded. Visitors to the Royal Menagerie in the Lion Tower at the Tower of London were admitted at no charge if they could produce a dog, cat, or other unfortunate to squeeze through the cage bars to feed the waiting lions and tigers. Bulls, badgers, and bears were baited. Dogs were made to fight. Animals who were to be eaten were routinely treated so miserably that a furious Alexander Pope wrote a letter of complaint to the *Guardian:* "I know nothing more shocking or horrid than the prospect of . . . kitchens covered with blood and filled with the cries of creatures expiring in tortures."[19]

London's masses, including nearly every free black, lived as weekly tenants in sparsely furnished rooms. Entire working class families occupied a single tiny room. Half a dozen people might sleep in the same stained bed. Houses were ancient, decayed, and in constant danger of collapse. In the sixteenth century, uncontrolled building outside the square-mile City had catalyzed fears that a larger population would, in turn, ignite disorder, disease, and a steep rise in the price of necessaries. Edicts flowed against the building of new houses, or at least the sorts of houses the poor might afford. This led to the shoring of houses that should have been demolished, to subdividing them into smaller and smaller units and, worst, to building flimsy, patchwork dwellings located as far from the attention of the authorities as possible and, in case they were discovered and had to be ripped down, constructed as cheaply as possible.

Owners who couldn't build up built down. If the poor didn't live in low-ceilinged garrets with windows so small they admitted negligible light and air, they inhabited deep, dark, dank cellars. Every inside room was infused with the smell of excrement. Not that the outside air was healthy. London was nearly surrounded by brick kilns that blackened the air. When a Dr. Lettsom began prescribing fresh air as a treatment for typhus around 1770, he ordered his patients to take it in the center of the Thames bridges, almost the only places where the air was even modestly fresh.[20] When a tax was imposed on houses with a certain minimum number of windows in 1696, many stopped up enough windows to bring them below the minimum required for the tax. When seven-windowed houses were taxed in 1766, their number plunged by two-thirds.[21]

By 1771, 2, perhaps 3, percent of London's people were black, most of them slaves. The highest published contemporaneous estimate of the slave population of all Britain, and it bordered on speculation, was a shade under 40,000, certainly too high. The lowest guess was 3,000, so low that it was immediately abandoned by its author in the face of Lord Mansfield's embrace of the number "15,000" in the *Somerset* trial.[22] The majority lived in London.

Many slaves were branded or collared with metal that could not easily be opened. The *Daily Journal* of September 28, 1728, carried an advertisement for a runaway wearing a neck collar engraved with the words "My Lady Bromfield's black, in London's Lincoln Fields." Collars of blacks belonging to the wealthy might be hammered from silver. A 1756 *London Advertiser* brought a notice to the public from one Matthew Dyer, goldsmith, working at the Crown in Duck Lane, Orchard Street, Westminster, that he forged "silver padlocks for Blacks or Dogs; Collars, &c."[23] Somerset was neither branded nor collared. But he may have stood out as significantly taller than the average, for American colonials, even their slaves, tended to be better fed and more disease free, having been raised—he from the age of eight—in the low-density populations that proved stony ground for the seeds sown by the waves of epidemics that endlessly rolled though the eighteenth century.[24] The French who would carry the Bastille two decades later would stand a mere five feet and weigh one hundred pounds.[25]

Somerset knew London and doubtless had made friends within its growing community of free blacks, self-sufficient, internally supportive, and so anxious to proselytize their enslaved brothers and sisters to increase their numbers that, in 1768, the blind magistrate, Sir John Fielding, brother of Henry, complained that they "enter into societies and make it their business to corrupt and dissatisfy the minds of every black servant that comes into England."[26] They were runaways, musicians, seamen, actors, boxers, and prostitutes; they congregated in the eastern parishes, the area around St. Giles, just west of St. Andrews, where the beggars among them were disparaged as "St. Giles' Blackbirds," and along the Thames near Wapping, just 2 kilometers to the southeast of the parish of St. Mary-Le-Bow, from where James Somerset had just fled.[27] Friendly whites, rich and poor, may have helped Somerset hide from Steuart's slave-catchers. Secreting a slave was not a crime, though Steuart could have sued anyone he caught at it for trespassing upon his goods. Nor was it a crime for Somerset to flee. Poor whites, whose miserable lives were no better than were the lives of escaped black slaves, were often friendly to poor blacks.

It took Steuart's slave-catchers fifty-six days to corner their man. They did not bring him home. Instead, on Steuart's orders, Somerset was shackled and thrown onto the *Ann and Mary*, anchored in the

Thames and ready to sail for Jamaica and the slave markets into which its captain, John Knowles, was to sell him. Had England sunk beneath its stern, Steuart's order would have proved Somerset's death sentence, for in the British West Indies' sugar plantations, field workers were "generally treated more like beasts of burden than like human creatures."[28] A third of Africans died within three years of their arrival. On one estate in Barbados, 5 percent of the slaves were replaced each year.[29] It was simply cheaper for planters to work the newcomers to death, then purchase replacements, than to care for the workers properly. Steuart knew the hell James Somerset would face in Jamaica.

But first Steuart had to get him there. And he would have succeeded, too, with nothing to have been done; but before the *Ann and Mary* could sail, three Londoners applied to Lord Mansfield for a writ of habeas corpus ordering Captain Knowles to produce Somerset before Mansfield in his chambers at Serjeant's Inn. These Londoners were probably Somerset's godparents, one or more of whom may have hidden him during his two months of freedom. Perhaps one had even witnessed his seizure and alerted the rest. We know nothing else about Thomas Walkin, Elizabeth Cade, and John Marlow, for their affidavits disappeared in an early twentieth-century housecleaning at London's Public Records Office. But they must have known that another London black, Thomas Lewis, had the previous year come within a few puffs of ocean breeze of being sailed over the horizon, out of the jurisdiction of the Court of King's Bench, and into West Indian bondage. And so they raced for the courthouse.

Somerset was captured on Tuesday, November 26, 1771. On Thursday, Lord Mansfield issued the writ of habeus corpus to Captain Knowles and required Somerset to designate "sureties," people who would bind themselves to pay a large penalty should he fail to appear for trial, at a cost of more than fifteen hundred modern pounds. These "recognizances" were presumably paid by one or more of Somerset's three godparents, though we don't know that. The writ sufficed to pry Somerset from the ship and place him under the authority of the Court of King's Bench, at least temporarily, until Captain Knowles could answer and a final hearing take place to decide Somerset's fate.

Because Captain Knowles produced Somerset in Mansfield's chambers in Serjeant's Inn, rather than in open court, we don't know exactly when it happened. The young lawyer, Francis Hargrave, who was to achieve enduring fame as one of Somerset's most junior barristers, would write that Captain Knowles produced Somerset on December 9. But he claimed that the writ was issued on December 3, which was wrong.[30] The Habeas Corpus Act of 1679 allowed three days for production after being served when a prisoner was within 20 miles of the issuing court, as Somerset was. Although that act literally applied only to imprisonment for crime, Mansfield and other judges modeled the common law of habeas corpus on it, and so it is likely that Captain Knowles was ordered to produce Somerset within three days. The average number of days between order and production was usually about four, which would have been consistent.[31] Because the last day of Michaelmas Term was December 10, Knowles had almost certainly produced Somerset by then. Lord Mansfield set the next hearing date for January 24, 1772. On January 13, 1772, Granville Sharp recorded in his diary that "James Somerset, a negro from Virginia, called on me this morning (with the compositor I employ at Mr. Beige's) to complain of Mr. Charles Stewart. I gave him the best advice I could."[32]

CHAPTER 2

Black Slaves in England

You have among you many a purchas'd slave,
Which, like your asses, and your dogs, and mules,
You use in abject and in slavish parts,
Because you bought them.

William Shakespeare,
The Merchant of Venice *(act IV, scene I)*

JAMES SOMERSET WAS PART of a third wave of English unfree. No one
is sure where English slavery came from or when it appeared, but English Christians were enslaving English Christians by early Anglo-Saxon
times in a first wave, and the practice was questioned neither by the writers nor didacts of the time.[1] A person enslaved through war, criminal conviction, or accident of birth was, under an English law modeled on the
Roman, a chattel, a thing lacking legal personality. The enslaved were
subject to being bought and sold and exported through one of the major
trading centers, Bristol or London, and any wrong done them was legally
perpetrated against their owners. By the tenth century, Anglo-Saxon law
had mellowed; slaves were allowed some few legal privileges, but were
generally still treated as things. Their legal "thinghood" was reflected in
an agreement between Anglo-Saxons and certain Celts that set out re-
placement values in the event of an animal's loss. A human slave was

worth twenty shillings, the same as a mare, though much more than a pig, a sheep, or a goat, but just two-thirds of a horse.

For millennia, human slaves had been treated as animals, their bondage modeled on the domestication of dogs, cattle, goats, sheep, pigs, and birds, which had begun in the distant Neolithic.[2] In ancient Mesopotamia and Homeric Greece, human slaves were priced in equivalents of oxen, horses, or chickens. Classical Greek slaves were "human livestock," an ox "the poor man's slave."[3] It was natural for the Portuguese to sell the black slaves they brought from Africa in the mid-fifteenth century as they had always sold cattle.[4] The fourteenth-century Tunisian historian, Ibn Khaldun, thought blacks excellent slaves because they "have attributes that are quite similar to those of the dumb animals."[5] Human and nonhuman slaves alike were sacrificed to the gods, and sometimes eaten; they were given the same names, selectively bred and transported the same way, subjugated through the same brutal applications of the collar, the branding iron, the whip, and the prod, and through castration, chaining, and ear-cropping. Human and nonhuman slaves were bought, sold, leased, mortgaged, and bequeathed. The neotenization, or juvenilization, of slaves was the object of many a master, for it increased slave submissiveness and dependence and decreased their aggressiveness.[6] Unlike those of animals, the genes of human slaves were not routinely manipulated, either indirectly or directly, but the slavery historian David Brion Davis is certain they would have been if the masters could have arranged it: Humans "fortunately have never been held long enough in distinct, isolated groups to undergo significant hereditary change."[7]

Eighteenth-century comparisons of human slaves to nonhuman animals were pervasive: One novel depicted the kinship display of a black man crying over the corpse of a black dog, and a 1731 Bristol fair featured a shaved bear, sitting in a chair, wearing clothes, and labeled an Ethiopian savage.[8] Of Francis Williams, an eighteenth-century black poet and classical scholar educated at Cambridge, the philosopher David Hume commented: "Likely he is admired for very slender accomplishments, like a parrot who speaks a few words plainly."[9] In 1744, a West Indies planter, Edward Long, argued that blacks resembled orangutans more than they did whites; and in 1773, his fellow planter, Richard Nisbet, echoing Hume, compared the black American poet Phyllis Wheatley to a parrot.[10]

As late as 1086, the Domesday Book recorded that between 10 percent and 25 percent of Anglo-Saxons were slaves. Most were ploughmen; in some counties, there were two slaves for every plough, which made sense because it took two men to handle the team of oxen necessary to operate a plough. Because the conquering Normans had no tradition of chattel slavery and, more important, believed that freemen could better develop their newly won lands, thereby increasing the rent the Norman landlords received, they set about freeing the slaves; by the beginning of the twelfth century, almost none remained, except a handful owned by the Catholic Church. In 1102, the Council of Westminster formally outlawed the slave trade: "No one is henceforth to presume to carry on that shameful trading whereby heretofore men used in England to be sold like brute beasts."

Though Anglo-Saxon chattel slavery disappeared within sixty years of the Conquest, many English were swept into a second wave of unfree. These were the villeins, and there were two kinds, villeins *regardant,* who were attached to land, and villeins *in gross,* who were joined to the persons of their lords. Historians disagree about the extent to which villeins were chattel slaves.[11] Lord Holt, the Chief Justice of the Court of King's Bench, who disliked black chattel slavery, didn't think so, and wrote in 1701 that "one may be a villain in England, but not a slave."[12] But neither did the deeply slaveocratic Georgia Supreme Court, which agreed, in the decade before the American Civil War, that "any analogy drawn from the villeinage of the feudal times, is utterly fallacious."[13] To the degree villeins were owned by their lords, they still enjoyed privileges that black chattel slaves were never given, such as the right to marry. At worst, they were owned outright by their lords, but they had legal rights against every other person in the world.[14]

Unlike a slave, whose hopes of freedom were limited either to voluntary manumission at the whim of his master or to escape, a villein might upgrade his legal status in numerous ways unavailable to black slaves, not just through manumission, but through his lord's conduct, residence in certain cities or boroughs for a year and a day without the lord's making a claim, ordination, knighthood, marriage, and others. In tandem with the developing common law presumption in favor of liberty, it became very difficult to prove that a man was a villein, for either he had to swear he was a villein in court, which happened infrequently, or it had to be proven that he had derived from villein stock from time out of mind, and that his line had not been broken by illegitimacy. Increasingly sympathetic juries, aghast at the spectacle of one Englishman attempting to exercise despotic power over another Englishmen, began stubbornly to refuse to brand anyone a villein. Together, these led to the extinction of villeinage by the end of the sixteenth century, not because it was formally abolished, for it never was, but because the river of villeins dried up and no more were created. The last law case involving a villein was decided in 1618, the jury verdict favoring the villein.[15]

Blacks had been living in London since 1555, when John Lok shipped back from Guinea with five Africans, though disagreement exists about whether they were slaves or freemen who had come to learn English, and whether they were free to leave.[16] There can be no ambiguity, however, about the intentions of one privateer, Captain John Hawkins. With the backing of the treasurer of the navy and the Lord Mayor of London, and the approval of Elizabeth I, who naively instructed him to remove only those blacks who desired to leave Africa, Hawkins, whose coat of arms would feature a shackled black woman, introduced British commerce in 1562 to the profits that Spanish, Portuguese, Italians, Flemings, Muslims, and Africans had long been enjoying by slaving the coast of Sierra Leone.[17] He returned in 1563 with a cargo of three hundred Africans obtained, "partly by the sworde and partly by other means." He mostly filched them from six boats that Portuguese slavers had filled with the intention of shipping them to the Cape Verde islands.[18] Hawkins traded the Africans in Hispaniola for five shiploads of "hides, ginger, sugars, and some quantity of pearls."[19] He turned such a substantial profit that the following year he set out again, backed once more by prominent personages, this time bringing with him Queen Elizabeth's personal ship, the *Jesus of Lubeck*. Seizing Africans after "burning and spoiling their towns," stealing more from

Portuguese ships, and trading for others, Hawkins sold them in present day Venezuela and Colombia, then returned triumphantly to Britain with a 60 percent profit in gold, silver, and pearls, or so he claimed.[20] Tolerance of this newest brand of unfreedom was no doubt facilitated by the fact that villeinage, though it had fallen into near total disuse, was not yet out of mind.

In 1618, Queen Elizabeth's successor, King James I, granted patents to Guinea coast traders, as did his successor, King Charles I, in 1631. After the restoration of the monarchy with Charles II in 1660, the Company of Royal Adventurers into Africa was created and granted a thousand-year monopoly on the English African trade. Among its investors were "four members of the royal family, two dukes, a marquis, five earls, two barons, and seven knights."[21] Three years later, a new charter was granted, with King Charles II, Queen Catherine, the Queen Mother, and the Duke of York among the new investors. This royal charter granted it "the whole, entire and only trade for the buying, selling, bartering and exchanging of, for or with any gold, silver, negroes, slaves, goods, wares, and manufactures." Some of the gold the Guinea coast slaves fetched was turned into the coins that came to be called "guineas."[22] The following year, the Committee of the Privy Council for Foreign Plantations found African slaves "the most useful appurtenances of a plantation."[23] Eight years later, the newly formed New Royal African Company was granted sole authority to "import any redwood, elephant's teeth, negroes, slaves, wax, guinea grains, or other commodities."[24] In 1677, Solicitor General Francis Winnington answered "yes" when asked whether "negroes ought to be esteemed goods or commodities intended by the Acts of Trade, which provide that no commodities intended by the Acts of Trade be imported or exported out of His Majesty's plantations, but in ships that belong to the people of England."[25] A decade later, the Privy Council refused to confirm a 1683 Jamaican law that fined persons who killed slaves, because a mere fine seemed to "encourage the wilful shedding of blood."[26]

Virtually every black in Britain was a product of the African slave trade. A few had been hauled in specifically for sale, or their forebears had been. Most had been transplanted for the same reasons as James

Somerset. After years of administering the colonies, securing the empire, or reaping its fruits, colonial officials, soldiers and sailors, and West Indies planters had decided to return "home," and they brought their slaves with them.

The British population explosion that closed the sixteenth century brought famine. Upon finding there were more than enough English mouths to feed, Queen Elizabeth proclaimed: "There are lately blackamoores brought into this realm, of which kind of people there are already too many." She then ordered that "those kind of people should be sent forth of the land." No one paid the Virgin Queen the least attention, and the black population continued to grow. Frustrated, Her Majesty in 1601 licensed a Lubeck merchant, Caspar Van Sended, to begin transporting blacks to Iberia. The Privy Council ordered local authorities to assist Van Sended, and Elizabeth insisted that the English should be served by their own countrymen rather than "those kinde of people."[27] She might have been Canute stopping the waves, for no one who owned black slaves cared. Domestic help didn't come any cheaper, and besides, having a black slave was becoming extremely fashionable.

Everyone had to have one and they seemed to be everywhere. At the Globe theatre, Iago mocked Othello as "His Moorship" before an audience familiar with black men, and Shylock scolded the Duke of Venice: "You have among you many a purchas'd slave, Which, like your asses, and your dogs, and mules, You use in abject and in slavish parts, Because you bought them."[28] By 1761, one London guide listed seventeen "black" places in London, among them Black Boy Court, Blackboy's Alley, Blackmoor's Alley, and Blackmoor Street.[29] The great majority of England's "Moors" were male, for that was the sex of choice for the West Indies planter who needed his sugar fields cultivated, and thus males became the primary targets of African slavers.[30]

By 1680, it was being written that a fashionable woman "hath always two necessary implements about her; a Blackamoor and a little dog."[31] Many English blacks began as page boys. Wealthy or noble Englishwomen accented their fairness by trailing young spoiled black boys, magnificently attired in silks and turbans, in their strolls along the Strand or at St. James's; the blacker the boy, the more stunning the contrast with madam and the more desirable the page. However, after five years or ten, on manhood's brink, no longer pageboy cute, and no longer permitted to care for madam, adolescent black males might be sold into domestic service or be shipped to the West Indies to a fate they could not imagine.[32] In 1690, John Dryden satirized the British attitude toward the Irish by comparing them to blacks and giving the Irish occupation troops a suggestion:

> Each bring his love a Bogland captive home;
> Such proper pages will long trains become;
> With copper collars and with brawny backs,
> Quite to put down the fashion of our blacks.[33]

Into this London, James Somerset escaped and was recaptured, and in this London twenty-nine-year-old Granville Sharp encountered a young slave named Jonathan Strong, by chance, on a morning in 1765, as Sharp was leaving the surgery of his brother, William. The meeting marked a new life for both and the beginning of the end of slavery.

CHAPTER 3

Granville Sharp Meets
Jonathan Strong

An event which has had very extensive effects.
Granville Sharp [1]

WILLIAM SHARP TREATED London's poor without charge each morning at his surgery on East London's Mincing Lane, which ran south from Fenchurch Street, an area Granville often visited. One day, he noticed a black youth, sixteen or seventeen years old, nearly dead, standing at the door, seeking advice along with the other sick paupers. Feverish, nearly blind, doubly lame, "ready to drop down," Granville would remember, Jonathan Strong had been struck so hard and repeatedly on the head with a revolver by his master that its butt had separated from the stock. Accurately believing Strong economically no longer useful to him, Strong's master, a lawyer named David Lisle, who had brought Strong to London from Barbados, cast him into the street to die.[2] Somehow, Strong had made his way to William's surgery.

Granville returned to ask William's help. William had assisted Strong just a day or two before, to little success. Now William had Strong admitted to St. Bart's Hospital. There he convalesced for four and a half months. After discharge, when Strong asked Granville for assistance, Granville found him employment as a medicine errand boy for a Mr. Brown, the owner of a nearby apothecary and surgery on Fenchurch Street. Strong worked and lived at the apothecary, receiving wages and board for the next two years and fleshed into a "good looking stout young man."

That happy period ended when Lisle chanced to recognize Strong attending Mrs. Brown behind a hackney coach and tracked him to the apothecary on Fenchurch Street. Delighted by the prospect of recouping some of his seventy-pound purchase price, Lisle promptly sold Strong to James Kerr, a Jamaican planter, for thirty pounds. Kerr, however, refused to pay for this "one Negro Man Slave" until Strong had been tucked safely aboard a Jamaica-bound ship belonging to Messrs. Muir and Atkinson, captained by David Laird. Lisle decided to kidnap Strong. He sent Strong a message saying that a person wished to speak to him at a certain public house. When the unsuspecting Strong arrived, he was horrified to find the brutal Lisle accompanied by two of the Lord Mayor's officers, into whose custody he was immediately delivered. They thrust him into the Poultry Compter (a compter being a prison under the supervision of a sheriff, this compter lying in that part of the Ward of Cheap called "the Poultry"). Not as notorious a prison as Newgate, the Poultry Compter was terrible enough. It was Saturday, September 5.

In the two and a half years since he had seen Lisle, Strong had been baptized. Terrified, he sent a distress call to his godfathers, John London and Stephen Nail, who were turned away at the prison's gate. Then Strong sent for Brown. But when Lisle intimidated the apothecary with the charge that he had illegally detained Lisle's property for the previous two years, Brown did nothing more than deliver Strong's written plea to Granville Sharp "imploring protection from being sold as a slave" on the following Saturday, September 12. That was enough. Years later, Sharp found the letter, signed "Jonathan Strong," and marveled that it had "such wonderful & unexpected consequences both in England & America & since in France."

At first, Sharp didn't recognize the name, for Strong's was merely one among numerous acts of charity he habitually performed. But he sent Brown's messenger, Poole, to investigate. Poole was greeted twice with a denial that Strong was being held at the prison. The next day, Sunday, September 13, a suspicious Sharp ventured, with another brother, James, to the compter to see what was happening. He demanded to see Jonathan Strong. As soon as Strong was reluctantly produced, Sharp recognized him and asked why he was there. When Strong explained, Sharp insisted the prison keeper hold him, not deliver him to anyone, until Sharp could obtain a hearing before the Lord Mayor of London, Sir Robert Kite, on the legality of Strong's imprisonment.

Sharp hurried to the nearby Mansion House, located just to the west of St. Paul's. On September 16, he was able to lodge a formal complaint that Strong was being held at the Poultry Compter without cause and demand that Kite summons his captors to justify his detention. As Lord Mayor, Kite was also Chief Magistrate of London, and the Mansion House was the only London residence with a court and holding cells. Kite promptly issued the summons and held a hearing on September 18. Neither Lisle nor Kerr appeared, just William MacBean, Kerr's notary public and attorney, and David Laird, captain of the ship *Thames*, which had been hired to sail Strong to the West Indies, and Sharp.

Sharp would write of the encounter that "[n]othing can be more shocking to human nature than the case of a man or woman who is delivered into the absolute power of strangers to be treated according to the new master's will & pleasure." MacBean produced the bill of sale for Strong that Lisle had given to Kerr. Jonathan Strong, who knew nothing of MacBean, Laird, or Kerr, but only what awaited him if they succeeded, was placed, wrote Sharp, "in extreme fear and anguish," which "deeply impressed [Sharp] with that extreme horror which the poor victims of the inhuman traffic generally experience."

"Trembling," ready "to sink down with fear," according to Sharp, Strong was unable to follow the intricacies of the legal dispute that was breaking over him, especially the interchanges between MacBean and Sharp. Then the Lord Mayor ruled. Strong had stolen nothing and was not guilty of an offense; he was at liberty to go wherever he pleased. Captain Laird then seized Strong's arm and declared that he was taking him "as the property of Mr. Kerr." And so Strong might have been dragged to the harbor but for the clear-headed presence of Thomas

Beech, the coroner of London, who stepped up to Sharp and urgently whispered into his ear, "Charge him!" Sharp, who lacked legal training, instantly grasped the coroner's meaning. He turned on Captain Laird and bellowed, "Sir, I charge you in the name of the King, with an assault upon the person of Jonathan Strong, and all these are my witnesses."[3] As Sharp recorded the scene: "The Captain thereupon withdrew his hand, and all parties retired from the presence of the Lord Mayor, and Jonathan Strong departed also, in the sight of all, in full liberty, nobody daring afterwards to touch him."

Lisle was furious. On the afternoon of October 1, he pounded on Granville's door at Old Jewry. Once inside, he upbraided Sharp, then challenged him to a duel. The short, gentle, mild-mannered ordnance clerk quietly reminded Lisle that he was a lawyer and suggested he therefore ought to be satisfied with his legal remedies. Within days, Kerr, frustrated in his attempt to gain possession of Jonathan Strong, sued Granville and James Sharp for 200 pounds, a substantial sum. The charge was trespass against his property, Jonathan Strong, in whom Kerr's lawyers claimed, Sharp wrote, "(a)s much private property as a horse or a dog."[4]

Kerr's writs were a mess. His lawyers, who included MacBean, were either incompetent or badly informed, for the writs were dated July 8, 1767, weeks before Lisle had seen Strong attending Mrs. Brown in the hackney, and weeks before Strong's bill of sale was dated. They erroneously claimed the Sharps had denied Kerr the use of Strong on June 1, made it appear that four slaves named "John Strong" were involved, and named John Doe and Richard Roe, instead of the brothers Sharp, as the defendants.

The brothers retained an eminent solicitor in the Lord Mayor's office to assist them in their defense, then consulted Sir James Eyre, Recorder of London, later Lord Chief Baron of the Exchequer. Slavery historian James Walvin claims that Eyre even consulted privately with Lord Mansfield before he gave his opinion.[5] Then the lawyers showed Granville an informal thirty-eight-year-old Joint Opinion, given by the realm's two highest legal officials at the time, both future Lord Chancellors, Attorney General Sir Philip Yorke, later Earl Hardwicke, and Solicitor General Charles Talbot, later created a baron in 1729. The two men had been invited by a contingent of West Indian planters for a convivial evening of food and drink at Lincoln's Inn. The evening had a serious purpose; the planters wanted the pair officially to negate the two principle arguments against black chattel slavery, baptism and the breathing of English air.

Most eighteenth-century blacks, and many whites, believed, against all the evidence, for the English courts had never actually freed a baptized slave, that baptism automatically conferred freedom. When Sir John Fielding, the blind magistrate, complained that free blacks were dissatisfying the minds of black servants, it was because they were telling them just that.[6] American colonials had wasted no time in putting the notion to rest. In 1667, Virginia made it explicit that "the conferring of baptisme doth not alter the condition of the person as to his bondage or freedome."[7] Nearly every British slave colony followed.[8] But, according to abolitionist Thomas Clarkson:

> Most of the slaves, who came [to England] with their masters, prevailed upon some pious clergyman to baptize them. They took of course godfathers of such citizens as had the generosity to espouse their cause. When they were seized they usually sent to these, if they had an opportunity, for their protection. And, in the result, their godfathers maintained that they had been baptized and that they were free on this account as well as by the general tenour of the laws of England.[9]

Ten-year-old Olaudah Equiano had himself baptized in February, 1759, at St. Margaret's Church in Westminster, 2 kilometers to the southwest from the church where James Somerset would be baptized twelve years later.[10] Sold in 1762 by his master to a ship's captain bound for the West Indies, young Equiano had boldly informed the captain that he was not for sale: "'I have been baptized: and by the laws of the land, no man has a right to sell me.' And I added that I had heard a lawyer, and others, at different times tell my master so." He was ignored. Equiano's friend, Ottobah Cugoano, would be brought by his master to England from the West Indies in 1772. At about the age of fifteen, Cuguano had himself baptized so that he "might not be carried away and sold again."[11] Like Equiano and Cugoano, James Somerset believed baptism would free him.

Christianity had long supported slavery of all kinds, as well as the slave trade, at least when infidels were the slaves. Here Britain's Anglican Church uncharacteristically stood shoulder-to-shoulder with Catholics, Presbyterians, Lutherans, and every other Christian sect. Levitticus 25:44 unambiguously sanctioned Hebrew slavery: "Both thy bondsmen, and thy bondsmaids, which thou shalt have, shall be of the heathen that are round about you; of them shall ye buy bondsmen and bondsmaids." The next two verses, however, enjoined Hebrews not to enslave each other: "Moreover of the children of the strangers that do sojourn among you, of them shall ye buy . . . and they shall be your possession. And ye shall take them as an inheritance for your children . . . to inherit them for a possession; they shall be your bondsmen forever," and there was more.[12]

The New Testament dispatched a more ambiguous and complex message, for inherent in Christianity was the demand for human equality, if not the temporal sort, then of spiritual equality before God. Because human slavery was part of God's punishment for man's fall, it was not only tolerated, but seen as justified, sometimes even deserved. There were scattered abolitionist Christian cries over the ages, but none was systematic or effective.

In Apostolic times, it had been no sin for one Christian to enslave another. That a non-Christian might enslave a believer, however, began to trouble. By the second millennium, baptism meant liberation and, by the middle of the next millennium, the enslavement of Christian by Christian was being censured, and had become rare. Medieval English Catholic doctrine preached the virtues of emancipation, even as the Church continued to own slaves. By the 1120s, the Church's Peterborough Abbey was the last known ground worked by slaves in England.[13]

However, the Christian enslavement of nonbelievers was thought to strike a blow at the enemies of Christendom, who deserved enslavement, and greatly to increase the likelihood of an infidel's conversion. Fifty years before Columbus sailed, a bull of Pope Nicholas V authorized the Portuguese to enslave Moors and allied unbelievers, and in 1488, Pope Innocent VIII actually accepted a gift of one hundred slaves from Columbus's Spanish sponsor, King Ferdinand. The enslavement of infidels remained acceptable, though the definition of one wobbled from a nonbeliever in Christianity to anybody who sprang from an infidel race or a place in which infidels usually inhabited, and that included Africa.[14]

At the turn of the eighteenth century, the English law of black chattel slavery was in chaos. The oldest case may even have been apocryphal. Supposedly, in 1569, one Cartwright returned to England with a Russian slave in tow. A court freed him with the pronouncement that "England was too pure an air for slaves to breathe in."[15] But no contemporaneous report of the case existed and it was known only because it had been mentioned, nearly in passing, during the seventeenth century in an unusual circumstance. In 1637, the notorious Star Chamber judges had imprisoned John Lilburne for libel. After the House of Commons impeached Lilburne's judges, the Commons managers quoted this mysterious Russian slave case, then more than seventy years old. How they learned about it, no one knows.

The first recorded slave case did not go well for the champions of liberty. In 1677, the Court of King's Bench, in *Butts v. Penny,* allowed a master to sue in trover for the loss of his black slave. Because trover was an ancient cause of action involving an owner of a thing, it is fair to infer that the judges thought a black slave was his master's thing, the reason being that commercial custom permitted the buying and selling of blacks "as merchandise" and because they were infidels.[16] Medieval rules of war had long given captors property rights in their captives until a ransom could be arranged, and Lord Coke had said in 1609 that, as perpetual enemies of Christians, infidels could be perpetually imprisoned. *Butts,* however, gave the slaveocrats only limited succor, for the Attorney General asked the King's Bench to postpone its decision to the following term; it agreed and never took up the matter again. Final judgment was never entered.

In 1690, one court did come perilously close to freeing a baptized slave. Katherine Auker, the slave of Robert Rich, a Barbados planter, was baptized at St. Katherine's, near the Tower and less than 2 kilometers east from where James Somerset would be baptized in 1771. Rich did not agree that Auker was free and, according to her appeal records in the Middlesex Sessions, he "tortured her and turned her out," refused to grant her a discharge to allow her to work, jailed her in the

Poultry Compter, and returned to Barbados. The court ruled that Auker was "at liberty to serve any person until such time as the said Rich shall return from Barbadoes."[17] Had Rich returned, Katherine Auker might have begun round two, but apparently he didn't.

Advantage returned briefly to the masters in the 1694 case of *Gelly v. Cleve.* A British court allowed compensation for the loss of a slave and "adjudged that trover will lie for a Negro boy; for they are heathens, and therefore a man may have property in them. . . . the court . . . will take notice that they are heathens."[18]

Three years later, however, the slave interests collided with the great Chief Justice of the King's Bench, Sir John Holt, who resembled Lord Mansfield in many of his legal attitudes and reputation for fairness and foresight. Holt, a superb lawyer and King's Serjeant, had antagonized King James II by resigning as Recorder of London because he could not, in conscience, sentence a peacetime army deserter to death. After James II fled England, Holt was appointed Chief Justice and was instrumental in restoring the reputation of the courts, which had suffered severely under the Stuarts. In *Chamberline v. Harvey,* a black argued that slavery couldn't exist in England because it violated the law of nature, the common law had a presumption in favor of liberty, and "being baptised according to the rite of the Church, he is thereby made a Christian, and Christianity is inconsistent with slavery."[19] The master riposted that 'it can't be denied but that trover will lie for a negro; for so was the case of *Butts v. Penny,*" and that allowing slaves to free themselves through baptism handed inmates the key to their prison. Who would squeeze the sugar from the cane once all the slaves had been sprinkled with holy water?[20]

Lord Holt denied that trover would lie for the taking of a negro anyway, no matter what *Butts v. Penny* said, and neither would an action for trespass, because both actions were available only to owners of chattels, and blacks weren't ownable. The black was not a slave, but, said Holt, "a slavish servant," a person akin to an apprenticed laborer. A master might invoke the ancient writ of *per quod servitium amisit,* to recover the servant's lost services, said Holt, but not the servant himself.[21]

In 1701, Holt was faced with a second challenge to the legality of English slavery in *Smith v. Brown and Cooper.* Smith sold a slave to the firm of Brown and Cooper in the Parish of the Blessed Mary of the Arches in the Ward of Cheap. When the firm neglected to pay for the slave, Smith sued. "[A]s soon as a Negro comes into England, he becomes free," Holt said. "[O]ne may be a villain in England, but not a slave."[22] A fellow justice, Powell, thought the owner of a villein or a ward might have a property interest in him, but "the law takes no notice of a negro"; a black was not in the same category as a ward or a villein and was to be treated as an Englishman.[23] Holt said the plaintiff should have alleged that the black was in Virginia at the time of the sale and that, under Virginia law, blacks were saleable, for English law did not extend to Virginia. Smith took nothing.

Holt was to confront slavery a third and final time. Six years later, a London jury awarded damages to a Mr. Smith (who may, or may not, have been the same Mr. Smith who sold the slave to the firm of Brown and Cooper) in an action for "a singing Ethiopian negro" and "other goods" he had bought from a Mr. Gould.[24] Gould claimed that, as one man could not own another, Smith could not sue in trover. Smith pointed to *Butts v. Penny*, though *Butts* wasn't his highest authority.[25] Exodus had said that a slave was a chattel, the same as his master's money, and Levitticus had given a master life and death powers over his slave. Negroes were simply "merchandize," Smith said, like "monkeys." A writ of habeas corpus could not be used to free a slave, for it applied solely to free men.

Unimpressed, Holt again "denied the opinion in the case of *Butts and Penny*," and said that "the common law takes no notice of negros being different from other men. By the common law no man can have a property in another, but [only] in special cases, as in a villain, but even in him not to kill him: so in captives took in war, but the taker cannot kill him, but may sell them for ransom: there is no such thing as a slave by the law of England."[26]

Holt's trio of antislavery opinions were terribly alarming to the West Indies planters, whose fortunes depended upon the continued cultivation of sugar cane by African slaves. It might seem unbelievable today that the reason for so much death and misery was the European craving for sugar. But the average European diet had long been so humdrum, boring, calorie-starved and bland, sugar being the sole province of the rich or the royal since its discovery by European crusaders in the Holy Land, that pent-up demand for it exploded into a mania. Because the tropical sugar-making process was so tedious, backbreaking, hot, and dangerous, freemen could not be induced to do it. It wasn't that black slaves were particularly fit for the task; only a slave could be forced to do it.

By 1729, the West Indians had grown so exceedingly worried that they invited the sympathetic legal officials Yorke and Talbot to dinner and asked that they declare slavery legal and that it should remain that way. The duo obliged. After explaining that their joint opinion had become necessary "in order to correct a mistake, that slaves become free by their being in England, or by their being baptized," the planters were assured that British law was consonant with Christian tradition: "Baptism doth not bestow freedom on [the slave], nor make any alteration in his temporal condition in these kingdoms." A slave coming into England or Ireland from the West Indies "either with or without his master . . . doth not become free; and that his master's property or right in him is not thereby determined or varied . . . [and] the master may legally compel him to return again to the plantations."[27] This was the opinion the lawyers showed Granville Sharp. Sharp had never heard of it. It "was entirely opposite to the ideas that induced [him] to liberate Jonathan Strong," Sharp wrote, and he "could not believe the law of England was really so injurious to natural rights as so many great lawyers for political reasons had been pleased to assert."

Sharp's was the voice of the future and it must have sounded odd. Whether he approved the Joint Opinion or not, it was law, his lawyers insisted, and had been law for nearly forty years. Gazing at the ordnance clerk with that patronizing mixture of pity and irritation lawyers display when a client insists the law must be more just than it is, they advised him to cut Strong loose and settle Kerr's suit on as favorable terms as he could beg; sloppy writs or no, the suit "could not be defended." The lawyers informed Sharp of one other thing: Following the Joint Opinion had been "the constant practice of the Court of King's Bench under Lord Mansfield, who strenuously persisted in delivering up all runaway slaves to their masters."[28]

CHAPTER 4

Granville Sharp, Abolitionist

> Men who submit to the Slavish Yoke of other men's
> depraved opinions or unreasonable customs . . . cannot be
> justly deemed men of Honour.
>
> *Granville Sharp,*
> A Representation of the Injustice and Dangerous Tendency of Tolerating Slavery,
> or Even of Admitting the Least Claim of Private Property in the Persons of Men, in England

WILLIAM WILBERFORCE, as responsible as anyone for abolishing the African slave trade, praised Granville Sharp as having "led the way" in the fight against the African slave trade. Thomas Clarkson, as great as Wilberforce, would characterize Sharp as "the first labourer" of abolition. Throughout history, some had criticized slavery as immoral or unchristian; Sharp alone "determined upon a plan of action in behalf of the oppressed Africans, to the accomplishment of which he devoted a considerable portion of his time, talents, and substance."[1]

Named for Queen Elizabeth's vice-admiral, Sir Richard Granville, Sharp was the twelfth of fourteen children of the Archdeacon of Northumberland, and the last of his five sons. His father dissipated most of the family's fortune on the oldest two sons, John and Thomas, both of whom became respected clerics. He spent the rest advancing the careers of his middle two sons: William, who became the surgeon to whom Jonathan Strong turned for help, and James, who became a respected and influential London ironmonger. When the money ran out, Granville was pulled from public school and sent to a small school that taught him little beyond writing and arithmetic. But his brothers never forgot his deprivation.

Granville was an intelligent boy who, it is said, read all of Shakespeare's plays while sitting in the bough of an apple tree.[2] As a boy, he loved animals and kept dogs, cats, jackdaws, bats, even lizards, and one of the last things he wrote was that "the inhumanity of constrained labour in excess extends no further in England than to our beasts. But thanks to our laws, and not to the general good dispositions of masters, that it is so; for the wretch who is bad enough to maltreat a helpless beast, would not spare his fellow-man, if he had him in his power."[3] In May 1750, at age fourteen, he was apprenticed to a London linen-draper, Mr. Halsey. Upon Halsey's death, he began work for Halsey's father-in-law, Henry Willoughby, who was also a justice of the peace. He completed his apprenticeship with the Irishman Mr. Bourke and, in August 1757, began work as a linen merchant, but disliked it and quit.

Sharp was extraordinarily persistent. While an apprentice, he argued theology separately with a Socinian and a Jew. Each got the better of him by claiming that Sharp had erred because he knew no Greek or Hebrew. Sharp painstakingly taught himself both languages, then finished the arguments. When he decided that his master, Justice Willoughby, was the rightful heir to a barony, Sharp learned everything he could about that arcane subject; his research led to Willoughby's being confirmed as a baron and seated in the House of Lords. The following year, 1765, Sharp used his extensive knowledge of Hebrew to challenge the interpretation given by the Rev. Dr. Kennicott, a respected Hebrew scholar and publisher of a Hebrew Bible, to the Old Testament texts of Ezra and Nehemiah. Kennicott had erred because he could read the Bible only in English, Sharp wrote, "which is not less injustice, than if a judge were to condemn a prisoner merely from his report given by others, without permitting him to appear before him to answer for himself."[4] Sharp's second publication, in 1767, explained the Anglican liturgy in both English and French.

He was a pacifist, but he paradoxically earned his living as a clerk in the ordnance office, a position so taxing that, in 1773, he would apologize to the Pennsylvania abolitionist Quaker, Anthony Benezet, for taking so long to respond to his letter, a lapse that had occurred, he said, "for want of proper leisure." He added: "I am really a sort of slave myself, being obliged to employ every day in the week, constantly, in the ordinary business of my office, and having no holidays but Sundays, as the branch I am in requires more attendance than any in the whole office."[5] He rigidly believed, and possessed an absolute moral sense and an unwavering Christian faith, that right makes might. He analyzed little, acted much, and lived oblivious to the potential for failure. His true north was the Bible and its prophecies, which he accepted as the unerringly accurate and divine source of every first principle of morality and law. He never doubted the correctness of those principles and his ability to interpret them accurately, nor did he question his duty to vindicate them.

When Sharp published the results of his investigation into the illegality of English slavery, *A Representation of the Injustice and Dangerous Tendency of Tolerating Slavery, or Even of Admitting the Least Claim of Private Property in the Persons of Men, in England* in 1768, lawyer Daines Barrington would write that Sharp was "inclined to make the law what perhaps it *should be.*" Barrington then stated his own preference: "[W]hereas being by profession a lawyer I rather endeavor to find out from precedent and authority, what the law *is.*" Sharp understood obeisance to authority, but believed lawyers and judges were worshipping false gods here. He had no patience with obsequious adherence to precedent: "Men who submit to the Slavish Yoke of other men's depraved opinions or unreasonable customs . . . cannot be justly deemed men of Honour."[6] If the most prominent lawyers and judges of England accepted the legality of human bondage, they would have to change their depraved opinions and he would show them why. That was why he wrote the *Representation.*

He knew he faced an uphill struggle. Not only did prominent judges and lawyers feel bound by the Joint Opinion, but English merchants had been slaving unmolested for two hundred years. Parliament had been heavily regulating the slave trade, granting concessions to slave traders that encouraged their work, and confirming masters' property in their slaves, often through Navigation Acts, for a century.[7] Perhaps 20,000 black slaves lived in England; an influx of blacks from the West Indies and American colonies would be unwelcome. But Sharp knew no world other than that of "should be," and he believed that lawyers, above all, should share his hatred of injustice. When they fell woefuly short, Sharp began to disdain the legal profession. If English black chattel slavery was not illegal, it should be, and therefore, it would be.[8]

Sharp's personality had an ugly, intolerant side, for he was a religious bigot who believed the references in the Books of Daniel and Revelation to a scarlet-coloured beast, a seven-horned beast, and a Great Beast, were to the Catholic Church, which he did not consider Christian. But once he concluded that human slavery was a moral evil and a legal wrong condemned by the Bible, he was incapable of abandoning Jonathan Strong or of settling Kerr's suit. Kerr would have to withdraw it. Because every lawyer he consulted thought his defense against Kerr's suit hopeless, Sharp felt "compelled, through the want of regular legal assistance, to make a hopeless attempt at self-defence, though [he] was totally unacquainted, either with the practice of law or the foundations of it, having never opened a lawbook (except the Bible) in [his] life,"[9] and would become certain that the outcomes of the cases of Strong and other slaves "could not have been effected without a peculiar interposition & blessing of Divine Providence considering the total ignorance of their first advocate to any knowledge of law."

Sharp obtained a copy of the indexes of a law library from his bookseller and tried to determine which books were available to neuter the Joint Opinion. When he had completed each day's ordnance department tasks, he set to studying the unfamiliar cases and authorities, taking notes in a folio common place book and working on the problem for much of the next year. Meanwhile, he continued searching for a lawyer who would urge the proposition that human slavery was illegal in England.

Browsing in a London bookstore, Sharp soon stumbled upon Anthony Benezet's *Short Account of That Part of Africa Inhabited by the Negroes*. This was the first he had heard of the man with whom he would correspond for twelve years, until the Quaker's death. Benezet was Sharp's American alter-ego, determined, indefatigable, finally influential. Abolitionist ranks always contained advocates who hated slavery, yet embraced other biases of their time. Sharp was one of them, not just in his fierce anti-Catholicism and anti-Quakerism, combined with unreasoning devotion to the Anglican Church, but also in his belief, shared by Hume, Voltaire, Gibbon, and Jefferson, that blacks were not the intellectual and moral equals of whites. The belief that blacks were inferior, even detestable, explains why some abolitionists failed to press for full equality, but employed "a be-kind-to-animals paternalism."[10] Sharp deeply believed that blacks were entitled to be treated as any other human being. But they had descended from Ham, Noah's dark son, and Noah had placed a curse upon them for having seen his naked drunken body.[11]

Benezet argued that blacks were not the "stupefied and malicious People some would have thought them to be," but the full moral equal of whites, "generally sensible, humane, and sociable, that their Capacity [was] as good, and as capable of improvement, as that of the White people," and his *Short Account* sewed together a wide range of writings about Africans that demonstrated it.[12] Like Sharp and that remarkable cadre of abolitionist Quakers that emerged from colonial North America, among them Benjamin Lay and John Woolman, who boycotted every product obtained from abusing humans or animals, Benezet combined compassion and political action that extended beyond black chattel slavery. Once asked by his sister-in-law to join her family for its chicken meal, Benezet demurred: "Would you have me eat my neighbors?"[13] Though he jotted in the margins of *A Short Account* that Benezet was "unhappily involved in the errors of Quakerism," Sharp was so moved by what he read that he edited Benezet's pamphlet, added a "Conclusion," and had it reprinted and distributed without Benezet's knowledge.[14]

By June 3, 1769, Kerr had struck again. That day, Sharp wrote to Mr. Mist, with whom Jonathan Strong was living and for whom he was working, that Kerr had sued Sharp again.[15] Nothing came of it. David Lisle, clueless as to what motivated Granville Sharp, attempted to persuade Sharp to hand Strong over. Sharp responded that because Strong was at liberty and he, Sharp, had no more right to deliver Strong up to Lisle than Lisle had to take him. Lisle was heard from no more.

Sharp returned to Kerr's first suit against himself and his brother, James. Then he stumbled upon Blackstone's 1765 *Commentaries on the Laws of England* and thought he had found his lawyer! And a well-connected lawyer Blackstone was. Lord Mansfield himself had been Blackstone's patron and mentor for almost twenty years. In 1752, the Chief Justice had recommended Blackstone for the position of professor of civil law at Oxford. Another received that post, but when Oxford's Vinerian professorship of civil law was created a few years later, Blackstone was chosen; it was in that capacity that, over thirteen years, he gave the unprecedented series of lectures, on nearly every aspect of the common law, that he was to fashion into his four-volume *Commentaries*. In an age in which the study of law was a dessicating, searing, hunting-and-pecking experience, the *Commentaries* was acclaimed. After reviewing the first two volumes, the *Annual Register* announced that it had "cleared the law of England from the rubbish in which it was buried, and now shew[ed] it in . . . a clear, concise, and intelligent form."[16] Lord Mansfield extolled the *Commentaries* for anyone wishing to learn English law: "There he may imbibe imperceptibly the first principles on which our excellent laws are founded." In the book's pages, Mansfield wrote, the student of law would find "analytical reasoning diffused in a pleasing and perspicuous style."[17]

Mansfield had advised Dr. Blackstone on what to include in the *Commentaries* at certain critical points and was almost certainly one of those "learned friends" whom the doctor gratefully thanked in the preface to the *Commentaries'* second edition for pointing out errors and supplying omissions in the first. Mansfield's influence was palpable in Blackstone's discussion of equity. At the end of the eighteenth century, English law and equity were almost entirely separate. One received the justice to which one was strictly due under the law in the Courts of King's Bench and Common Pleas, leaving equitable justice to be dispensed on a case-by-case basis, according to the demands of good faith, fair dealing, and the Lord Chancellor's conscience. This was not to

Mansfield's liking. The Chief Justice struggled to leaven and moderate the often rigid common law with what he thought was fair to the individual litigants before him, to the delight of many, and the displeasure of some, such as Jeremy Bentham and Thomas Jefferson, who accused him of making the law whatever he liked. Blackstone wrote that because equity depended upon individual circumstances, there could be no fixed ways of dealing with a problem, though it should not be abused by leaving "the decision of every question entirely in the breast of the judge."[18]

However, the deeply conservative Dr. Blackstone approved of how mid-eighteenth-century English society was structured and believed English law resonated almost entirely in harmony with nature, which was his touchstone of justice.[19] It was true that English law might swing a miscreant into the Great Beyond for trivial criminal offenses. But the beauty and justice of English law lay not in its draconian potential, though it had plenty of that, but in how it was practiced in British courtrooms, especially by juries, who often engaged in "pious perjury," as Blackstone gamely put it, to the extreme of finding a 5-pound note worth less than a shilling to spare a thief the gallows for grand larceny. Blackstone professed to value above all life, in the sense of benevolence and a concern for the sufferings of others, and liberty, meaning the protection of the rights of individuals, said to mean "nothing more than his freedom to do whatever the law allowed him to do." But one value occupied the apex of Blackstonian English law, and that was property, especially commercial property, and the freedom of a property owner to use it any way he pleased.

The *Commentaries* only briefly discussed black chattel slavery. Blackstone had been strongly influenced by Montesquieu, the chief rooster in the Enlightenment's awakening to the injustice of that institution. The French philosophe had demolished many of the standard arguments in favor: It was a legitimate alternative to killing in wartime, one might sell oneself into slavery, one's children might be enslaved, religions might empower their adherents to enslave unbelievers, slave labor was superior to free, and blacks were not really human.[20] Montesquieu's chief weapon in his 1749 *Spirit of the Laws* was irony: "The Europeans, having extirpated the Americans, were obliged to make slaves of the Africans." Africans were "all over black, and with such a flat nose that they [could] scarcely be pitied." No one could believe that God "should place a soul . . . in such a black ugly body"; further, Montesquieu wrote, it was "impossible . . . to suppose these creatures to be men, because, allowing them to be men, a suspicion would follow that [whites] are not Christians."[21]

To Sharp's delight, Blackstone, citing Holt's 1701 decision in *Smith v. Brown and Cooper*, stirringly proclaimed that the English "spirit of liberty is so deeply implanted in our constitution, and rooted in our very soil, that a slave or a Negro, the moment he lands in England, falls under the protection of the laws, and with regard to all natural rights becomes so *eo instanti* a freeman."[22] In another section, Blackstone wrote the following:

> [I have] formerly observed that pure and proper slavery does not, nay cannot, subsist in England; such I mean, whereby an absolute and unlimited power is given to the master over the life and fortune of the slave. And indeed it is repugnant to reason and the principles of natural law, that such a state should subsist any where. The three origins of the right of slavery, assigned by Justinian, are all of them built on false foundations [here Blackstone repeated Montesquieu's arguments]. . . . Upon these principles the law of England abhors, and will not endure the existence of slavery within this nation. . . . And now it is laid down [here Blackstone again cited *Smith v. Brown and Cooper*] that a slave or negro, the instant he lands in England, becomes a freeman; that is the law will protect him in the enjoyment of his person, and his property.[23]

Sharp had a problem with the next, contradictory, sentence:

> Yet, with regard to any right which the master may have lawfully acquired, by contract or the like, to the perpetual service of John or Thomas, this will remain exactly in the same state as before; for this is no more than the same state of subjection for life, which every apprentice submits to for the space of seven, or sometimes for a longer term.

Sharp was not alone. In his 1785 *Dialogue Between a Justice of the Peace and a Farmer,* Thomas Day's bewildered farmer would complain that "I cannot say I perfectly understand that last passage, how the negroe is a free man, and yet his master may possibly have a right to his service."[24] Edward Christian, editor of the *Commentaries'* 1820 seventeenth edition, couldn't understand it, either: "I do not see how the master's right to the service can possibly continue; it can only arise from a contract, which the negro in a state of slavery is incapable of entering into with his master."[25] Blackstone lined up with Talbot and Yorke on whether baptism affected a black's legal status:

> Hence too it follows, that the infamous and unchristian practice of with-holding baptism from negro servants, lest they should thereby gain their liberty is totally without foundation, as well as without excuse. The law of England ... will not dissolve a civil contract between a master and servant, either express or implied, on account of the alteration of faith in either of the contracting parties: but the slave is entitled to the same liberty in England before, as after, baptism; and whatever service the heathen negro owed to his English master, the same is he bound to render when a Christian.[26]

Eventually it dawned on Sharp that more than one edition of the *Commentaries* was circulating. When he consulted the second edition, he was disturbed to find that the spirit of English law and liberty which, just one year before had been so deeply implanted in the constitution as to make a slave free the moment he landed in England, had become so shallowly rooted that "the master's right to his service may probably still continue."[27] In the fourth edition of 1770, Blackstone regretted going so far and changed "probably" to "possibly," where it remained until his death in 1780.[28] Sharp immediately fingered the responsible party: "The learned author [Blackstone] having been induced (as it is said) by the sentiments of the Chief Justice of the King's Bench to withdraw that opinion."[29]

Sharp lacked hard evidence that Blackstone had taken his marching orders on slavery from Mansfield. Infamously however, Blackstone was not above altering the *Commentaries* for political reasons. The most famous example occurred when the doctor became tangled in the shenanigans of the notorious John Wilkes. Unsavory, ungrateful, wolfish, a spendthrift, and a member of Parliament, Wilkes occupied the center of numerous first-rank political, legal, and legislative controversies throughout the 1760s that embroiled England's finest legal talent, including many who would play key roles in the *Somerset* case: Serjeant John Glynn, barristers John Dunning and James Mansfield, and Lord Mansfield. Wilkes was outlawed, then expelled from the House of Commons twice in early 1769. Three times over the next three months he was returned by Middlesex voters to the House of Commons by large majorities. Each time, he was expelled again. In the last election of April 13, 1769, one Colonel Luttrell managed to garner 296 votes to Wilkes's 1,143. The Commons then voided every Wilkite vote and declared Luttrell the winner.

Blackstone argued in the Commons that the common law disqualified Wilkes from taking his seat. George Grenville rose, the *Commentaries'* third edition laid open to page 162, and read Blackstone's list of common law grounds for disqualification. None fit Wilkes. One opponent recorded "a pause of some minutes in the House, from a general expectation that the Doctor would say something in his own defence; but . . . his faculties were too much overpowered."[30] When the fourth edition appeared, the common law suddenly permitted disqualification from the House of Commons upon conviction of a crime, a condition that fit Wilkes nicely, as we shall learn.[31]

Perhaps recognizing their mutual reliance upon Montesquieu, Sharp instructed his lawyer to ask Blackstone to join Eyre as his co-counsel. A few days later, they met. Sharp left believing that the round-faced, jowly, extremely near-sighted civil law professor "had no objection to make to this answer, but only warned him that it would be 'uphill work in the Court of King's Bench.'"[32] Knowing of the long relationship between the doctor and the Chief Justice, Sharp would have figured Blackstone knew why. Now Sharp asked him to arrange a consultation with the solicitor general of England to discuss Kerr's case.

That man was John Dunning and he would serve as a mercenary in Sharp's war against slavery for the next four years, though on both sides. Thirty-seven years old, Dunning was the head of the common law and equity bars.[33] He was widely admired, a popular figure with all sides in Parliament, acclaimed as witty and sharp. Fellow lawyer and member of Parliament, John Nicholls, thought Dunning "the quickest man" he "ever knew at the Bar. If an objection was to be taken or answered . . . he did it on the instant."[34]

Dunning must have been extraordinarily competent, for he was said to be "the ugliest man of his day, without being in any way what could be called deformed. His figure was short and stumpy. His complexion was sallow, his face was adorned with a snubbed nose, giving remarkably plebeian expression to his countenance. His whole frame was infirm and weak. He labored also under an affection of the nerves, which occasioned his head to be in a state of perpetual oscillation."[35] A client once missed Dunning at his chambers and tracked him to the coffee house where the barrister often whiled the evenings away. When the waiter claimed he didn't know who Dunning was, the client instructed the man to go upstairs and look for a "gentleman with a face like the knave of clubs." The waiter easily located Dunning.[36] On another occasion, Dunning was cross-examining an old woman about a man's identity when he asked, "Was he a tall man?" "Not very tall, your honour—much about the size of your worship's honour." "Was he good-looking?" "Quite contrary—much like your honour, but with a handsome nose." "Did he squint?" Dunning persisted. " A little, your worship; but not so much as your honour by a good deal."[37] Dunning probably failed to understand the laughter, for he was said to be fond of admiring himself in the mirror.[38] Unless he was painting the barrister as the man saw himself, a painter from the studio of Sir Joshua Reynolds didn't find Dunning repulsive, for an oil reveals a ruddy and stout man, rectangular-faced, with full lips and a prominent nose, large eyes that conveyed some private amusement, and a prosperous double chin, not at all unattractive.

Then there was the matter of Dunning's voice: It was "almost repulsive . . . His throat was always half-choked with phlegm, as though he were labouring under a chronic catarrh; and when a member of the Parliament, he always gave intimation of his intention to address the house, by violent and incessant efforts to clear his throat. All his efforts were unavailing, to render his voice otherwise than husky and unpleasant."[39] But he was exceedingly fluent and persuasive, a powerful orator who "spoke with such rapid fluency 'that he was the terror of the (court) reporters,'" with sentences complex, complete, exquisitely grammatical, delivered rat-a-tat-tat.[40]

For six or seven years, Dunning practiced the anonymous and sporadic law of the scrambling young lawyer. However, Serjeant Glynn, who would oppose Dunning in the *Somerset* case, noticed him. In 1762, Glynn, struck by one of his occasional gout attacks, was debilitated and had to refer his briefs. He gave them to Dunning, who handled them so expertly that he immediately began to attract business that brought him a huge leap in income.[41] Four years later, he was appointed Recorder of Bristol, which made him that city's chief judicial magistrate.

Solicitor General Edward Willes soon rose to what would prove to be an unhappy position on the Court of Kings Bench, where he would sit in judgment of James Somerset four years later. On January 29, 1768, Dunning took Willes's place and, with Serjeant Glynn and Dr. Blackstone, became a member of the House of Commons. Eight months later, he would meet with Sharp, Blackstone, and Eyre to discuss Kerr's lawsuit against the brothers.

While Sharp and his two lawyers were waiting for Dunning, they naturally began to chat about the case. The conversation quickly devolved into a remarkable, if brief, debate between the greatest legal commentator and greatest abolitionist of the age. In harmony with the second edition of his *Commentaries,* Blackstone insisted that Jonathan Strong's relationship with Lisle had been in the nature of an apprenticeship and, because he owed Lisle service in the West Indies, Strong owed him the same in England. Blackstone had a reputation for sternness and aloofness, as well as "a certain irritability of temper, derived from nature, [which] increased in his latter years by a strong nervous affection," and, the tardier Dunning was, the moodier he would have become, for "punctuality was in his opinion so much a virtue, that he could not bring himself to think perfectly well of any who were notoriously defective in it."[42] Still, Sharp stood his ground.[43] Following Montesquieu, he insisted that a valid contract required the free assent of both parties. Because no slave could freely enter into an agreement with his master (and Strong was also a minor), he lacked the legal capacity to enter into a binding slavery contract, and any contract he made was void.

Enter Dunning, who listened to the story and promptly sided with Blackstone. Sharp did not argue further, on that day, in that room, with Dunning and Blackstone arrayed against him for, in his mind, he was "no speaker," and he was in the presence of two powerful and experienced orators. But he was not cowed; he left unpersuaded, undaunted, and entirely determined to place his arguments before the courts—and to win.

CHAPTER 5

John Hylas: The Test

They usurp an absolute authority over their fellow man, as if
they thought them mere things, horses, dogs, etc.

Granville Sharp,
A Representation of the Injustice and Dangerous Tendency of Tolerating Slavery,
or Even of Admitting the Least Claim to Private Property in the Persons of Men, in England

As the Strong case ground on, John Hylas asked Sharp to
help him gain the return of his wife, Mary, from the West Indies.
The couple had sailed to London from their native Barbados in 1754,
John with his mistress, Judith Alleyne; Mary, with her master and mistress, Mr. and Mrs. Newton.[1] With the consent of both masters, they
married in 1758, whereupon Alleyne formally set John free. The two
lived together until 1766, when the Newtons had Mary kidnapped and
shipped back to slavery in the West Indies. For the next two years, John
had no idea where to turn. Then he learned of Granville Sharp.

Sharp was angered by John's story. Not only would victory right a
terrible wrong, it could be the test case he was seeking to attack English
slavery. He drafted a memorandum for Hylas based on the arguments
he was developing in *A Representation*; John had a right to "very considerable damages, as well by the Habeus Corpus Act as by the common
law and common justice."[2] Sharp also asserted that, if John were free,

Mary must be free, for under the common law, husband and wife were one, the husband, and John, was indisputably free. But John's lawyers were too cowed by the Joint Opinion to demand Mary's return. Instead, their Court of Common Pleas writ against Newton sought only money damages. At nine o'clock on December 3, 1768, Lord Wilmot, Chief Justice of the Court of Common Pleas, began trying the case just off the nave of Westminster Hall. The Hall had been the site of many important trials: William Wallace, St. Thomas More, Guy Fawkes, and, most notoriously, King Charles I. Construction had begun in 1097 by William Rufus, the Conqueror's son.[3] By 1178, judges were sitting and, when King Edward I ascended the throne in 1272, the Hall had already come to symbolize British justice. Nearly 240 feet long and 68 feet wide, it housed all four of England's central royal courts: the Court of King's Bench, which convened at the southeast end and tried cases that touched the sovereign; the Court of Common Pleas, which heard private suits in the northwest corner; the Court of Exchequer, in which revenue matters were litigated in a building that adjoined the west side of the Hall; and the Chancery, where the Lord Chancellor dispensed equity on the southeast side, directly opposite the Court of King's Bench. About 1740, the Court of Common Pleas moved into the room off the west wall.

Sharp passed the thicket of public houses and coffee houses—some physically attached to the Hall—where lawyers met clients and interviewed witnesses, strode beneath the colorful standards once seized on civil and foreign battlefields—now hanging from the rafters—pushed past the booths of booksellers, linen-vendors, toy sellers, mathematical instrument-makers, seamstresses, and haberdashers that lined its edges, and entered the Court of Common Pleas through its huge Gothic doorway. It was darkish inside the Hall. For illumination, the Hall depended principally upon what natural light sifted through its twenty-odd-foot-high windows. Twenty-five years before, candles had been introduced, but they were not usually lit until late afternoon; it would be another fifteen years before large hanging lamps would be installed. Heating stoves did not arrive until 1793; until then anyone not wearing an overcoat or layers of robes in the winter froze. If the winter was severe, the Hall might flood, the Thames occasionally leaving fish behind.

Wilmot was fifty-nine years old and deeply respected. He had been appointed to the Court of King's Bench in 1755, a year before Mansfield became its Chief Justice, where he sat for eleven years, until being made Chief Justice of the Court of Common Pleas. He and Mansfield remained close. Mentor and friend to the younger Scotsman, who sometimes asked him to review draft opinions, as Mansfield was mentor and friend to Blackstone, Wilmot had never once in ten years differed from Mansfield on any matter that had come before the Court of King's Bench.

One of Newton's lawyers was Sir Fletcher Norton. He had entered Parliament in 1761, become Solicitor General in 1762, Attorney General the year after that, and served until 1765. He was such an overbearing, intimidating personality, and was alleged to accept fees from both sides, that newspapers sometimes referred to him as "Sir Bull Face Doublefee." Mansfield despised him. In a case involving manorial rights, Norton responded to an argument, "My Lord, I can instance that point in my own person. Now my Lord, I have myself two little manors," at which Mansfield interrupted, "We are well aware of that, Sir Fletcher."

Mansfield thought Norton's chief strength the misleading of judges and juries; he wrote: "[A]nd with him I found it more difficult to prevent injustice being done, than with any person who ever practiced before me."[4] Characteristically, at the Hylas trial, Sir Fletcher implied that John really didn't care for Mary; he wanted money. Hylas's timid lawyers had left him vulnerable; after all, he had sued only for money! That John didn't even care for his wife enough to seek her return, Norton argued, should be factored into the amount of damages awarded. Wilmot questioned John: Would he have his wife or damages? His wife, John replied.

At the beginning of the trial, Norton told Wilmot that the case involved the great and difficult question of the legality of English slavery and he wanted Wilmot to decide it. Sharp recorded that one of Newton's lawyers, likely Fletcher Norton, asked Wilmot again to determine the issue. But Wilmot didn't address it. Instead, he awarded Hylas one shilling in damages and ordered Newton to return Mary to London by the first available ship, and, in all events, no later than six months hence. Sharp was outraged: "[W]hy this cruel alternative? If he had a right to his wife, which cannot be denied, he most certainly had a right also, in consideration of the violent and unpardonable outrage committed against himself in the person of his wife, for which no pecuniary allowance whatsoever can make him amends." He was also going to require another case.

Sharp aimed *A Representation* at English slave holders, "for they usurp an absolute authority over their fellow man, as if they thought them mere things, horses, dogs, etc."[5] But his legal arguments varied in strength. His claim that every human being in England was the king's subject and entitled to his protection was strong. Unless a master could prove that a slave was "neither man, woman or child," there could be no slave. "True justice makes no respect of persons, and can never deny to any one that blessing to which all mankind have an undoubted right, their *natural liberty*." His argument that, if liberty could be denied to blacks, anyone could be enslaved in the American colonies, then imported into England; mulattos, American Indians, even "a Hungarian, Pole, Muscovite, or alien of any other European nation," was stronger.

Sharp referred to two old Guildhall cases, one he learned of after he "accidentally met with a gentleman who was present at this trial . . . about thirty years" before, where the judge declared a black "to be free on his setting foot on English ground"; the other, almost forty years old, he claimed was a verdict in favor of one who "protected a poor negro woman, claimed by the plaintiffs as their slave."[6] Sharp had told Blackstone in Dunning's anteroom that English slavery had to be voluntary and therefore the Joint Opinion wasn't wrong, just exceedingly narrow, though Yorke and Talbot had not been invited to dinner to declare English slavery optional.[7] Barring that, "there are many instances of persons freed from slavery by the laws of England, but (God be thanked) there is neither law, nor even a precedent (at least I have not been able to find one), of a legal determination, to justify a master in claiming or detaining any person whatsoever as a slave in England, who has not voluntarily bound himself as such by a contract in writing."[8] Sharp overlooked Yorke's 1749 attempt, as Lord Chancellor Hardwicke in *Pearne v. Lisle*, to make the Joint Opinion law: Black slaves, he said, were "as much property as any other thing." They "wore out with labour as cattle, and other things," and were fungible; one slave being "as good as another."[9] But he also overlooked *Shanley v. Harvey*, in which Lord Chancellor Henley had said that "[a]s soon as a man sets foot on English ground he is free: a negro may maintain an action against his master for ill usage, and may have a *Habeas Corpus* if restrained of his liberty."[10]

On October 4, 1768, Sharp sent *A Representation* to Blackstone for comment and informed him that he had rejected the suggestion of the trial judge, Justice Welch, that Sharp settle Lisle's case by apprenticing Jonathan Strong to Mr. Mist.[11] Blackstone asked to keep Sharp's manuscript for two weeks and ended up retaining it for four months. On February 20, 1769, he returned it, attached to a curt note.[12]

Miffed that Sharp had cited Lord Holt and the first edition's claim that negroes became free as soon as they stepped into England, Blackstone complained that he had altered the *Commentaries* because it "had been misunderstood both by yourself and others." He went on: "[I] never peremptorily said, that 'the Master hath acquired any right to the perpetual service of John or Thomas,' or that the Negro did owe such service to his American master. I only say that if he did that obligation is not dissolved by his coming to England and turning Christian. It did not become me to pronounce decisively on a matter which is *adhuc sub judice*: whatever the inclination of my own Opinion might be." Sharp inserted Blackstone's explanation nearly verbatim into the final version of the *Representation*.[13]

The potential for mischief in applying the law of villeinage law to black slavery was so great that Sharp devoted a great deal of the *Representation* to denigrating any relationship between the two. At least Sharp and the doctor saw eye-to-eye on this for, in his letter to Sharp, Blackstone agreed that villeinage was "a thing totally distinct from that of negro slavery." Sharp had written:

I have frequently had the mortification to hear very sensible and learned persons refer to the old villeinage doctrines, in their examination of the present question, concerning property in slaves; and from thence they have insinuated a sort of legal propriety in the pretensions of the modern West-India slave holders, as if they could suppose, that a state of slavery might still exist in this kingdom according to law. This has happened not only in private conversation, but also lately in open court, and is therefor become a matter of very serious consideration.[14]

Blackstone discussed villeins in the *Commentaries'* section on "things" rather than on "persons"; the Normans had placed villeins in "a kind of estate superior to downright slavery, but inferior to every other kind of condition," so that they "could not leave their lord without his permission; but if they ran away, or were purloined from him, might be claimed and recovered by action, like beasts or other chattels."[15] But he cautioned Sharp: "[T]he only argument that can be drawn from it against you, is, that as villeinage was allowed by the common law, it cannot be argued that a state of servitude is absolutely unknown to and inconsistent therewith."

As far as Sharp was concerned, anyone who relied on villeinage to support black slavery implicitly conceded that "neither the present laws in force, nor the present constitution and customs of England, can afford . . . the least justification for such opinions, or they would not be obliged to go so far back for precedents." He warned those seeking to revive villeinage in order to enslave English blacks that they jeopardized every Englishman's freedom. "The pernicious effects of reviving the doctrines of villeinage, at first, perhaps would be felt by none but the poor wretched Negroes themselves, and therefore, the subsequent evils may (like objects at a distance) seem less, at first sight, than they really are." But if blacks could be enslaved on authority of villeinage, their English-born children and ensuring the flood of mulattos would also be condemned to perpetual bondage and that would only be the beginning: "[A] foundation would be laid for a more dangerous vassalage, in which the poorer sort, even of the original English themselves, might in time be involved." If a rich landowner detained some peasant born on his land as his villein, it would be nearly impossible, and quite expensive, for her to prove she was free. The customs and doctrines that supported villeinage were unnatural, unreasonable, and immoral. Because reason, morality, and the law of nature beat at the heart of the common law, villeinage was null and void, and Sharp applauded customs that favored liberty and restrained villeinage.

Sharp saw the rise and fall of villeinage as a dramatic struggle in which the detestable custom had been confronted by a common law determined first to cabin it, then stamp it out. The heroes of this tale were "the ancient lawyers" of the middle and late Middle Ages who had worshipped liberty and created, then stubbornly defended, one legal roadblock after another, undermining villeinage at every opportunity, even at feudalism's height just after the Conquest:

> The King's courts in those ancient times were so manifestly disposed to favor liberty, that is seemed to be their endeavor to render the [rights of the lord] as difficult and precarious as possible, when, at the same, the villein's suit [for liberty] was indulged with as many advantages as the lawyers could well venture to give it, considering the severity of the times in which they lived. Nay, their humanity and justice even outwent the temper of those rude times.

As the common lawyers and judges slowly gained the upper hand, Parliament, controlled by the barons whose livelihoods depended upon villeinage, enacted statutes to hobble the ability of villeins to obtain their freedom. But "the ancient patriotic lawyers" interpreted these statutes nearly out of existence: "At length, by the repeated discouragements which villeinage met with in the courts of law . . . this detestable practice of holding men in an involuntary state of bondage became entirely out of use in this kingdom, insomuch, that a single villein . . . has not been known for many ages."

At the end of the seventh decade of the eighteenth century, wrote Sharp, "every lawyer who is a well-wisher to the civil liberties of mankind [should] take the first opportunity of disclaiming and publicly professing against all doctrines which may tend to the introduction of the West India Slavery, or the least right or property in the involuntary servitude of our fellow-subjects." He was appalled that the professional descendants of yesteryear's freedom-loving legal champions could produce a Talbot and a Yorke. What, he asked, could possibly "excuse the very different behaviour of our modern lawyers in attempting to revive the oppressive doctrines of villeinage which their honest predecessors always laboured to abolish?" Some modern lawyers remained "as thoroughly sensible of the injustice and impropriety of tolerating Slavery in this kingdom, as their predecessors," Sharp conceded. "Nevertheless those gentlemen of the law, whose contrary doctrines I am unfortunately obliged to oppose are numerous, eminent, and learned: and some of them (with respect to the proceedings of a late trial) have so far prevailed, as to give me every just reason to dread a confirmation by judicial authority of those doctrines against which I contend."

Sharp continued his argument with a comment about local customs in the Indies: "The only excuse which can be alledged for tolerating this iniquitous and disgraceful bondage, even in the West Indies, is a presumed necessity, arising (as interested persons tell us) from the excessive heat of the climates where our colonies are situated; but as the said supposed necessity is merely local, so ought to be the toleration of it likewise, if we might allow, that any necessity whatsoever can justify it." The customs and laws of the colonial plantations were as different from England's as were their climates, "which, in truth, is so many degrees, that the least right or title to the inheritance of the old English villeinage cannot possibly be admitted." As the only thing that plantation slavery and villeinage had in common was their "cruel oppression and apparent immorality . . . it will certainly be a stain of everlasting infamy on the present lawyers (as well as on the age in which they live), if they do not demonstrate the unlawfulness of admitting the least claim of property in the persons of men by this very similarity."

The *Representation* offered some decidedly odd, and occasionally erroneous, legal arguments. For one, Sharp warned everyone involved, however indirectly, in the Jonathan Strong kidnapping—"1st. The buyer, and 2ndly, The seller of the Negro; 3rdly and 4thly, The two city officers, who apprehended and confined him; 5thly, The notary-public who drew up, witnessed, or negotiated the bill of sale, and 6thly, The master of the West India ship, who demanded him in the name of the buyer, in order to transport him beyond the seas"—that they had violated the 1679 Habeas Corpus Act, which prohibited sending prisoners beyond the seas. The prescribed penalty was a stupendous minimum 500-pound fine, as well as treble costs and permanent disability from holding office in England.[16] Sharp assured that he was inclined not to prosecute anyone who acknowledged his errors, in writing, and gave sufficient security for his future good behavior so that others with the same inclinations might be deterred "and for the vindication and right understanding of English liberty."

But the 1679 Act didn't apply to Kerr or any of the others.[17] In the centuries immediately following the Conquest, habeas corpus was merely a Crown judge's order to a sheriff, or perhaps a private person, usually made in conjunction with some more powerful writ, to produce someone in court. It wasn't until the middle of the fourteenth century that a command to explain the cause of the detention could be included.[18] Only in the sixteenth century did common law courts begin using the writ to attack imprisonments ordered by the executive.[19] By 1670, the Chief Justice of the King's Bench could write that habeas corpus was "the most usual remedy by which a man is restored again to his liberty, if he have been against the law deprived of it," either by public or private action, anywhere English law and power could reach.[20]

Habeas corpus writs were not intended to punish, but were a straightforward demands that courts summarily remedy unlawful restraints of liberty. They could not be used to decide property disputes, and were neither criminal nor civil. Anyone showing probable cause that he or she was unlawfully restrained could use them. They were heard *ex parte*, meaning the petitioners, or someone applying for them, went before judges without the persons accused of illegal restraint attending, or even necessarily knowing that a writ was being sought.

This common law writ had its deficiencies, unconscionable delays in releasing prisoners, refusals to issue between court terms, and shipping prisoners overseas to escape the jurisdiction of British courts (Lord

Chancellor Clarendon favored Tangier). After passage of the 1679 Act, major defects remained, especially the inability to investigate the truth of a writ's return and the Act's application almost entirely to those committed on "criminal or supposed criminal matters."[21] Jonathan Strong had been held in the Poultry Compter while awaiting shipment to the Jamaican slave markets. He was not accused of a crime, and Sir Robert Kite said he was guilty of no offence, so the 1679 Act didn't apply to him.

Beginning in the seventeenth century, writs of habeas corpus were occasionally used to challenge military impressments, bankruptcy jailings, and enslavements.[22] The 1777 case of Millichip, a Thames waterman, suggests these suits were still uncommon. When Millichip was pressed by a gang into the Royal Navy, London's Lord Mayor asked the Admiralty for the man's release. After a refusal, the city solicitor obtained a writ of habeus corpus from Lord Mansfield. Millichip was released, then, two weeks later, pressed again.

"You will be surprised," Mansfield said,

> when I say, that I believe this is the first return to a writ of *habeus corpus* upon a man's being pressed, that ever existed. I never met one. . . . We are upon untrodden ground. . . . It is a late time of day, indeed, never to have had a precedent. But it is a matter of great consequence to the public service to put it in a right way; that whoever ought to be pressed may be pressed without litigation; and whoever ought not to be pressed, and are pressed, may have a speedy way of getting their liberty.

Only Mansfield seemed to have a good idea how to proceed. He solicited the opinions of the Attorney General, barrister James Wallace, and his puisne judges, Willes, Aston, and Ashurst. Finally, he suggested that the Crown lawyers

> "return the writ of habeas corpus, that Millichip, being a liveryman serving upon the river Thames, had been impressed into his majesty's service, having no legal exemption." That, his Lordship said, would give the

gentleman on the other side an opportunity of suggesting, that he had an exemption, such as the charter of the City, constant, invariable, immemorial usage, or whatever pleas might be alleged. This being entered on record, might lead to a complete investigation of the whole matter in view to which proposal all parties seemed to acquiesce.[23]

In 1758, the House of Commons might have extended the 1679 Act to Jonathan Strong and Millichip, both imprisoned for reasons other than crime. But Lords Mansfield and Hardwicke fiercely opposed any alterations in the House of Lords, and these would not be enacted until 1816.[24] Thus, Strong was left to whatever protection common law writ of habeas corpus might give him, and this did not include either damages or penalties for Kerr or any of the others involved.[25]

In an even shakier argument, Sharp claimed that Strong could not be Kerr's property, as a horse, dog, or cat was, for the law regarded those domestic animals as having a base nature. But Strong was no worse than a wild beast, which the law declared had a noble nature. Born free, Strong had parents with "as much right to their natural liberty, as the wild animals with which their native country (Africa) abounds."

[T]herefore if this negro should unjustly be denied all human privileges, yet, as he is not of a base nature, he ought at least to enjoy as much privilege as bears, hawks, or any creature ferae naturae, which have been taken and made tame: because in these we have only a property . . . so long as they remain tame, and do not regain their natural liberty, and have not a custom of returning; for otherwise they cannot be claimed as an absolute property (such as one has in "hens, geese, peacocks, &c.").

This was in line with Blackstone, who insisted that, by natural and divine right, humans had an absolute property interest in any animal they "occupied," which he defined as "taking possession of those things which before belonged to nobody," and that included every wild animal not reserved to the king.[26] If a wild animal managed to regain its natural liberty, all property interests in it were lost.[27] It was a felony to steal occupied animals fit for food, but not those kept solely "for pleasure, curiosity, or whim, as dogs, bears, cats, apes, parrots, and singing-birds," because their value was not intrinsic, but rested on the feelings of the owner.[28]

But wild creatures enjoyed no privileges Sharp wanted for Jonathan Strong. Foreign travelers, ambassadors, and royalty had for centuries been treated to the English spectacle of bear-baiting, in which a de-fanged, declawed, pathetic bear was tethered to a stake at the Bear Garden in London, at a palace, village fair, or alehouse yard, and set upon by dogs, one at a time or all at once, until the field was a bloody mess.[29] The century before, elephant white ivory had been grouped with Negro "black ivory" as "commodities" over which the New Royal African Company held an import monopoly, both being treated the same in law. Traders scoured Africa for tusks to turn into billiard balls, combs, business cards, and letter openers; they used black ivory to barter for white and to haul the white to the coast for sale, each pound of white finally costing a life of the black.[30]

If Strong really was akin to a wild animal, it had been no crime to re-move him from nature and no felony to steal him from Kerr. If he es-caped, he regained his natural freedom, but only until re-occupied. This implied that Strong's capture in Africa had been legal and Kerr had every right to occupy him. Once he escaped, he regained his natural lib-erty. Once occupied again, Strong belonged to his occupier, Kerr or anyone else. Sharp's conclusion that "it must appear, that the plea of private property in a Negro, as in a horse or dog, is very insufficient and defective" simply didn't follow.

By May 1769, *A Representation* was complete. Sharp presented a copy to Dr. Blackstone, who blandly offered his best wishes in the third person: "Mr. Blackstone presents his compliments to Mr. Sharp and is much obliged to him for the valuable present which he found on his table on his return to town. He sincerely wishes him success in his hu-mane undertaking."[31] Over the next eighteen months, Sharp circulated about twenty manuscript drafts of the *Representation* among London legal lights, "particularly among the Professors of the Law," whom he wished to persuade and hoped would carry his arguments into court, and gathered encouragement and support while he continued to troll for the test case that would lay the problem of English slavery to rest forever.

Meanwhile, Kerr's suit continued. The rules of the Court of King's Bench required that cases be concluded within three terms of being filed. Kerr's lawyers failed to advance his case for eight. Sharp's *Representation* may have intimidated them, as some claim, but this is unlikely. Sharp frankly admitted the number, fame, and power of his opponents. With one exception, we have no evidence that lawyers were impressed by Sharp's legal reasoning or offered any substantive assistance. Sharp's lack of legal training showed, and it would be unsurprising if the lawyers reading the *Representation* thought his arguments a bit simplistic or even off the mark.

The exception was Francis Hargrave. Educated at Oxford, he had been called to the bar of Lincoln's Inn in 1764, the year before Jonathan Strong bumped into Granville Sharp. On May 17, 1769, the hawk-nosed, curly-haired, twenty-eight-year-old Hargrave wrote Sharp that he was "very much obliged . . . for the favor of [his] ingenious & elaborate considerations on the toleration of slavery in this country" and hoped, through a second reading, to imprint them "more strongly on [Hargrave's] mind." Hargrave had been pondering slavery, but other than the rough outline he had sent Sharp, which he now thought so imperfect that "he [was] really ashamed of having troubled Mr. Sharp with it," Hargrave "had not had an opportunity of putting into form his ideas of the subject; but if at any future time he shall reduce them into writing, he shall be happy in having an opportunity of communicating them to Mr. Sharp."[32] Sharp would hear from him again on the eve of the *Somerset* trial.

Every lawyer knows someone like Kerr, an enraged hothead who sues, becomes obsessed with some other injury, or comes to resent his suit, and the lawyers bringing it, for consuming so much time and money. When nothing happened for eight terms, the case was dismissed and Kerr ordered to pay treble costs, almost 20 pounds. By 1774, when Sharp received the money, Jonathan Strong had been dead a year (he was twenty-five when he died), and *A Representation* and the *Somerset* case had vaulted Sharp to the first rank of black champions. In 1770, slaves around England were seeking his help, Sharp was doing what he could, for as many as he could, while sifting their complaints for the next test case. Now Thomas Lewis emerged.

CHAPTER 6

The Next Test: Thomas Lewis

Being wicked and evil disposed persons and
devising and intending to violently seize one Thomas Lewis
and to transport him to the Island of Jamaica in parts
beyond the sea and there wickedly intending to sell
and dispose of him as a slave.

Middlesex Grand Jury indictment of Robert Stapylton,
Aaron Armstrong, and John Maloney, July 10, 1770

IN THE EVENING DARK of Monday, July 2, 1770, Thomas Lewis was seized near the Chelsea docks in the parish of St. Luke, beside the garden of the mother of the renowned biologist, Sir Joseph Banks, whose idea to feed breadfruit to West Indies slaves would later cause the British Admiralty to send Captain Bligh and the *H.M.S. Bounty* to Tahiti. Mrs. Banks's servants excitedly informed her that Lewis had been dragged aboard the *Captain Seward,* anchored in the Thames. She immediately brought the news to Granville Sharp, whose reputation for saving blacks was now well known, and offered to underwrite the prosecution of the kidnappers if the *Captain Seward* could be stopped.

Both knew every moment counted. Sharp and Mrs. Banks hurried to Justice Welsh, Jonathan Strong's judge, and obtained a warrant from the Rotation Office demanding Lewis's return. Sharp rushed the warrant to Gravesend, enlisting the mayor's aid, in hope of intercepting the ship as it was carried down the Thames, before it could reach the open sea. Because the *Captain Seward* had been cleared for sailing when the warrant arrived, its captain felt free to ignore it, and the ship continued toward the Downs.

Next day, Thursday, July 4, Sharp appealed for a writ of habeus corpus to the Lord Mayor of London, to Justice Welsh again, to Justice Willes on the Court of King's Bench, and to Baron Smith. He got it. By Saturday, July 6, one of Mrs. Banks's servants had arrived with the writ at Spithead, where he delivered it to the appropriate officer. This was truly Lewis's last chance. The *Captain Seward* was already under way, pushing deeper into the sea, though very slowly, for the winds that day were all wrong off the Downs. Abolitionist Thomas Clarkson set the scene in his history of the abolition of the slave trade:

> In two or three hours [the ship] would have been out of sight; but just at this critical moment the writ of habeas corpus arrived on board. The officer, who served it on the captain, saw the miserable African chained at the mainmast, bathed in tears, and casting a last mournful look on the land of freedom, which was fast receding from his sight. The captain, on receiving the writ, became outrageous; but knowing the serious consequences of resisting the law of the land, he gave up his prisoner, whom the officer carried safe, but now crying for joy, to the shore.[1]

By Sunday, July 7, Lewis was back in London where, from that day forward, he conducted himself as if he were free. His purported master, Robert Stapylton, who was responsible for Lewis's kidnapping, never challenged him on it, never even filed a return to Sharp's writ of habeas corpus, and we don't know why. Perhaps he didn't anticipate that Sharp would seek a habeas corpus and, when it suddenly appeared, calculated that surrender was the cheaper response.[2]

Neither Sharp nor Mrs. Banks, however, had any intention of letting the matter rest. With the assistance of Mrs. Banks's solicitor, a Mr. Lucas, they initiated a criminal prosecution against Stapylton and two watermen, Aaron Armstrong and John Maloney, who had assisted in the kidnapping. On Tuesday, July 10, a Middlesex grand jury indicted the three men on four counts. First, the defendants, "being wicked and evil disposed persons and devising and intending to violently seize one Thomas Lewis and to transport him to the Island of Jamaica in parts beyond the sea and there wickedly intending to sell and dispose of him as a slave," were charged with assaulting Lewis on July 2, 1770, in Chelsea, violently seizing him and forcing him into a boat on the River Thames and "cruelly and inhumanely gagg[ing] the mouth of the said Thomas Lewis," and imprisoning him without legal authority and against his will for seventy-six hours, thus causing him "great bodily pain and anguish of mind." Second, the defendants were charged with unlawfully assembling and making a riotous assault on Lewis. Third, they were charged with assaulting him; and fourth, of falsely imprisoning him.[3]

These indictments were handed down, Sharp wrote, "without the least demur or doubt on account of the plaintiff's complexion, or idea of private property."[4] Had he succeeded in spiriting Lewis to Jamaica, Stapylton might have exposed himself to the "very heinous crime" of kidnapping, which Blackstone had defined as "the forcible abduction or stealing away of a man, woman, or child from their own country, and sending them into another."[5] On the offense of false imprisonment, Blackstone gave this opinion: "The most atrocious degree [was] sending any subject of this realm onto parts beyond the seas, whereby he is deprived of the friendly assistance of the laws to redeem him from such his captivity."[6] But the defendants claimed Lewis was Stapylton's property and therefore, like other property, he could be seized and removed to the West Indies if Stapylton so wished.

Having defended Lisle's prosecution, Sharp knew how unpleasant and stressful a lawsuit could be and how much a prosecution might cost Mrs. Banks. Every paper filed, every person who handled every paper, as well as the hall keepers, door keepers, bar keepers, tipstaffs, jurymen, clerks, criers, and marshalls, cost, sometimes shillings, sometimes pounds. Then there were the lawyers. We don't know exactly what an eighteenth-century English lawyer charged, but a couple guineas, 2 pounds, or 20 shillings, appeared to be roughly the going rate for a run-of-the-mill felony case. This was at a time when a laborer earned from 10 to 12 shillings a week, a journeyman in a lesser-paid profession such as masonry earned about 15 shillings a week, and a journeyman printer earned about 24 shillings a week.[7] In a 1779 forgery case prosecuted by the Bank of England, Justice Willes, of the Court of King's Bench, ordered the bank to pay the indigent defendant ten guineas to furnish him with a solicitor and defense counsel.[8] The anonymous author of the 1773 *Attorney's Compleat Guide to the Court of King's Bench, Containing the Whole Modern Practice of the Court* warned: "The practitioner, in drawing his brief, cannot be too concise, for he preserves perspicuity."[9] Not to mention his client's funds for, according to the *Compleat Guide:* "It is now usual to give your leading counsel . . . a guinea per sheet, if a matter of importance, and tried by a special jury. This mode of feeing is extended sometimes to five or ten guineas. The junior counsel is usually paid half a guinea every brief sheet."[10] It was no wonder that, in the eighteenth century, lawsuits had become the privilege of the affluent.

Sharp repeatedly urged the solicitor Lucas to offer Stapylton a compromise. To Mrs. Banks, Sharp wrote: "I shall use my best endeavors to intimidate the defendants and their attorney, by every fair method and argument." He could devise "that they [might] be induced to submit to the accommodation proposed."[11] All Stapylton need do was publicly acknowledge that Thomas Lewis was not his slave, give sufficient security to keep the peace, and pay all outstanding charges. But Stapylton would have none of it, and switched lawyers. On July 16, Sharp learned the new lawyer had asked the Court of King's Bench, which had general superintendence over all inferior criminal courts, to remove the case from the sessions to itself. That would increase Mrs. Banks's costs.

Sharp also had Lewis inform the Court that he was not "desirous that the law should be enforced in its utmost rigour, which he apprehends would absolutely ruin the several offenders. He only wishes that this Court may make them truly sensible of the heinousness of their offence, and oblige them to make public acknowledgment thereof, that others may be deterred from committing such unlawful and dangerous outrages."[12] But nothing budged Stapylton, and Sharp relayed this news to Mrs. Banks: "Stapylton and his attorney still seem obstinately determined to stand trial. I am very uneasy about the risk of a trial," Sharp went on, "especially as you have already incurred such heavy charges: and as I am chiefly to blame for this continuation of expenses, by being too easily persuaded to consent to an indictment." He offered what little money he had from his work in the ordnance department. "[M]oney," he said, "has no value but when it is well spent; and I am thoroughly convinced, that no part of my little pittance of ready money can ever be better bestowed than in an honest endeavor to crush a groaning oppression, which is not only shocking to humanity, but in time must prove even dangerous to the community."[13] Mrs. Banks declined the offer.

The case was ordered tried before Lord Mansfield in February 1771. It was Hilary Term, one of four judicial terms that together lasted just three months of the year. Michaelmas Term, which began November 16, and Hilary Term, which commenced on January 23, each lasted three weeks and a day. Easter Term commenced the Wednesday fortnight after Easter and ran three weeks and six days. Trinity Term began immediately after Trinity Sunday and ran to the Wednesday, a fortnight after it began, unless that Wednesday happened to land on June 24, in which event it ended the following day.

The Court of King's Bench was the only Westminster central court able to conduct original criminal trials, and its jurisdiction, at least since the 1720s, had been limited to misdemeanors, of which it saw a few dozen each year.[14] Criminal trials comprised a minuscule part of Manfield's Westminster docket, indeed a small portion of English trials in general. In London and Middlesex county, trials of felonies, those crimes punishable by death or transport to the colonies, and many serious misdemeanors, were usually held at the Old Bailey in central London.

The most common misdemeanors over which Mansfield presided at the Court of King's Bench were assault and false imprisonment, precisely the crimes with which Stapylton was charged.[15] Mansfield was experienced in trying criminal cases, for the four judges of the Court of King's Bench rotated at the Old Bailey for ten of the first eleven years he served as Chief Justice. In addition, all twelve central court judges trudged into the countryside "on assize" every Lent and summer, moving from town to town, trying every sort of allegation of criminal wrongdoing. Mansfield was widely seen as fair to the criminal defendants who were paraded before him, though according to Lord Campbell, "he did not allow the guilty much chance of escaping, and, for the sake of example, he was somewhat severe in the punishments he inflicted."[16] Of the 110 known criminal trials over which he presided at the Old Bailey, thirty ended in acquittal, eighty in conviction, with Mansfield sentencing nearly half of the convicted, thirty-nine defendants, to death.

Sharp told Mrs. Banks that he had instructed solicitor Lucas quickly to prepare a brief for their barrister, also named Lucas; he wrote: "[A]s it is the safest way to have two counsel, our next step must be to retain a proper person to take the lead in the Court of King's Bench."[17] This lead was the man who would run the trial. Preeminent candidates were Serjeant John Glynn and John Dunning. They knew each other well, Glynn, as we have seen, having given the young Dunning the professional break of his life after suffering one of his recurring bouts of gout in 1762 and transferring his files to Dunning. Both were outspoken political enemies of Lord Mansfield in the House of Commons.

Some claim Sharp chose Dunning, others say it was Mrs. Banks. She is the more likely, for Dunning had, just two autumns before, advised Sharp to pay close attention to Dr. Blackstone when he said they should view Jonathan Strong as similar to an apprentice bound by an implied contract for perpetual service. Once chosen, however, Dunning abandoned his proslavery position and transformed himself into a powerful antislavery advocate.

He was no longer Solicitor General. The end had recently come, on January 9, 1770, when Dunning spoke in the House of Commons against the government, then voted for a bill urged by Mansfield's nemesis, Lord Chatham, that demanded a general inquiry into the cause of English discontent. Mansfield so hated Chatham, who disliked lawyers and nearly everything about the Royal Law Courts that, when Chatham collapsed eight years later during a speech on the floor of the House of Lords, nearly every peer but Mansfield rushed to him, and

Mansfield failed to attend the funeral. When Chatham's bill failed, Dunning resigned his post. Blackstone was offered it, but refused.

Lord Camden, then the Lord Chancellor, also stood with Chatham against the Duke of Grafton's government. Mansfield advised the government to sack Camden and he was dismissed. Then no politically acceptable substitute could easily be found. The Duke of Grafton and King George III several times asked Mansfield to assume the post and each time he refused. After he demanded that the Chancellery be run by commission until a suitable man could be appointed, Mansfield ended up acting as Chancellor in all but name.

Lord Campbell would write that Dunning had been the best candidate for Lord Chancellor. But, because he was "enemy both to the Chief Justice and to his principles," Dunning was never offered the post.[18] Dunning's act was courageous, and taken with full knowledge it would probably destroy his chance for that place on the bench that almost certainly would have been his, for three-quarters of the Attorneys General and Solicitors General between 1680 and 1819 were made judges, with nearly three-fifths being appointed to a senior position, such as Chief Justice or Lord Chancellor.[19]

Despite their enormous political differences, when Dunning first appeared in Westminster Hall after resigning as Solicitor General, Mansfield generously announced that, out of respect for his former position as Solicitor General and because of Dunning's high business rank, he would, from that time on, call on Dunning immediately after he recognized any King's Counsel, the King's Serjeants, and the Recorder of London.[20] Courtroom lawyers generally addressed the court by order of rank, the two highest King's Serjeants taking precedence over all. The Attorney General followed, then the Solicitor General, followed by the other King's Serjeants, wearing gowns with black lace and tufts. The King's Counsels, whose rank was professional, not social, were next, followed by the Serjeants-at-Law, whose rank was socially equivalent to a knighthood or an academic doctorate; their badge was the white silk or line coif, or covering, over their wigs, and in court they wore long blue-and-white robes and fur hoods.

Fewer than a thousand serjeants were created over six hundred years, beginning in the fourteenth century; Chaucer mentions one in his *Canterbury Tales*. They were made by judges, after Crown nomination; barristers emerged from the Inns of Court. Only serjeants could appear before the Court of Common Pleas; from their ranks, all England's judges were formally chosen, though, by the seventeenth century, this requirement had become largely symbolic, with many, including Lord Mansfield, being invested as a serjeant, then a judge on the same day. By Mansfield's time, the actual class of serjeants had fallen so low that he was said to laugh when presiding over the elaborate ceremony that created them.[21] Between 1740 and 1800, not one practicing serjeant was made a senior judge, as opposed to seventeen King's Counsels; and only ten gained even junior judgeships, compared to seventy-eight KCs. Finally came the ordinary barristers, such as Dunning. All the King's Counsel, serjeants, and barristers knew each other well, for not more than two dozen or so lawyers, out of a total of several hundred in the Greater London area, regularly practiced before the Court of King's Bench, and there were probably not more than six hundred practicing barristers in the entire country.[22]

In maturity, Dunning would confide to Sir Joshua Reynolds his long-held admiration of Lord Mansfield: "[I] well remember when I used to attend the court of law, as a student, for instructions; and always made a point of going whenever I understood Murray was to speak. This was as great a treat to me, Sir Joshua, as a sight of the finest painting by Titian or Raffaele would be to you! Sometimes when we were leaving the court, we would hear the cry, 'Murray is up,' and forthwith we rushed back, as if to a play or other entertainment."[23] He thought Mansfield "exceedingly difficult to answer . . . when he was wrong, and impossible when he was right."[24] Yet Dunning was not cowed by him and was one of the few barristers confident enough to challenge Mansfield's habit of reading of newspapers and books during oral argument. Dunning would stop. "Pray go on, Mr. Dunning," Mansfield would say, to which Dunning would reply, "I beg your pardon, my Lord, but I fear I shall interrupt your Lordship's more important business. I will wait until your Lordship has leisure to attend to my client and his humble advocate."[25]

However, Dunning despised Mansfield's handling of seditious libel jury trials and would prove a stout opponent, first of the coercive policies of Lord North against the American colonies, then the war itself, and especially Britain's hiring of Hessian and Hanoverian troops to war against the colonists, all policies Mansfield strongly endorsed. Undoubtedly Mansfield, trying cases by day in the gloom of Westminster Hall, crossing swords with Lord Chatham by candlelight in the House of Lords, was central to the government's decision to snub Dunning for the post of Lord Chancellor, and Dunning knew it. In December 1770, incensed by the manner in which Mansfield had conducted one seditious libel trial, Dunning rose in the House of Commons and charged Mansfield with having "committed a bold robbery on justice" through "[h]ints, and looks, and half words . . . by skulking and concealment."[26] Dunning joined Serjeant John Glynn's motion to inquire into the conduct of the judges. As this parliamentary fight raged, Sharp and Mrs. Banks had to decide who would take the lead in the trial of Thomas Lewis before Lord Mansfield. They chose John Dunning.

CHAPTER 7

Lord Mansfield

The learned judge before whom this cause will come, is said to have given an opinion, formerly, that Negro slaves continue such even when brought to England, or something to that effect. But I have too high an opinion of his Lordship's Justice and good sense to conceive that he will still persist in that sentiment.

Granville Sharp,
Trial memorandum written for barrister John Dunning, February 20, 1771

ON TUESDAY, FEBRUARY 19, 1771, Granville Sharp and Thomas Lewis traveled to Westminster Hall for Robert Stapylton's trial. As Lewis and one of his lawyers retired to a nearby coffee house, a press gang, commanded by a Royal Navy lieutenant, burst in, seized the black man, and would have carried him away had they not been stopped by his lawyer.[1] We don't know how they were stopped. If they were physically stopped, it was unlikely to have been by stubby, pasty, weak, infirm John Dunning. If they were persuaded to abandon their impressment of Lewis, or were threatened with some Draconian legal writ, it may have been he. Whoever it was, Dunning was irate. The trial was rescheduled for the next morning.

Minutes before the trial began, Sharp took a seat in a nearby coffee house and sketched out some arguments for Dunning.[2] Sharp was certain that Stapylton's only possible defense was that Thomas Lewis was his chattel, with the pecuniary value, Sharp estimated, of a "good horse," 30 to 50 pounds. Echoing John Locke's argument that "every Man has a property in his own Person," Sharp wrote that an African, being human, has natural title to his own person.[3] Any man's legal right to himself towered above any master's pecuniary claim, for "surely [an African's] Liberty to him is inestimable; at least the English law presumes it so." Sharp conceded a master suffered a wrong when denied his property, but the alternative inflicted a worse wrong upon the slave. "[E]very claim of property is absolutely unjust . . . if it interferes or is inconsistent with that natural and equitable claim to personal security which the Law of this Kingdom hath always favored." Sharp believed Stapylton's counsel would never dare "to venture to contradict these maxims because such a behavior would necessarily draw upon them . . . just censure and contempt."

Sharp then joined Lewis, the three prosecuting lawyers, barristers Dunning, Lucas, and Davenport, and defense counsel Walker, in Westminster Hall. Of the defendants, only Stapylton appeared. Sharp, hopeful the case would finally test the legality of English slavery, hired a professional stenographer, William Blanchard, to take down the proceedings in shorthand and transcribe them. Mansfield, ruddy, round-faced, short even for his day, dark eyes bright and piercing, took his place on the bench in the Hall's southeast corner, presiding beneath three of the thirteen stone statues of British kings, from Edward the Confessor to Richard II, that had been placed within niches in the south wall four centuries before. The courtroom was not large, a square with sides of about twenty-five feet.

Sharp knew that Mansfield's view of slavery, moral and legal, stood to be the most important in the realm. In his brief memorandum to Dunning, Sharp gave this advice:

The learned judge before whom this cause will come, is said to have given an opinion, formerly, that Negro slaves continue such even when brought to England, or something to that effect. But I have too high an opinion of his Lordship's Justice and good sense to conceive that he will still persist in that sentiment, if the case is fairly stated and compared with [the maxims of the common law Sharp sketched].

Mansfield was the first Scot to become a powerful English lawyer, legislator, politician, and judge. He was convinced early in his judicial career that he could achieve justice only when equity, which demands uprightness, rationality, common sense, good conscience, high principle, fairness, and natural justice, leavened the often hidebound, rigid, absolute, fragmented, and unjust common law. He had studied Roman and Continental law which, like the law of his native land, were marinated in equity. Watching Lord Chancellor Hardwicke dispense equity over many years had transformed him. Once he reached the bench, he slowly refashioned the entire field of commercial law by insisting that parties act in good faith. He often prodded juries to reach for equity in their verdicts.[4] As a young chief justice, he once listened to a lawyer cite case after case on the meaning of the words with which an old woman had filled her will. "Pray, sir," Mansfield asked, "do you think that this old woman ever heard of these cases? And, if not, what construction do you think common sense points to?" He proceeded to construe the will as common sense required.[5] In deciding a copyright case, he wrote, "[t]he whole must finally resolve in this question, whether it is agreeable to moral justice and fitness," and he believed that mercantile disputes ought to turn "upon natural justice and not upon the niceties of the law."[6]

He possessed vast, remarkable, and unparalleled judicial, legislative, and executive experience, as Chief Justice of the King's Bench, leader in the Houses of both Commons and Lords, and King's minister (in some years serving in several capacities simultaneously). He was confident he could cut through Gordian knots and he inspired such confidence in his fellow judges that, in the hundreds of reported cases in which he took part, during more than thirty-two years as Chief Justice, there are recorded just twenty dissents, or disagreements, by his colleagues on the Court of King's Bench to his decisions.[7]

For all this he became, for some, notorious. In its infancy and before it petrified, the common law had been more than a little equitable. As it grew rigid, it pulled apart from equity and the two became provinces of different, ferociously competing, courts. The common lawyers came to despise equity, "a roguish thing," groused the seventeenth-century legal historian, John Selden: "For law we have a measure, know what to trust to. Equity is according to the conscience of him that is chancellor, and as that is larger or narrower, so is equity." The common lawyers "would tolerate a 'mischief' [a failure of substantial justice in a particular case] rather than an 'inconvenience' [a breach of legal principle]."[8]

The virulent anonymous writer, "Junius," raged against Mansfield in a letter, published November 14, 1770, just two months before Stapylton's trial: "Instead of those certain, positive rules by which the judgment of a court of law should invariably be determined, you have fondly introduced your own unsettled notions of equity and substantial justice. . . . The Court of King's Bench becomes a court of equity; and the judge, instead of consulting strictly the law of the land, refers only to the wisdom of the court, and the purity of his own conscience."[9] Junius's wasn't a crank opinion. Thomas Jefferson shared it. In a 1785 letter, Jefferson wrote:

> Mansfield, a man of the clearest head & most seducing eloquence coming from a country where the powers of the common law & chancery are united in the same court, has been able . . . to persuade the courts of common law to revise the practice of construing their text equitably. The object of former judges has been to render the law more & more certain. That of this personage to render it more incertain under pretence of rendering it more reasonable.[10]

Legal certainty derived from adherence to precedent, and Mansfield had little use for it. "The law of England," he would declare two years after freeing James Somerset, "would be a strange science indeed if it were decided upon precedents only. Precedents only serve to illustrate principles and to give them a fixed authority."[11] Precedent, seeing justice as furthering stability and certainty, and principle, understanding justice as doing what is right, were two of the three great visions of common law justice, with policy, justice as promoting the good, being the third.

Most judges invoke all three visions at some time. But the great judges, and Lord Mansfield was one of the greatest, may ignore precedent as anachronistic or seize on it for the purpose of molding it into something so different, modern, and moral, that their predecessors would scarcely recognize their contributions. At Mansfield's retirement, the Chief Justiceship passed to Lord Kenyon, and Mansfield was disgusted when Kenyon declared, "I cannot legislate, but by my industry I can discover what our predecessors have done, and I will servilely tread in their footsteps."[12]

For Mansfield, lawyer Daines Barrington's letter to Granville Sharp criticizing Sharp's inclination "to make the law what perhaps it *should be,* whereas being by profession a lawyer [he] rather endeavor[ed] to find out from precedent and authority, what the law *is,*" marked him a mediocre common lawyer, as Kenyon implicitly confessed to being a mediocre common law judge. Mansfield acknowledged the wisdom of his predecessors, but understood their rules had been laid in another age, for another age, another king, another world. Exuding self-confidence and intellectual vigor, he was unafraid to innovate and he was unafraid to correct his own errors. Concluding he had given an incorrect jury instruction, he once suggested to the losing party's lawyer that he seek a new trial. When other judges expressed surprise, Mansfield told them, "It is, after all, only showing the world that you are wiser today than you were yesterday."[13]

Believing the common law tended to "work itself pure," Mansfield routinely pared it to first principles which, if he thought them unjust, illogical, or anachronistic, he made just and up-to-date. A married woman living apart from her husband could be sued, he ruled, for breach of contract to protect unsuspecting merchants who thought they were doing business with single women from being cheated, despite the fact that, at common law, husband and wife were one, the husband. This was because "as the usages of society alter, the law must adapt itself to the various situations of mankind."[14]

Of course, he sometimes felt fettered by the past, writing Garrick that "[a] judge on the bench is now and then in your whimsical situation between Tragedy and Comedy, inclination drawing him one way and a long string of precedents the other."[15] "Whimsical," in the sense of comical or fanciful, aptly conveyed the slackness in the pull Mansfield sometimes felt between precedent and principle, rather like the difference in power between the forces of gravity and electromagnetism.[16] It did indeed take a long string of precedents before he felt himself bound. When the precedents were simply too numerous, consistent, or overpowering, he might grudgingly yield, for the time being, the issue being at the time "too fully settled to be . . . gone into."[17] Holdsworth would write: "There is no doubt that occasionally mansfield went beyond the province of the judge and usurped the province of the legislators."[18] More commonly, Mansfield whittled a precedent to its never-to-be-repeated facts or, when the weight of the cases was funneling him toward obvious injustice, might beg the lawyers to dig deeper into the reports; perhaps they had missed an important case. Or he challenged the accuracy of what they unearthed. It was generally agreed that court reporting was abysmal; indeed, the ineptness of some reporters, Lord Holt had growled, "will make us appear to posterity for a parcel of blockheads."[19] "We must not always rely on the words of reports, though under great names," Mansfield said. "Mr. Justice Blackstone's reports are not very accurate."[20]

His most powerful emotional clashes were between principle and policy, right versus good, the former often overwhelming the latter, unless Mansfield's natural sympathies for party, that is Whig, and Crown, which manifested clearly in the seditious libel cases, or free commerce overwhelmed it. He knew a great deal of ethics and philosophy, especially classical philosophy, and a superb classical education had taught him to speak and write a fluent and elegant Latin. He had been taken under the wing of Alexander Pope, a religiously tolerant Roman Catholic, who was often immersed in the classics and would celebrate Mansfield in classical verse (to Venus, "direct your doves, / There spread round Murray all your blooming loves"), will him a marble bust of Homer, make him an executor of his estate, and introduce him to many of the wits with whom, Samuel Johnson would observe, he drank champagne.[21] Mansfield routinely translated Horace, Sallust, and Cicero into English, then back into Latin, and memorized volumes of their writings. His full-length portrait, painted late in life, for which Mansfield wears the robes of the earldom he was granted in 1786, hangs at Oxford's Christ Church College; his right hand rests on a book by Cicero. Like many of his time, he was mesmerized by Cicero, whose orations he scrutinized and writings, especially on ethics, he commended to others. These were greatly to influence his ideal of the common law as the embodiment of moral right, and helped propel him to become the great, inventive, often daring, judge into which he evolved.[22]

At the center of Ciceronian ethics flowed mainstream Stoicism. Cicero's principal ethical writing, "On Duties," enjoined his son to hew closely and consistently to the universal and immutable nature that underlies natural justice and law: "True law is right reason in agreement with nature; it is of universal application, unchanging and everlasting."[23] Right was not just the highest, it was the only, good and "we ought invariably to aim at morally right courses of action."[24] Indeed, "we ought to aim at nothing other that what is right."[25] Advantage and right could never clash, for no wrong action could possibly be advantageous, and anyone who thought otherwise was deluded, mistaken, and immoral.[26]

This principle was at work in Mansfield's determination to rein in the bias against non-Anglicans, especially Catholics, who could not hold public office, say or attend Mass, or practice a profession. In 1748, the Corporation of London began levying fines of from 400 to 600 pounds on anyone who refused to serve as sheriff. For six straight years only Dissenters, who could not take the required oath to fill that post, were appointed. Naturally, they refused to serve and were fined so heavily that the Corporation was able to erect the new Mansion House in which Jonathan Strong would be freed by Sir Robert Kite.

In 1754, three Dissenters finally refused to pay and sued. The ensuing litigation lasted thirteen years, reaching the House of Lords, where Mansfield delivered a long and memorable speech.[27] "[T]here is no custom or usage, independent of positive law, which makes nonconformity a crime," he said (a similar statement would form the backbone of his *Somerset* judgment). "If someone reviles, subverts, or ridicules the eternal principles of natural religion," that person might be punished at common law. "But it cannot be shown from the principles of natural or revealed religion, that, independent of positive law, temporal punishments ought to be inflicted from mere opinions with respect to particular modes of worship." Legions of English bigots neither forgot nor forgave; when, in 1780, the Gordon Riots erupted in response to the passage of the Catholic Relief Act, a primary target of the mob was Mansfield's home in Bloomsbury Square.

In determining English slave law, Mansfield would have to confront the clash between principle and policy. He walked the streets, visited the wealthiest and most dignified homes, and knew there were blacks everywhere, many of whom belonged to friends and social equals, even to his betters. Setting them free in their thousands might be viewed as little more than judicial robbery and might make England, especially London, a magnet for every oppressed African in the English-speaking world. Such a judgment might burden the wards and intensify the economic struggle in an underclass already groaning beneath an influx of Irish.

If he cast his lot for principle over policy, he would have to reconcile, or choose between, paramount legal principles, the two most important rights possessed by the English people, personal, or bodily, liberty, the power of "moving one's person to whatsoever place one's own inclination may direct, without imprisonment or restraint, unless by due course of law," and the right to possess private property undisturbed.[28] Both were fundamental natural rights that Blackstone had discussed is his *Commentaries*.[29]

Slavery destroyed a man's bodily liberty. Yet, Blackstone had written, there was "nothing which so generally strikes the imagination, and engages the affections of mankind, as the right of property; or that sole and despotic dominion which one man claims and exercises over the external things of the world, in total exclusion of the right of any other individual in the universe."[30] This right came from God Himself and was "the only true and solid foundation of man's dominion over external things, whatever airy metaphysical notions may have been started by fanciful writers upon this subject."[31]

Almost two hundred years later, British philosopher Sir Isaiah Berlin would identify two of the most important senses of "liberty": "negative liberty," or "freedom from"; and "positive liberty," or "freedom to." "Freedom for the pike," Berlin said, "is death for the minnow."[32] As the American Civil War entered its bloody endgame, Abraham Lincoln would tell the nation that "[t]he shepherd drives the wolf from the sheep's throat, for which the sheep thanks the shepherd as a liberator, while the wolf denounces him for the same act as the destroyer of liberty, especially as the sheep is a black one."[33] Positive liberty was the right of the wolf to the sheep, negative liberty the sheep's right to be left alone. Liberty and property were at war in slavery, which might trouble Mansfield, if not in the abstract, then one slave at a time. But so did the destruction of the slaveholder's property rights. Sharp was going to require Mansfield to square that circle.

Mansfield's judicial philosophy suggested some antipathy to disturbing the slave trade. He harbored a keen, deep, and abiding interest in developing and rationalizing commercial law in general, especially British commercial law, and sought to adhere to merchants' customs whenever possible in order to fulfill their reasonable expectations and customs. Because slaves were treated as property, and property law was one area in which Mansfield desired certainty, he might be loathe to upset the commercial customs that the merchants had so carefully constructed.

He was a strong mercantilist, nearly a free-trade fanatic, going so far, as Solicitor General, to oppose a proposal put forth in the House of Commons to forbid English firms from insuring enemy ships in time of war! The once and future enemy, of course, was France. Murray argued that the French had become so reliant upon English insurance that they had never bothered to develop their own insurance industry. If the English stopped insuring the French, the French would be forced to create a home-grown insurance industry that they would carry on during peacetime, to the detriment of British commerce.[34]

Mansfield's Whiggish politics also bolstered judicial predispositions to maintain English slavery. A century later, Senator Sumner of Massachusetts, an ardent abolitionist, would fume that Mansfield "was not naturally on the side of liberty, as becomes a great judge, but always, by blood and instinct, on the side of prerogative and power."[35] The problem of British judges' acting as their sovereign's tools had been acute in the seventeenth century, most painfully in the treason trials that followed the Civil War and when King Charles II had removed judges whose rulings displeased him. Public revulsion against biased judges who served at the sovereign's pleasure had been a catalyst for the Glorious Revolution of 1688–1689.

Mansfield's predecessor during those last Stuart years, George Jeffreys, had been a notorious royal toady. When made a serjeant, he inscribed his ring *A deo rex, a rege lex,* "From God the King, from the King the law," and, during one trial, expressed the hope that he would "never lose [his] heart nor spirit to serve the government."[36] The English people did not forgot such things.

At the time of Stapylton's trial, judicial life tenure in England was not one decade old, and Mansfield had done a particularly poor job of emphasizing his judicial independence. From 1757 to 1763, while serving as Chief Justice of the Court of King's Bench, he served the Crown in a cabinet post, as Chancellor of the Exchequer as late as 1767, and as Lord Chancellor in all but name in 1770. It was a sore point for many that he consistently acted the arch-royalist in every seditious libel trial over which he presided.

Then there was the problem of Dido. On August 29, 1779, Thomas Hutchinson, the deposed royalist governor of colonial Massachusetts, would dine with Mansfield at his country home, Kenwood. In his diary, Hutchinson would remark on an extraordinary scene: "A Black came in after dinner and sat with the ladies, and after coffee, walked with the company in the gardens, one of the young ladies having her arm within the other." Mansfield explained that his nephew, Sir John Lindsey, had taken Dido's mother prisoner in a Spanish ship and brought her to England, where she had given birth to Dido.

Mansfield was childless, and his affection for this grand-niece became so strong, open, and well-known that Hutchinson would relate how, during the *Somerset* case, a Jamaican planter, asked to speculate on how Mansfield would rule, replied, "No doubt he will be set free, for Lord Mansfield keeps a Black in his house which governs him and the whole family." Dido would have been about eight years old. The judge, Hutchinson recorded, "knows he has been reproached for showing a fondness for her." That evening, Mansfield asked Dido to do "this thing and that, and she showed the greatest attention to everything he said." During the after-dinner stroll about the grounds, wrote Hutchinson, Dido acted as "a sort of Superintendent over the dairy, poultry yard, &c."

Dido was Dido Elizabeth Belle.[37] The Mansfields had raised her at Kenwood alongside her cousin, Lady Elizabeth Murray, the daughter of another of Mansfield's nephews, David, 7th Viscount Stormont. Both were born in 1763. A painting of the cousins walking arm in arm, as Hutchinson saw them, hangs at Scone Palace, Mansfield's ancestral Scottish home. Dido, who is holding a bowl of fruit, wears a long silver satin gown and a turban with an ostrich feather. She is dark and pretty. Mansfield treated her well, giving her expensive asses' milk for medicine, a mahogany table, and a bed hung with glazed chintz. Sometimes she acted as his amanuensis.[38] Sharp never mentioned Dido, and we have no evidence that he knew anything about her. But a Jamaican planter knew, and the unusual domestic situation of the Chief Justice of the Court of King's Bench must have been the subject of gossip in the City.

Mansfield's royalist leanings, his intimate involvement with a government that did not oppose slavery, his service in the Privy Council until 1760, and in the House of Lords subsequently, his hard-nosed support of seditious libel prosecutions, his yen for free trade and commercial stability, his respect for the customs of merchants, his admiration for Lord Hardwick, his reputation, deserved or not, for enforcing the Joint Opinion, and his ownership of a slave, must have caused Sharp sleepless nights. Yet Sharp realized that Mansfield possessed a powerful sense of individual justice and a store of good sense. He saw that Mansfield's desire to rule in morally correct ways could lead him to drench his decisions so deeply in equity that they brought him public obloquy and that principled argument could persuade him. The Chief Justice obviously possessed an independent mind, and he was no one's servant: Six years before, he had famously struck down general warrants issued by a Privy Council colleague. Finally, after two years researching and writing the *Representation*, Sharp knew the legal case against slavery was strong, if not as strong as he believed.[39] Stapylton's would be the next test.

Lewis v. Stapylton *Begins*

[T]hey have taken it into their heads to say he was not under the protection of the laws of this Country, and that they have a right to treat him as their property, or whether or not their property, they had the right to treat him as a horse or a dog to carry him where they pleased and do what they pleased with him.

Opening argument of John Dunning for Thomas Lewis

EIGHTEENTH-CENTURY ENGLISH criminal trials little resemble twenty-first-century Anglo-American trials. Prosecutions brought by the state today were undertaken privately by the victims then. Thomas Lewis, as the private prosecutor, had the right to have barristers conduct direct and cross-examinations, make opening statements and, if the defendant presented evidence, make closing statements to the jury, and argue legal questions.[1] But unless the prosecutor was an institution, such as the Mint, the Post Office, or the Bank of England, a barrister rarely appeared. Most judges believed prosecution counsel unnecessary, in the absence of special circumstances, for the defendant's guilt often appeared obvious, as when he was caught red-handed or confessed, or so they believed.

Though Stapylton was charged with a serious crime, it was a misdemeanor, not a felony, and so he was entitled to defense counsel.[2] Both prosecutors and misdemeanor defendants were entitled to counsel, though defendants charged with the most serious capital felony, except treason, were not.[3] In State trials, which might involve an allegation of treason, the Crown was routinely represented by counsel, usually the Attorney General or Solicitor General, from the sixteenth century on. Treason defendants could employ defense counsel after 1696. As late as the 1730s, only prosecutors were permitted counsel at the Old Bailey's felony trials.

There were no defense lawyers at the Old Bailey in the 1720s; the first appeared in a handful of cases scattered throughout the following decade, acting at the sufferance of individual trial judges. But within twenty years, judicial sufferance had hardened into a defendant's right, though one conditioned on counsel's staying clear of factual disputes, sticking to cross-examination, and arguing questions of law.[4] It would not be until 1836 that defense lawyers were permitted to address felony juries directly. By 1770, felony defendants were rapidly gaining access to trial lawyers, though neither side used them much. Of the 578 felony cases tried at the Old Bailey that year, prosecutors retained counsel in just five, defendants in twelve.[5] As late as 1840, only 4 percent of prosecutors and a quarter of felony defendants had trial counsel.[6] The number of barristers employed for misdemeanor trials, lesser crimes that might leave defendants pilloried, whipped, fined, or imprisoned, but neither transported nor hung, were probably even less.

Private prosecutions, such as Thomas Lewis's, were not very common, for the victim/prosecutor could incur hefty legal and court costs. Legislation would make it possible for prosecutors to recover some, but only some, of those expenses. Recall how Granville Sharp was consumed with guilt for having been "too easily persuaded to consent to [Stapylton's] indictment," leaving Mrs. Banks saddled with "heavy charges." She had borne not just the cost of retaining the three prosecuting barristers, but solicitor Lucas, too. As solicitor, his job was to investigate and prepare the case, locate the witnesses, prepare a brief that described the case to the barristers who were to try it, then attend the trial to sit mute. A solicitor who represented the prosecution had the responsibility to obtain the necessary subpoenas. Barristers often received their solicitors' instructions at the eve, perhaps the very day, of trial. But Sharp, thinking ahead, had advised solicitor Lucas to place his brief into the barristers' hands even before Dunning was retained.

One reason private prosecutors began to hire trial counsel was that more defendants began doing it, and their barristers quickly demonstrated how effectively they could blunt an unrepresented prosecutor's case. Another reason was that a private prosecutor might be very highly motivated to win his case. And sometimes the issues might be too complex for a private prosecutor fully to understand or competently to present. Lewis was no Olaudah Equiano or Ottobah Cugoano, the prominent African autobiographers brought to England as slaves in the middle of the eighteenth century. Perhaps Stapylton had hired counsel first. Sharp intended the case to test the legality of British slavery, and he wanted to win. The facts might not be difficult, but the legal arguments would require an extensive knowledge of numerous aspects of the common law and legal history. Had Sharp not assisted Lewis and been financially supported in turn by Mrs. Banks, Lewis could never have prosecuted Stapylton.

Stayplton's trial would not last long. In the 1730s, one court session usually ran from two to five days and disposed of fifty to one hundred felony cases and a few serious misdemeanors. In the second half of the eighteenth century, some courts disposed of fifteen felony cases a day.[7] Not until 1794 did a British trial for a serious crime, other than treason, last more than a day. It was even worse for unrepresented defendants: In 1833, one experienced barrister calculated that the average Old Bailey felony trial lasted less than nine minutes, with some so quick-fire "it [was] not, indeed, uncommon for a man to come back, after receiving his sentence on the day appointed for that purpose, saying 'It can't be me they mean; I have not been tried yet.'"[8]

It is hard to know exactly what barrister Walker's job would have been for Stapylton in a 1771 King's Bench misdemeanor trial, for little is known about how misdemeanor trials were conducted then. We know much more about Old Bailey felony trials, because of the Old

Bailey Session Papers, which reported most of the criminal trials that took place in that court between the 1670s and 1913, though often in a highly condensed form. We even know more about British treason trials, rare though they were, because so many were recorded in the nineteenth century series known as Howell's *State Trials*. This was the major place in which the *Somerset* case would be reported.

Some argue that, in a misdemeanor trial of the time, only the defendant personally could examine and cross-examine witnesses and address the jury; others claim his lawyer could do both, even that his primary responsibility was the cross-examination of Crown witnesses.[9] Walker would examine defense witnesses, but he would never address the jury and never cross-examine the only Crown witness, Thomas Lewis himself; and we have no way of knowing whether these were Walker's strategic decisions or handcuffs that Mansfield clicked on. It certainly hobbled Stapylton's defense.

When only the prosecution could open and close to the jury, and only the private prosecutor had trial counsel, a "duty of restraint" had evolved by which prosecution counsel was expected not to exploit his great advantage. His job was to lay out the facts he intended to prove, then leave it. When barristers for both sides could address the jury, prosecuting counsel did not consider himself restrained. As we shall see, John Dunning felt unfettered, which implies he believed Walker could address the jury.

Dunning began. The kidnapping of Thomas Lewis was, he croaked, a "very gross and outrageous assault . . . accompanied with the actual imprisonment of his person for the space of seventy-six hours and with a great deal of malice and outrage . . . a violent outrage to the laws of this Country."[10] Worse, Stapylton's invidious purpose had been to sell Lewis into West Indian slavery. Dunning sarcastically detailed Stapylton's perfidy and bogus legal justification:

> Thomas Lewis, the prosecutor, has the misfortune as he finds it to be in point of colour a Black, and upon the ground of that discovery made by them, his having a darker complexion than the now defendants, they have taken it into their heads to say he was not under the protection of

the laws of this Country, and that they have a right to treat him as their property, or whether or not their property, they had the right to treat him as a horse or a dog to carry him where they pleased and do what they pleased with him. But I trust by your verdict they will find themselves mistaken, for by the laws of this country they have no such right.

Dunning scoffed at the very idea one human might own another: "[T]he laws of this Country admit of no such property. I know nothing where this idea exists, I apprehend it only exists in the minds of those who have lived in those countries where it is suffered."

Dunning strained to make himself heard. Six years later, a newspaper reported that Dunning could not be heard in a courtroom so noisy "it was difficult to know what the business was about." The Great Hall was a hustling, bustling place, buyings and sellings occurring at its north end, loiterers hanging about with their dogs, lawyers studying the proceedings, thieves slicing purses, witnesses waiting to be called and sometimes selling perjured testimony, friends meeting, the fashionable displaying expensive clothing, and hopefuls, as Samuel Pepys had recorded a century before, trawling for sexual partners. The Court of King's Bench had conducted its business entirely in the open until 1739, when identical two-story Gothic stone screens, complete with ogee windows and pinnacles, were installed over both it and the Court of Chancery, leaving them encased in a space twenty-five feet square. The judges presided in benches raised up against the south wall. Beneath them sat the chief clerk and his two clerks, the clerk of the Crown, the clerk of the papers with his clerks, thirteen filacers, who processed writs and issued process, the marshall, criers, and ushers. Until 1755, the courtrooms lacked roofs.

Dunning was still seething over the attempt to press his client the previous morning; foreigners couldn't even legally be pressed, and only sailors and other workmen were even eligible.[11] Since Lewis had been rescued seven months before, Dunning said, "there have been frequent attempts made by the defendants to remove the prosecutor that he might not give evidence against them and no longer ago than yesterday some of the party had him seized on and impressed [into the Royal

Navy]." Mansfield would have none of this. "You can't go into that. . . . I will not try anything but this indictment. We have business enough."

Unlike Dunning's, Mansfield's voice was sweet, charming, and polished, the product of practice reaching back to the time when Alexander Pope had coached young Murray before a mirror at Lincoln's Inn, though he sometimes wandered into grammatical mazes and thickets of run-on sentences. Mansfield had only partially succeeded in erasing every linguistic trace of his native Scotland. He carefully pronounced every letter, with some of his words sounding decidedly odd to English hearers. When he ruled in open court that "precedents only serve to illustrate principles and to give them a fixed authority," the audience would have heard the last word as "awtawrity." "Attachment," he pronounced "attaichment." "Bread" was "brid," "regiment," "regment."[12]

Dunning persisted. "[T]hese people should understand, and I hope will be made to understand, that whatever idea they may have the prosecutor would be safe in coming into this Court to give testimony, for no longer ago than yesterday fresh experiments were made to prevent his coming here to give evidence." The jurors knew that men were sometimes pressed upon information given by informants who, out of jealousy, spite, hatred, or calculation would be delighted to learn they would be gone for years, perhaps forever.[13] The defendants act, Mansfield retorted, "at their peril," but whatever they might have done to interfere would have to be the subject of another complaint. Dunning reluctantly dropped the subject and moved to the main business.

If Walker had anything to tell the jury in Stapylton's defense, now would have been a good time. But he did not rise. Dunning quickly called Thomas Lewis as the Crown's first and only witness and began methodically to prove that Lewis was, and always had been, free. Mansfield began to jot in his trial notebook.[14] In the 1690s, judges had begun taking trial notes, primarily to stimulate their recollection when it came time to sum up the evidence for the jury and to instruct them.[15] The notes were rarely extensive—Mansfield's were no exception—because only the rare judge couldn't recall the meager evidence presented, and Mansfield's memory was prodigious. But the notes were also a reminder of what had occurred in the event post-trial proceedings that took place weeks or months after the verdict.

Lewis testified that he had been born on the Gold Coast, precisely where, he could no longer remember. When he was five or six, his father died, and so his uncle had raised him. Both had been free men. Mansfield must have glanced at Walker, looking for an objection. But there was no objection; Walker would object to nothing Lewis was asked. Mansfield interrupted the questioning anyway: "You don't prove his being free by himself." This might have signaled an early serious, even fatal, obstacle to the prosecution. It depended upon what Mansfield meant.

He might have considered Thomas Lewis a party to the lawsuit. Until 1898 in England and 1962 in the American state of Georgia, parties in a criminal case were incompetent to testify, because judges feared their self-interest made perjury inevitable. But the formal parties in criminal prosecutions were defendant and Crown, even though a private prosecutor might be eligible for a reward or government reimbursement of some of his prosecution costs if a conviction resulted. Despite that, victim-prosecutors were usually seen as ordinary witnesses able to testify. The defendant, Stapylton, could make an unsworn statement, but he was permitted neither to testify under oath nor to be cross-examined, a potentially crippling handicap in light of the medieval practice of giving equal weight to all, but only, sworn evidence; some jurors simply refused to believe unsworn statements.[16]

If Lewis wasn't an interested party, he might still be an interested witness. But the common law disqualified witnesses only if they were financially interested. The victim of a crime such as forgery or usury might be prohibited from testifying because acquittal would allow him to avoid liability on a contract, promissory note, or bail surety. It usually didn't matter how strong someone's nonpecuniary interest was. The exception was that one spouse could not testify in a trial involving the other, because the common law considered the spouses one. Jeremy Bentham detested the irrationality of this pecuniary/nonpecuniary distinction. "If you believe the man of law, there is no such thing . . . as filial, no such thing as parental, affection. . . . For a farthing for the chance of gaining the incommensurable fraction of a farthing, [there is] no man upon earth, no Englishman at least, that would not perjure himself. This in Westminster Hall is science; this in Westminster Hall is law."[17] A man who would be delivered into perpetual slavery and an early death in a West Indian sugar field if the case went badly might have had a pecuniary interest in Mansfield's mind.

Even so, Mansfield, a leader in the movement against the blanket disqualification of interested witnesses and in favor of allowing the jury to hear the testimony of interested witnesses and sort it themselves, might have allowed the jury to hear Lewis, and permit them to assess his credibility, rather than disqualify his testimony wholesale.[18] For some time, he had been referring civil cases for arbitration with an order to allow the parties to testify.[19] But his was just a leaning, for his trial notebooks reveal that he often disqualified interested parties and witnesses, noting with an "IC" that he had disqualified them as "incompetent."

Mansfield might have assumed Lewis was not a Christian but a pagan who believed neither in God or an afterlife. The Joint Opinion had declared that baptism did not affect one's status as slave or free, though it might affect one's competency to testify.[20] The worst possibility for the prosecution was that Mansfield might consider disqualifying Lewis simply because he was a slave, property, a commodity, merchandise, a thing. If that should happen, then Mansfield accepted that blackness meant servitude and Dunning's fine sarcasm—Lewis's misfortune of being black was enough to remove him from the law's protection—had been entirely lost.

The possibility that Mansfield might disqualify Lewis because he was a slave would have been most frightening for Sharp and Dunning, for it would reverse the great presumption of English law that every English subject was free, and place the burden on Lewis to prove he was free, rather than on Stapylton to prove Lewis his slave. Sir John Fortescue, Mansfield's fifteenth-century predecessor, had written: "Servitude was introduced by men for vicious purposes. But freedom was instilled in human nature by God. . . . The laws of England favor liberty in every case."[21] For four centuries the common law had been *in favorem liberatis* (in favor of liberty) with all presumed free until proven otherwise. Even the burden of proving a villein had rested with the feudal lord.[22] If Mansfield disqualified Lewis because he was black, Sharp would have grounds for fearing that worse was coming. The Habeas Corpus Act of 1679 had extended the Great Writ's umbrella over "any person or persons." If Mansfield thought Lewis was a slave because he was black, a black might not be a "person," but a thing no more entitled to invoke the protection of the Great Writ than a dog or a horse. "You don't prove his being free by himself," Mansfield had said. Dunning had better have a good response.

He didn't. "This boy has always understood himself to be free," Dunning said. This lame reply failed to address any of Mansfield's likely concerns. Disaster loomed, for it appeared that Mansfield might actually disqualify Lewis from testifying and that would have been the end of the case, for Dunning had no other witnesses ready to prove Lewis free. Then, unexpectedly, Mansfield backed down. Instead of disqualifying Lewis's testimony, or implying that he had ever been a slave, he wrapped Lewis in the cloak of traditional English liberty. "I shall presume him free," Mansfield declared, "unless they prove the contrary."[23] Stapylton would have to convince the jury that Lewis was his slave, and that was going to be exceedingly difficult.

Barrister Lucas took over the questioning of Lewis from Dunning. Lewis had lived with his uncle about a year after the death of his father, becoming a servant to the local English-speaking governor and general, when he was aged six or seven. Asked whether he would like to go abroad, Lewis leaped. The governor placed the youngster aboard a ship bound for Santa Cruz. There he was passed to a ship's captain, who died, then to another ship's captain, to a nobleman, who also died, to his cooper, who died as well, then to the nobleman's clerk, who eventually took him to an English merchant. "What was his name?" Dunning asked. "His name was Bob Smith." Lewis said. "To an English merchant?" Mansfield asked. "To an English merchant of the name of Robert Smith," Dunning said.

Lewis had lived with Smith half a year, until Smith asked him whether he wanted to go abroad with Stapylton: "I told him I should like it very well as I never had been in any parts of the world." Stapylton's brig was heading "to a place called Carolina." But they never made it: "[W]hen we came there" Lewis said, "the brig was taken by a Spanish privateer."

"What," Mansfield asked, "Stapylton's brig?" "Yes," Lewis replied. "You was taken prisoner?" Lucas asked. "Yes, from Stapylton I was taken . . . then they carried me to Augustine and then to Savannah," where he stayed for four or five weeks, then to Havannah, Cuba, where another English merchant took him to a tavern, where he became a waiter. There he stayed for three weeks. "At what place?" Mansfield asked. "At the Havannah," Lewis repeated.

A man at the tavern gave Lewis wages, victuals, and drink. The wages were important, for Dunning was doggedly trying to demonstrate that Lewis had never been treated as a slave. One evening Stapylton came to the tavern for dinner: "I went and [spoke] to him and he said he did not know me." St. Peter–like, Stapylton repeatedly denied knowing Lewis. That was a ruse for, when Stapylton left the tavern at a late hour, he took Lewis and brought him to the town: "[He] said nothing to me, but told the merchant I belonged to him and insisted upon having me away." Stapylton put Lewis aboard a ship sailing for Philadelphia. "The ship was going to Philadelphia?" Mansfield asked. "Yes, the sloop was going there," Lewis said. Then on to New York, where Lewis began working for a wine merchant, who paid him wages. Then it was back to Santa Cruz for another year and a half with Bob Smith, until he died. From Santa Cruz, Stapylton took Lewis to Pensacola, where he lived for almost three months with a judge who, again, paid him wages, until the judge's hairdresser brought him to New England.

Mansfield was starting to get restless. "All this minuteness can never be material," he complained. Dunning and Lucas disagreed. What he wanted the jury to know, Dunning said, was where Lewis had lived and, which was important, that he "had wages and was not a slave but free." "It does not show he was free," Mansfield said. It was a warning growl that Dunning should have heeded. Instead, he resumed questioning Lewis about where he had lived and what he had done.

Stapylton arrived from Pensacola, seized Lewis from the hairdresser, and sailed again for Carolina. This time they made it. Then it was on to Jamaica, back to New York, and finally to England, where Lewis lived with Stapylton in Chelsea. But Lewis's travels were not over. When Stapylton kidnapped Lewis near Mrs. Banks's garden, it was the second time he had done it! The first time Lewis had been thrown onto a ship that was wrecked. This allowed him to escape back to England. Lewis was launching into the story of the shipwreck when even Dunning felt enough was enough. "I don't want to know the particulars of the wreck. After that you came to London?" He did, Lewis said. Stapylton had found him and took him again by force to his house in Chelsea. "Since that time you have been in Stapylton's house?" Dunning asked. "Yes, and he kidnap me again," Lewis replied. "Tell me how you were kidnapped this last time," Dunning asked. "It was a Monday night," Lewis said, "Between ten or eleven, twelve o'clock." "After you was wrecked you came to England and lived again with Stapylton?" Mansfield asked, perplexed. "Yes, Sir," Lewis said.

The kidnapping began to unfold. "Stapylton one night he says I have got some illegal gin and tea down by the water side, by Mrs. Banks' wharf." Stapylton said he was afraid a customs officer had discovered it. But Mansfield was still struggling with what had happened after the shipwreck. "You had not left him?" "No Sir." Lewis continued. Stapylton had told him to fetch the gin and tea: "[B]ut come the back way, not through the College for fear the Custom House Officer take it from you." "Where was it you went to?" Mansfield asked. "Down by Mrs. Banks. The water side at Bull Wharfe," Lewis replied.

Stapylton sent two men with Lewis to the wharf: "[O]ne behind me and the other before me," Lewis said. "I did not know all this and some waterman was hiding in a passage there and three men and the waterman that come and lays hold on me." "Do you know who they were?" Dunning asked. "I know three of them," Lewis said. "Name them," Dunning ordered.

One was John Maloney, the other Aaron Armstrong, and Michael Coleman. When I went there they seized me directly, then I begun to call out for help. I called to Mrs. Banks for help. I told them the same persons took me away before, the same person going to trespass me on board a ship. Then they began to fight with me and I would not go and I fought about a quarter of an hour with them in the way. And at last they drag me about a hundred yards upon my back upon the ground and when I got to the water side they shoved me into the water instead of the boat because I would not go and then they put me into the boat and then put the cord around my leg.

Lucas interrupted. "Did you call out?" "Yes, Sir. I cry out all the time, and then they put a stick across my mouth and gag me. I struggled and got it off, then when I got past Chelsea College, then I hold my tongue then," Lewis said. "Did anybody give directions about tying or gagging you? Did you hear anybody?" Dunning asked. "Yes, I heard some people, I heard him cry out, 'Gag him,' says he," Lewis said. "Who cried out, 'gag him'?" Dunning asked. "I think it was Stapylton," Lewis replied. "You knew his voice?" Dunning asked. "Yes, Sir. He was somewhere upon the side of the shore crying out, 'Gag him!'" Lewis said. Dunning wanted no confusion. "Did not you say you knew his voice?" he asked. "Yes, Sir," Lewis replied. Mansfield wrote: "Defendant on the side shore cried, 'Gag him'" into his notebook, and scrawled "Stap." in the margin opposite.

Then Mansfield spoke. "Where was you sent then?" "I was sent on board the *Snow*," Lewis replied. The questioning resumed. "Where were you carried to, first in the boats?" Dunning asked. "First to Gravesend. Mrs. Banks sent down to Gravesend for me. I was out on board the ship there. The Captain refuse twice to give me up . . . then when he would refuse to give me up, the mayor come on board, they would not deliver me up. The mayor ask me, is it not better to go abroad? I said I don't huye to it," Lewis said. "Did the captain give any reason why he would not deliver you up?" Dunning asked. "He said he had a Bill of Sale from Stapylton, then they take me down to Gravesend. Mrs. Banks send the Corpus and sent after the Captain and he would not deliver me up till such time as he went on shore and had further notice," Lewis replied.

Walker began to cross-examine. "You said you were born at Guinea?" he asked. "Yes, Sir," Lewis replied. "And you was put on board a Danish ship when you left your uncle?" Walker asked. "Yes, Sir," Lewis said.

Walker turned to Mansfield. "My Lord, what I mean to prove is that he was the servant of those people when they sent him away." Mansfield was unimpressed. "Very likely. Nothing he has said is inconsistent with that one way or another."

Servants were everywhere in London and a slave was a kind of servant. But there were many other kinds and no others were their masters' property. In *Chamberline v. Harvey*, Chief Justice Holt had written that a black man could be a "slavish servant," but not a chattel, akin to an apprenticed laborer.[24] Walker returned to Lewis. "What was Stapylton at the time you first came home?" he asked. "He was Captain of a merchantman," Lewis replied. "What was he when he came over to England?" Walker asked. "He was blind," Lewis said. "He continues blind now?" Walker asked. "Yes, Sir," Lewis replied. "Very old and incapable of carrying on any business?" Walker asked. "Not very incapable," Lewis replied. Mansfield jotted "Defendant Stapylton blind & old" into his trial notebook.[25]

"Have you not been out of order, ill?" Walker asked. "Yes, since I came into England," Lewis replied. "Who took care of you?" Walker asked. "He did a little time and then got a letter to get me into the hospital . . . to St. Georges Hyde Park Corner," Lewis said. "All the time you was in England he took care of you?" Walker asked. "No, Sir, not always," Lewis said. "Only when you was with him? But not when you was away from him?" Walker asked. "Yes, when he used me ill, he always paid for my victuals when I was with him," Lewis said. Prodding him to the point, Mansfield asked Walker whether he had any evidence that Lewis was actually Stapylton's property. "My Lord," Walker said, "I have a title under which we can prove him the servant of the defendant."

Now Mansfield announced how the major issues in the trial would be decided.

> I tell you what I think to do. The general question [of the legality of slavery] may be a very important one and not in this shape ever considered, as I know of. If you have any title of property, I shall first leave it to the jury to find whether he is his property as a slave, and then put it in some solemn way to be tried. His being black will not prove the property. The

only excuse for the prosecution is that he [Lewis] is not Stapylton's property, but he was sent as their servant is what we shall prove.

This meant a special verdict.

Mansfield was departing from how he usually handled disputed questions of law. His practice was to take a general jury verdict, guilty or not guilty, then present any dispositive legal issue to the full Court of King's Bench, who either accepted or overturned the verdict depending on how the four judges viewed the law. Eighteenth-century judges who wanted to force a jury to rule a certain way or to remove its ability to make the usual general verdict sometimes deployed the special verdict. Its use became notorious in seditious libel cases after juries repeatedly displayed great hesitancy to convict on a general verdict. Judges began to insist that the jurors decide only whether the defendant published the offending material. If he did, the judges convicted them.

Stapylton's jury would not decide Stapylton's guilt, at least not immediately. It would simply answer the question propounded by Mansfield: Was Thomas Lewis Robert Stapylton's property? This was the cautious, conservative Mansfield at work, the man who might have advised Chief Justice Wilmot to dither in the *Hylas* case. He was dithering now in the hope that the question of the legality of English slavery would not arise, for then he would have to decide it, alone, or by referring the momentous question to the four judges of the Court of King's Bench, or the twelve judges of the Court of King's Bench, Court of Common Pleas, and the Exchequer who, in half a dozen or a dozen cases each year, wrestled with the really difficult legal issues. But no one would have to wrestle with slavery until, and unless, the jury found Lewis was Stapylton's property, and Mansfield had no intention of allowing them to do that.[26]

Mansfield mortified Sharp, already reeling from the decision to force the jury to a special verdict, as if it were a seditious libel case, for it meant he didn't trust the jury and had decided to keep control. "I have granted several writs of habeas corpus upon affidavits of masters for their Negroes, two or three I believe," he said, "upon affidavits of masters deducing sale and property of their Negroes upon being pressed. I have granted habeas corpus to deliver them to their masters: Whether they have this kind of property or not in England never has been solemnly determined."[27]

This confirmed what Sir James Eyre had told Sharp at the beginning of the Jonathan Strong case: Mansfield's Court of King's Bench invariably delivered "all runaway slaves to their masters." But Mansfield's use of habeas corpus to free pressed slaves was ambiguous, for a pressed slave was, for Sharp, a slave twice over, chattel and naval impressment. Sharp thought Mansfield's use of the writ to free blacks from naval impressment entirely admirable, "[a] clear acknowledgment from his Lordship of the illegality of pressing . . . [and] very proper relief from that illegal oppression."

But Sharp was furious that Mansfield redelivered pressed blacks into chattel slavery. It didn't have to be. Writs were granted for pressed apprentices, to the master's cold comfort, for the apprentice would be ordered free to go, and the master left to the poor remedy of suing the press gang for the apprentice's wages.[28] Blackstone's *Commentaries* equated slaves and apprentices, slavery being "no more than the same state of subjection for life, which every apprentice submits to for the space of seven years, or sometimes for a longer term."[29] But Mansfield treated them differently. When a father sought a writ of habeas corpus for his son against his aunt, Mansfield ordered the boy released, but told him to go where he pleased; the father's rights had to be decided in another action.[30]

Sharp thought habeas corpus should never be used "to deliver up a poor wretch, against his will, into the hands of a tyrannical master, who rates him merely as a chattel, or pecuniary property, and not as a man." If Mansfield did, he would be "guilty of a three-fold injury"; he would "deprive the country of a useful sailor (Sharp thought it "well known that negros, in general, turn out able & hardy sailors"), "cruelly injure the poor negro himself, by dragging him from the King's service (in which he was content) in order to deliver him up, against his will, into the hands of a cruel private tyrant," and injure English law "by perverting a constitutional writ to purpose entirely opposite to its original use, meaning, & intention!" Mansfield did not share Sharp's view that naval impressment was slavery: "[A] pressed sailor is not a slave; no compulsion can be put upon him except to serve his country; and, while doing so, he is entitled to claim all the rights of an Englishman."[31]

"I shall presume him free," Mansfield had said. He had used the writ to release pressed blacks, which meant he believed, at least, that they possessed the liberty habeas corpus was meant to protect. But the writ, which was heard without a jury, did not secure one's right to property, for only a jury could do that.[32] Yet Mansfield returned blacks to masters who could prove their "sale and property." This was all nonsense. If a black was his master's property, Mansfield should never have issued the writ of habeas corpus in the first place. If the writ applied, the forcible return of the black to his master violated its spirit and letter, as Sharp claimed. Mansfield was either befuddled, which would have been unlike him, or grimly determined to avoid what Sharp was resolved to force upon him, a ruling on the legality of English slavery.

"My Lord, we have from Captain Smith a regular transfer to Stapylton and at all the places he has claimed him, at Havannah, at New York and Pensacola, he has never denied it," Walker told Mansfield. "There is a great chasm before you took him at New York, for he was at Santa Cruz with Smith again and then with the judge there," Mansfield said. "From Mr. Smith we have him," Walker said. "No," Mansfield said, "he is twice with Smith." "It was in the year 62 we first purchased him," Walker said. "If you have any evidence of the fact you allude to it will acquit them," Mansfield replied. In a surprise move, Walker then called Richard Coleman, who had testified before the grand jury for the prosecution, as his first witness.[33]

CHAPTER 9

Sharp Fails, Again

Ever since that trial I have had a great doubt in my mind, whether
the negro could prove his own freedom by his own evidence.

Lord Mansfield, June 17, 1771

WALKER SHOWED COLEMAN a document. "Look at that
paper." "I can't read," Coleman replied. "You can't read it, you
say?" Walker asked. "No, Sir. I can't read. I own I can't read." "Do you
know the handwriting?" "No, Sir, I don't know that." "Nor you can't
read?" "No, Sir," Coleman repeated. "Nor you can't read writing?"
Walker's instructing solicitor had apparently advised him to have a man
who could not read as his first witness. "No, Sir." Was this paper the bill
of sale for Thomas Lewis?

Davenport jumped up. "Do you know Robert Stapylton of Chelsea?"
"Yes, Sir," Coleman said. "Do you know Thomas Lewis the black before
you?" "Yes, Sir." "What are you, Coleman?" "A waterman." "Was you
applied to any time by Stapylton concerning this black?" "Yes, Sir." "Tell
us when and how." And Coleman began the tale.

It was Friday, June 29, 1770, when Stapylton asked Coleman to per-
form a task. "I said what is it about and he said he should not tell me
then, but that he would come and let me know." At 9:00 P.M., Stapylton

97

told Coleman he would not be needed that night. He returned Saturday. "I shall want you tonight. . . . do you know what it is upon? I said no. Says he, you can guess can't you? Say I, I can't, unless it is to carry the black down again." Stapylton appeared about 9:00 P.M. and said the kidnapping had been postponed to Sunday. This was repeated on Sunday night. On Monday, Coleman said, Stapylton "came again and he sent the black man to me to fetch some things."

"Who did he send him to?" Lucas asked. "To me," Coleman said, "then I was to lay in ambush and they sent a man with the black under pretence to help him and he was to seize him and put him on board the boat and then, at that time they seized him, I was away at a distance from the shore, and I heard a strange noise. I judged what it was and I went to them. I heard him say, Mrs. Banks come help me, for God's sake, they are going to take me on board the ship, and he hallowed out for the coachman."

"Who put him into the boat?" Lucas asked. "One Maloney, a red-headed man, and one Armstrong," Coleman said. "In what way was he put on board the boat?" "In the hold." "Did they put him on the water?" "In getting him into the boat they shoved him in. He said he could not swim and he would jump over board and be drowned sooner than go. I then tied his leg with a rope." "Did they do anything to his mouth?" "He hallowed out prodigiously when he was in the boat. There was one man tried to put a stick in his mouth. I was going to put a string round his mouth, but he got that off." "Did anybody say, gag him?" "I heard somebody say 'gag him.'" "Do you know Stapylton's voice?" "Yes, I believe I do." "Did you take it to be his voice?" "He made such a noise that I could not tell." "Did somebody interpose about their taking him away?" "One of Mrs. Banks' servants spoke to me."

Dunning took up the cross-examination. "Did they say they had any authority?" "He pulled a paper we had advertised him in," Coleman said. "Under the pretence of property I understand they said they had a warrant from Lord Mayor which prevented the people interposing," Dunning said. That interested Mansfield. "Who produced it? Was it Armstrong that said it?" "No," replied Coleman. "Was it Maloney?" Mansfield asked. "No, my Lord." Dunning broke in. "It was one of those who assisted, I suppose. We have several people that stood on the shore that saw the transaction of putting him into the boat, but I believe it is sufficiently proved already."

Walker turned to Mansfield:

My Lord, I can say no more in the defense of my client than this, that this negro has been a servant and as a slave aboard by Smith to him. He has all the accounts to produce in evidence that he has been his slave and that as such he brought him into England and as such he has been in England and as such he has continued ever since he has been in England. He has run away from him at times and has been advertised and then he has returned again as his slave . . . and I can only submit it to the jury that we can prove him to be the property of the defendant Stapylton.

"I dispute the fact and the possibility of his being anybody's property here in England!" Dunning cried. Walker ignored him. "This paper I have in my hand [presumably the bill of sale Coleman had been unable to read] is to show that he was transferred to Stapylton by Smith, the black knows it, and I can prove by the witnesses I shall call that he has always acknowledged it."

Mansfield told Walker what he needed to do. "Can you call any witness to prove the conveyance?" "My Lord, I cannot, for want of the person that made the conveyance." Dunning jumped in. "Any man may treat his servant then as this man has been treated, if this is the case." Mansfield agreed: "To be sure, it will be expected you should prove the property very clear," he warned.

Walker called one George Roach and asked if he knew whether Stapylton had purchased Lewis from Robert Smith. "I know very well he had a boy was called August." "Was your name August?" Walker demanded of Lewis. "Yes, but there was two or three besides me of the same name," Lewis said. Now Roach chimed in. "He was thought by everyone there that he was his property." "That he was Stapylton's property?" Walker asked. "Yes," Roach said. "You don't know the boy [Lewis]?" Walker asked. "No," Roach said, "I don't." Mansfield jotted that down.

Walker called ship's captain, Philip Sawyer, who had nearly succeeded in carrying Lewis to Jamaica in the *Captain Seward*. Sawyer,
who had known Stapylton and Lewis for three years, identified Lewis
as the boy Stapylton had brought from New York. "Who was his master?" Walker asked, "Stapylton, he called him his boy," Sawyer said.

Dunning was irritated with Sawyer for defying the warrant issued in
London for Lewis, backed by the mayor of Gravesend, and heading for
the Downs and the open sea. "Did [Mrs. Banks's servant] not tell you
he had an order from the mayor of Gravesend?" Dunning demanded.
"No, he never told me anything about it," "For what purpose was he
brought on board your ship?" "To be sent to Jamaica," Sawyer admitted.
"For what purpose was he to be sent there?" "As a servant." "What was
he to do when he got there?" "Why, he was to be sold at Jamaica." Dunning leaned toward Sawyer. "Did you find it any difficulty to bring that
out?" Dunning paused. "Because you gulp'd at it." "No, sir," Sawyer said.

Dunning showed Sawyer a letter he had written: "[Y]ou assure Mrs.
Banks you are perfectly innocent of Mr. Stapylton's intentions with regard to the negro." "I do not know what [Stapylton] did with [Lewis]
before he got on board . . . I knew he had a mind to sell him," Sawyer
said. "But did you mean to say that when you wrote this letter?" Dunning asked. "I sent the boy on shore by the habeas." "But what did you
mean by this, I am perfectly innocent of what Captain Stapylton had an
inclination to do with the Negro? Take another gulp and let us have another rise now. What was his inclination?" "I told you it was to sell
him," Sawyer insisted. "From whence I should conclude you were not
perfectly innocent. What did you mean she should understand by it?"
Dunning asked. "I did not understand or mean anything by it," Sawyer
said. Dunning let him go.

Walker called Miles Stapylton, Robert's brother. He said Lewis had
come to England with his brother, lived with him, and always acknowledged being his servant. "You say [Lewis] always acknowledged his
being [Robert's] servant?" Dunning interrupted. "He means his slave in
the capacity of his servant," Mansfield said. "To be sure," Dunning said,
"according to their opinion a man acquires a property to a man with a
black face by coming over with him, but when he is white he does not."

"Mr. Walker," Mansfield said, "you are calling all them witnesses to a fact not disputed. It is agreed by the boy and nothing is said by the boy inconsistent." Everyone agreed that Lewis had been Robert Stapylton's servant. The question was, what kind of servant? "We can prove [Robert Stapylton's] being at great expense on account of the boy and that he always acted as the defendant's servant," Walker said.

Walker called one William Watson, who testifed that Lewis had belonged to Robert Stapylton. "How do you know that?" Walker asked. "I was acquainted with his brother Bryant at Chelsea College some years." Dunning objected. Watson was apparently going to tell the jury that Bryant Stapylton had said something that demonstrated that Lewis was Robert's slave. "What you said to him or he to them is nothing to the purpose."[1] "I'll tell you," Watson said, "the point I know this to be Captain Robert Stapylton's boy, if you please to let me tell you the truth." Dunning would have looked to Mansfield. "He is going on with the conversation between himself and Bryant Stapylton, which is nothing to the purpose."

Watson changed the subject. "I went and got a letter for the boy to go into St. George's Hospital where he was admitted there. General Hudson said to me, will you . . . take him away if he does well, after that I went to see him and I heard this black fellow say he belonged to Mr. Stapylton." "The Negro belonged to Defendant," Mansfield wrote in his trial notebook.

"All this would have happened if he had been your son," Dunning said. Dunning meant that the hospital would have done the same for a patient of any color. But it was the wrong thing to say. "My son, a negro! What! A negro! My son!" Watson said fiercely. "Don't be angry, my friend," Dunning said soothingly, "What's all this ferment about? It might have happened to you. They never have admitted people to the hospital in any other way." "I can't tell whether they do or not," Watson said.

"Who did he belong to?" Walker asked. "He belonged to Captain Robert Stapylton. He always called him master." "How did he say he belonged to him?" "As his property and that he brought [him] from abroad when he run away and came to him again. He always allowed him to be his master," Watson said.

Dunning leaped to the offensive. "Did you ever hear him say he was Stapylton's property?" he demanded. "Yes, sir, I have," Watson said. Dunning turned sarcastic. "A thousand times I will give you credit for." "I have heard him several times say he was Captain Stapylton's property," Watson said, not giving an inch. "Do you venture to swear you ever heard him say once he was Captain Stapylton's property?" "I heard him say that he was his master," Watson said. That was all Dunning needed. "But not the word property. You want to bring in some other word?" "No, Sir." Then Dunning would make him: "But you shall not bring in no other word but the truth. Did you ever hear him say he was his property?" "That he was his master. There was a advertisement with a reward in the newspapers for him and he always come back to his master."

Walker showed Thomas Burke the document Richard Coleman had found unreadable. "Is that your handwriting?" he asked. "No, Sir," Burke said. "Is that Captain Smith's handwriting?" "Give me leave to look at it again." Walker gave Burke time to study the document. "Is that Captain Smith's writing?" "I can't say. I can't swear to it." "Did you ever see him write?" "Very often," Burke said. "Do you believe that to be his handwriting?" "I believe it may be. I have often seen him write." Walker was getting irritated. "Do you know anything of this black?" Walker asked. "No, sir." "Is your name William Burke?" "No, sir," Thomas Burke replied. "I am not one of the witnesses to this paper." Dunning leaped up. "But this gentlemen represents you as if you was." Walker must have been thinking dark thoughts about his instructing solicitors.

Now he questioned Bryant Staplyton. "Did you ever hear [Lewis] object to his being your Brother's property?" "No, sir. He never deny'd it." "He never deny'd it?" "No, sir." "You never heard that black boy object to his being your brother's property?" "No, sir."

"You are upon your oath?" Dunning reminded Bryant. "I am, sir." "Do you mean to speak the truth?" "I mean to say the truth and nothing else." "Do you mean to say you heard the boy call himself your brother's property?" Dunning asked. "Where?" Bryant asked. "In your own house or any where else," Dunning said. "Yes, sir, I do, sir," Bryant insisted.

Dunning reentered the area Mansfield had warned him against. "A word more with you sir, if you please. You have been . . . trying to get [Lewis] pressed?" "No, Sir. I deny it," Bryant said. "Was it you that put the press gang after him?" "No, sir." "Was it not you that sent the press gang after him yesterday to stop him coming here?" Dunning demanded. "No, sir. I don't know what you mean, sir." "Was it not you that sent for those that are ready bye and bye to take him?" "No, sir. No, sir." "I am told it was you, though you pretend to know nothing of it. I am told it was the Old Soldier [Robert Stapylton]." "No, not one of us." Bryant said, "And you know of no such people attending?" Dunning asked. "No, sir. I do not, sir." "I do not believe one word you say, sir," Dunning snapped. Stapylton shrugged. "It is indifferent to me, sir, whether you do or not, sir."

It was time to sum up. Dunning said he didn't need to discuss the legality of English slavery, for "there [was] no proof that [Lewis] was ever the property of the defendant." Lewis may have been Stapylton's servant, but never his slave. Mansfield reminded Dunning that the jury was considering just one thing: Was Lewis Stapylton's property? "I don't myself see what the evidence is upon which that question can be construed," Dunning said. "Yes, there is evidence," Mansfield replied.

In that case, Dunning would argue that Lewis was not Stapylton's property, "reserving to myself an opportunity of . . . insisting that no such property can exist . . . in any place and in any court in this kingdom, leaving to myself a right to insist that our laws admit of no such property." If the defendants were not entitled to treat Lewis so badly, "then it seems to me to be material whether there exists that sort of property or not? But if not I submit this clear result to you, that the boy is born as free as any man, and can never be otherwise than free, but by some act of those, that have power over one another, by captivity in war, or in other circumstance of that sort."

Walker "would have foisted upon me, if I had not been a little attentive about it, a paper which they would talk about, as if it conveyed some title, which they had acquired in the boy." But because Lewis was a regular servant, Stapylton could have no title, despite Stapylton's belief that Lewis's color made him more his property than if he were white:

> Is it to be distinguishable only by colour that such right is to exist? And with regard to capacity that it creates property in the one and not in the other, or does one tittle of evidence make it stronger in one than in the other? It would be very extraordinary if in this age upon his coming into this part of the world, in company with a man, who upon the single ground of coming here with him, says you are my property.

He asked the jurors not to "suffer any man in a free country like this to be sold and conveyed to the place where he would be treated like a horse or a dog, or be treated with more inhumanity than would be applied to a dog."

Neither Walker nor Stapylton addressed the jury; Mansfield delivered the jury's charge. He said nothing about a presumption of innocence, because Stapylton didn't have one, at least not in its modern form.[2] Judges and juries of the time didn't so much view a defendant as innocent until proven guilty as think that an innocent man ought to be able to demonstrate that innocence.[3] There was "no question" Lewis had been assaulted, Mansfield said. The jurors were specially to decide whether he was Stapylton's slave. Only if he was would Mansfield decide whether Lewis could possibly be Stapylton's slave in England.

Mansfield had no intention of allowing the jurors to place him in that position. Stapylton's claim would have to be proven "strongly and clearly," and that was impossible. "There is no evidence of a bill of sale," he told the jurors, "no evidence to show [Stapylton] bought [Lewis] . . . so that it is manifest they did not prove the contrary." In his notebook, Mansfield recorded the most important evidence he told the jurors they should consider: "I laid stress upon the capture by the Spaniard." Even if Lewis had been Stapylton's slave, he became the property of the Spanish captain who captured him at sea, "like a bale of goods." If Lewis was not Stapylton's slave, the jury should find him guilty. If he was, "that will leave it for a more solemn discussion concerning the right of such property here in England."

Only the boldest, or most obtuse, jurymen could turn a deaf ear to this. When James Boswell asked Mansfield whether juries decided cases the way he wanted them to, Mansfield replied, "Yes, except in political causes where they do not at all keep themselves in right or wrong" (probably referring to the seditious libel trials he tried throughout the 1760s).[4] When occasional juries wandered from the right, judges had ways to obtain the correct verdict. The century before, they clapped recalcitrants in the Tower until they changed their minds; the unfortunates temerous enough to acquit William Penn of unlawful assembly had been the last to suffer that fate.[5] Eighteenth-century judges might reject verdicts and instruct the jurors to deliberate again, help a defendant obtain a pardon from the king or, if they thought a jury was leaning in the wrong direction, stop the trial, dismiss the jurors, and start all over again with more pliant jurymen.[6]

Eighteenth-century criminal verdicts arrived swiftly. Often jurors didn't leave the courtroom to deliberate, but would "gather round their foreman, and in about two or three minutes, return their verdict." It was common for a jury to hear several criminal cases, then retire to deliver verdicts on them all.[7] As late as the latter half of the nineteenth century, fewer than 5 percent of English criminal verdicts emerged from a jury deliberation room.[8]

The Stapylton jury had no trouble reaching its verdict. "We don't find he was his property," the foreman said. "No property, no property!" other jurors said. "Then you will find he is guilty," Mansfield ordered, and they did, the jurors crying, "Guilty, guilty." Sharp thought the jurors so enthusiastic in the delivery of their verdict that they would have found every black in England "no property" if they could have. Disappointed, he recorded "the jury had it not in their power to find a verdict [against slavery] for the honour and dignity of the human species, as could have been wished, or indeed as the honest jurymen themselves really seemed to intend." But they could do no more.

However, the larger question, made irrelevant to Thomas Lewis, still weighed on Mansfield. "Mr. Dunning, you will find more in the question that you see at present." "My Lord, I shall never find ideas that could have gone further than master and servant." "It is no matter mooting it now," Mansfield said, "but if you look into it there is more than by accident you are acquainted with. There are a great many opinions given upon it."

He began warming to the question:

> I am aware of many of them, but I know that Justice Foster, Lord Hardwicke, and Lord Talbot had several discussions concerning the right of property in negroes and one of them quotes a text of St. Paul, which I don't immediately think of, that shows their being Christians don't vary the case [St. Paul had instructed slaves to obey their masters and made it clear that Christians could hold other Christians in slavery, even returning one escaped Christian slave to his Christian master].⁹ Perhaps it is much better it never should be finally discussed or settled. I believe you will find them still slaves after they are Christians. You will not find they are upon the footing of contract servants. In that opinion I am confident you will not.

Dunning was rooting about for a copy of the Joint Opinion. "It is a short opinion. Here it is, my Lord." Mansfield turned to the jurors; the ultimate question would remain undecided. "I think you have done very right. I should have found the same verdict." Back to Dunning. "I don't know what the consequence may be if they were to lose their property by accidentally bringing them into England." Back to the jury. "I think you have done very right to find him not the property, for he was not the property, and you have done right, according to the evidence, to find it so."

The abstract issue of the legality of human slavery in England having been evaded, for the moment, there remained a pressing problem. Another gang was waiting for Thomas Lewis outside the courtroom, inside Westminster Hall. Dunning implored Mansfield's protection. "If anybody dares to touch the boy as he is going out of the Hall," Mansfield said, "especially now as the jury have found the boy not the property of the defendant, tell the officer to take them into custody and bring them before me."

"I have found the opinion, my Lord." Dunning said again, the Joint Opinion before him. "Well," Mansfield said, "am I not right as to my opinion that their being Christians don't take away the right of property?" "It does not, my Lord," Dunning said. "I was sure it did not," Mansfield said. "I hope it will never be finally discussed, for I would have all masters think they were free and all negroes think they were not, because then they would both behave better."

Sharp was disappointed. But he thought Dunning had done an excellent job and, in a letter to Mrs. Banks two days later, said that he was sending her a copy of the proceedings "because a view of the diligence and adroitness of her counsel on that occasion will probably afford her both entertainment and satisfaction."[10]

At least four days were required to pass between verdict and sentence, and it was the prosecutor's responsibility to see the defendant was present at sentencing. If the defendant was in the courtroom when he was pronounced guilty, he would be taken into custody. Stapylton was not there. It wasn't until Monday, June 17, 1771, that Lewis's lawyers moved that Stapylton, Maloney, and Armstrong, be sentenced.

"What is it about?" Mansfield asked. "It is about the black, if your Lordship remember," replied Elijah Impey. Was Impey another of Lewis's attorneys? One expert, Ruth Paley, isn't sure. Marveling at the large number of lawyers who materialized at this hearing, she wonders whether some just so happened to be in the courtroom that morning and decided to join in.[11] The defendants were called; none answered. Impey asked their recognizance be withdrawn and demanded their defaults.

But something had continued eating at Mansfield in the four months since the verdict. "Ever since that trial I have had a great doubt in my mind, whether the negro could prove his own freedom by his own evidence. . . . Ever since the trial, I have had a doubt about it." Again, Dunning failed to meet any of Mansfield's possible objections. Instead, he blandly assured that the question of Lewis's competency to testify need not be reached. "I don't believe it will come at all before your Lordship, for the people do not appear." Mansfield didn't care whether the defendants appeared for sentencing; a burden was lifting: "I am glad I mentioned it. He was led on by degrees to give a history that came at last to prove that by which the jury found him free. I speak from memory what occurred to me a very few minutes after the trial. The man was led into the evidence improperly. At first I started at it, but the counsel did not make the objection to his giving such evidence of his own freedom, which came at last to be the only fact to prove him free." Mansfield was forgetting he had declared he would presume Lewis free, unless Stapylton proved the contrary, and neither Dunning nor any of Lewis's other lawyers reminded him.

"There was no manner of doubt of his having had wages," Mansfield continued,

> he was taken in the last war and the capture I thought changed the property. The capture was proved and that the ship was carried into port and there was a long account given of himself when he went to Jamaica and other places. I remember I left it to the jury to find whether he was a slave or free and in case he had been found by them to be a slave the question (of the legality of English slavery) would have come properly before the court.

The evidence that Lewis had received wages and been captured by the Spanish captain might have been clear, but its only source was Lewis, Mansfield said. "Afterwards I had a doubt in my mind whether a slave may be a witness to prove himself free."

Mansfield was not going to enforce the verdict. But he was not inviting Stapylton's lawyer to seek a new trial; he was simply refusing to impose sentence. The question was why. There had been at least four possibilities—Lewis was a party, Lewis was an interested witness, Lewis was a heathen, and Lewis was a chattel slave. Mansfield appeared to be relying on the last, and that was Granville Sharp's nightmare.

"He was taken in the last war and the capture I thought changed the property." "Changed the property" meant Lewis had once been Stapylton's property, then had become the property of the Spanish captain when captured on the high seas. Black slaves, Christian or not, were incompetent to testify. But the jury was supposed to say whether Lewis *was* a slave. Only if he was would Mansfield decide whether there could be such a thing in England. If slavery was illegal, Lewis was no slave, no matter what the jury said. Mansfield had once assumed Lewis free, unless otherwise proven. Now he assumed Lewis had once been Stapylton's property, thereby leaving the issues of the legality of English slavery a bigger mess than he had found it.

Still, Stapylton had failed to prove that his ownership of Lewis survived the black's capture by the Spanish captain. "There was no evidence before the court that he was the defendant's property, which was the ground upon which he acted," Dunning said. Amazingly, Mansfield agreed, "You say right." Yet without Lewis's testimony, Dunning could not prove that Lewis was not Stapylton's slave, just as Stapylton failed to prove he was. In short, neither side had proved anything material. Whoever had the burden of proof was going to lose.

Mansfield continued his unburdening. "I am glad of an opportunity of mentioning it, as I have a great doubt in my own mind whether he can be sufficient evidence of his freedom. . . . The point I left to the jury was that the capture made an end to the property of the defendant in this cause. . . . That was proved all by himself and nobody else that was with him." He was implying that Lewis had the burden of proof and, because he had failed to carry it, Mansfield would refuse to pass sentence. Sharp prodded Dunning to try again. At ten o'clock that Wednesday evening, Dunning did try gain, but neither the defendants nor Lord Mansfield appeared. Justice Aston, presiding, said, "The judgment must be respited . . . as we have no report of the cause." But Sharp was not finished.

On November 28, the last day of Michaelmas Term, Dunning made a final attempt to induce Mansfield to enter judgment and sentence Robert Stapylton, but Mansfield would have none of it:

I am surprised that Stapylton was brought up! I did not expect they would bring him up again! I was in great doubt, and so were my brother Judges, & many of the [Privy] Council, whether the black could be a proper witness of his freedom, he being the only witness; and I wish any body could satisfy me of that doubt. But I did not think they would have brought him up; and I should advise the Prosecutrix not to bring him up, as she has got the black in her possession."[12]

With that, Stapylton's case sputtered to a close. Three months later, in the middle of the *Somerset* case, Sir Joseph Banks still failed to comprehend it, and wrote to Granville Sharp: "You know, I suppose Mrs. Banks's cause is put off until this general question is determined."[13]

CHAPTER 10

The Struggle for the
Body of James Somerset

Somersett's Case . . . in which Lord Mansfield held
that slavery did not exist under the common law of England,
was a writ of habeas corpus.

Lehman v. Lycoming County Children's Services
(United States Court of Appeals for the Third Circuit, 1981)[1]

MANSFIELD'S ATROCIOUS AND cowardly fiddle-faddling in
Stapylton's case was so unbefitting a great judge that Granville
Sharp felt terribly betrayed. Soon after Dunning's final unsuccessful attempt to persuade Mansfield to sentence Stapylton, Sharp began drafting
a memorandum on the case. It was, he wrote, "merely intended to prevent
[the Stapylton] trial from being used as a precedent, & not to injure the
character of the judge," and he did not intend to show it to anyone "unless absolutely necessary." Stapylton had been indicted for violent acts
that plainly violated English law. Mansfield had the duty to enforce
that law in the absence of some legitimate exception. If none existed,
Stapylton's "plea of private property never ought to be admitted, or even
named," Sharp insisted.

This was cutting. Without bothering to invoke an exception, Mansfield had "absolutely refused to give judgment on a clear verdict, which was 3 times publicly approved by himself! He seems to think the bare mention of 'a doubt in his mind' a sufficient excuse." In June and November 1771, Mansfield had six times expressed "doubt," without giving any grounds, that Thomas Lewis could prove his freedom through his own testimony. This was a legal question restricted to Lewis's competency to testify, and Sharp wondered how the Scot could rely upon the king's laws for protection "if the said laws were really liable to be rendered *ineffectual*, even in England, by a mere groundless doubt of *one single* judge."

> A doubt is certainly a very insufficient excuse for an *arrest of judgment*, in any case whatever, unless *"strong and probable grounds"* are alleged to justify it; but a *groundless doubt* upon the present question would be particularly criminal; because it would, probably, tend to the introduction of the diabolical tyranny and injustice of the West Indian Colonies, whereby *human nature is vilified and degraded to the rank and level of brute beasts . . ."*

Sharp was incensed by Mansfield's exclusion of Lewis's testimony. Had the Chief Justice found an exception "or even an Act of Parliament, made expressly for the purpose of holding such unnatural kind of property in the Kingdom," Lewis's uncontradicted testimony ought to have been considered "because, it is, and ever has been the constant practice of the courts of law to allow, even to a felon, the benefit of his own evidence in his own cause."

Of course, the defendant Stapylton could not have given evidence under oath, though he might have made an unsworn statement to the jury. But Sharp had a point that, if it was Stapylton's burden to prove Lewis was his property, he had failed miserably, and Lewis would have been "entitled to a judgment in his favor even in the most tyrannical court of the West Indies." Mansfield had, "without the least foundation, either in reason, equity, or law," refused to impose sentence. Instead, the Chief Justice had dangerously subordinated the law to his own "will and pleasure." The action was dangerous because it could ul-

Granville Sharp (1735–1813), by George Dance

(Courtesy of National Portrait Gallery, London)

Charles Talbot, 1st Baron Talbot of Hensol (1685–1737),
by an unknown artist

(Courtesy of National Portrait Gallery, London)

Shown bottom opposite page:

Philip Yorke, 1st Earl of Lord Hardwicke (1690–1764), copied
by Joseph Wright of Derby after a work by Thomas Hudson

(Courtesy of Art & Visual Materials, Special Collections Department,
Harvard Law School Library)

Charles Steuart
(1725–1797)
(Courtesy of Colonial
Williamsburg Foundation)

John Dunning, 1st Baron Ashburton (1731–1783),
by Sir Joshua Reynolds

(Courtesy of National Portrait Gallery, London)

William Murray, 1st Earl of Mansfield (1705–1793),
by John Singleton Copley
(Courtesy of National Portrait Gallery, London)

The Honourable   Mr Just.^{ce} Ashhurst.

William Ashurst, Justice, Court of King's Bench (1725–1807)

(Courtesy of Professor James Oldham)

Singular Habiliment of

GEO: HILL ESQ.

The King's Antient Sergeant.

Published by Alex. Hogg & Co. at Paternoster Row May 1, 1804

George Hill, Serjeant-at-law (1716–1808), by an unknown artist, published 1804

Dido and Lady Elizabeth Finch Hatton, by Johann Ziffany
(Courtesy of the Earl of Mansfield)

timately "render all trials and laws useless and trifling" and drive men "to seek some other means of settling their differences"; it was so dangerous that Sharp thought it "ought to be esteemed an open contempt of the Legislature, as well as a notorious breach of the laws."

Mansfield, Sharp claimed, had demonstrated a

> "deplorable hardness of heart and abandoned spirit of justice," for when a notorious outrage and breach of the peace is committed under the pretence of any such *groundless claim of service*, the Magistrate who neglects to relieve the person oppressed, and *to punish* the offenders, is certainly a partaker of their guilt; and no upright and conscientious judge (who does not set up his *own will above the laws of the land*) can possibly entertain *any doubt in his mind* about the punishment of such offenders: for when the laws of the land, and especially the Habeas Corpus Act, are expressly and clearly *on one side of the question* (without the least exception whatever concerning any difference or distinction of persons), and when the *only plea* on the *other side of the question* is absolutely without foundation whether in natural equity or the established law and customs of this country, what room can there be for doubt? And how would a Judge be able to justify and arrest of judgment in such a case?

Had Parliament repealed the Habeas Corpus Act and enacted the worst of the West Indian slave laws, it would not matter, for "[n]o legislature on earth ... can alter the nature of things, or make that to be lawful, which is contrary to the law of God, the supreme Legislator and Governor of the World."

Mansfield's refusal either to sentence Stapylton or vacate the judgment against him was indefensible. If he felt sorry for a sick old man, Mansfield could have punished him lightly. Perhaps he believed that Walker, and Walker's briefing solicitor, had done such an awful job defending Stapylton that he slipped into the ancient position of the British judge who acts as counsel for the unrepresented accused. Maybe he really had reconsidered and concluded he erred in allowing Thomas Lewis to testify, because he was a slave. But that would have assumed the very issue being tried, circular reasoning to which Mansfield was not usually prone. Perhaps he wanted to avoid a ruling on the legality of British slavery because he believed it was a linchpin of British mercantilism. Whatever the reason, Mansfield had numerous legitimate arrows in his judicial quiver that he could have used to shoot down a jury verdict with which he disagreed. One of them was not bullying John Dunning into abandoning his client.

Then, the very afternoon in which he finally rid himself of Lewis's case, Stapylton, and the vexing question of the legality of British slavery, the petition for habeas corpus that James Somerset's three godparents had filed arrived at Mansfield's chambers at Serjeants Inn on Chancery Lane. This was the first time he had been directly confronted with a plain and forthright demand for a slave's freedom. Sometime between 6:00 P.M. and 8:00 P.M., the hours in which the judges of Court of King's Bench judges conducted business in chambers when Court was in session, Mansfield studied the petition and the accompanying affidavits, by candlelight and a heating fire. Though the king's subjects generally had the right to have a writ of habeas corpus issued on demand, as a practical matter, Mansfield did not have to grant it.[2] He had refused to sentence Stapylton that morning, and, had he been so determined, Mansfield could have avoided deciding the legality of English slavery at the outset of Somerset's case by refusing to issue the writ.

Some judges, not wishing to deal with the messy consequences of the *Somerset* decision, would later refuse. Mansfield's judgment spawned an epidemic of masters forcing black slaves to sign bogus apprenticeship agreements or indentures in a transparent offer to pass them off as apprentices or indentured servants. In 1799, one "apprentice," John Hamlet, was charged with violating the terms of his apprenticeship by "unlawfully absenting himself." As had James Somerset, Hamlet escaped. By affidavit, he informed the Court of King's Bench that he had flown because of the cruelties he had endured and the threat of his master to return him to the West Indian slave markets. By that time, however, the Court of King's Bench was Lord Kenyon's, not Mansfield's, and its judges refused to look behind Hamlet's spurious apprenticeship agreement, and refused to issue the writ that would bring Hamlet's body, and his vexing legal question, before them; they thereby doomed him to bondage.[3] In 1812, ten imprisoned black crewmen on a Portuguese ship in Truro Harbor alleged they had not contracted to be slaves, had been in England, and wished to remain. As with John Hamlet, the judges of the Court of King's Bench refused to issue the writ of habeas corpus with no explanation.[4]

Mansfield might have questioned whether a proper person had even sought the writ on Somerset's behalf. This problem arose every time a master demanded the return of his impressed apprentice or slave, for the servant had not applied for the writ, couldn't have if he wanted to, because the Admiralty was not in the habit of allowing a pressed seaman shore leave to petition the Court of King's Bench for his release.[5] A third party had to petition for him, and that person had to be an agent, or at least a friend, of the detained person, and the petition had to reflect the prisoner's desires. Wives and husbands could petition for each other, parents for minor children, children for aged parents, guardians for wards, brother for sister. Except in unusual circumstances, judges usually refused to consider petitions filed by strangers and, if some busybody managed to haul a prisoner into court, he might be sued. Mansfield could have ruled Somerset's three godparents strangers to the case and refused to issue the writ, but did not.

Habeas corpus was supposed to be a quick procedure, intended summarily to decide the lawfulness of a person's detention, on agreed facts, usually after oral argument, without a full trial, and without a jury. Not until 1816 could the truth of the reasons given for the detention even be challenged, in the absence of some outrageous falsehood.[6] When a genuine dispute existed over whether a black was a slave, as Somerset and Steuart were disagreeing, every American Southern court simply dismissed the petition, all the way up to the American Civil War. Mansfield could would have ruled that, as Somerset was property, he was not entitled to a writ of habeas corpus, but did not.

Perhaps, he had told John Dunning nine months before, the legality of English slavery should never be settled, in the interests of both slave and master. Now Mansfield dramatically increased the likelihood that the issue would be settled, and that he would settle it. He signed the order requiring Captain John Knowles to produce, "at Chambers . . . immediately after the receipt of this our Writ the body of James Summersett being detained under your Custody (as is said) together with day and cause of the taking and detainer of him the said James Summersett."[7]

We don't know who drafted Somerset's habeas corpus petition, but he knew what he was doing, for it was simple and direct. Somerset might be a slave in Africa and Virginia, but not in England. Captain Knowles had imprisoned him on Steuart's order to sell him in Jamaica.[8] Absent was any mention of Somerset's baptism or allegation that he had been freed.

It may have been the work of Serjeant William Davy, who led Somerset's legal team, though he would have been a rather odd choice. "Bull" Davy was probably the first of the five barristers enlisted. He was not always scrupulous, even as a barrister, and had been imprisoned after going spectacularly bankrupt as a druggist in Exeter. One elderly woman whom Davy was cross-examining about how she managed to recall an event that had happened on a long-ago day, rejoined, "Why, Sir, by a very remarkable token, that all cry of the city went that Mr. Davy, the drugster, had that morning shut up shop and ran away." The amused judge suggested, "I think, brother, that you want no further proof of the witness's memory."[9] And when a gentleman appeared before the Court of Kings Bench to give a 3,000-pound bail, Davy asked, "And pray Sir, how can you make out that you are worth 3,000 pounds?" The gentleman detailed property that amounted to 2,940 pounds. "That's all very good, Sir. But you want 60 pounds more to be worth 3,000 pounds." "For that sum," he said, "I have a note of hand of one Mr. Serjeant Davy, and I hope he will have the honesty to settle it soon."[10]

Davy had been admitted to the Inner Temple in 1741, attained the rank of Serjeant in 1752, King's Serjeant in 1762. He was unpopular with the attorneys who were the source of barrister's briefs. After claiming in 1765, in open court, that "out of the many mistakes that happen in the management of cases, 19 out of 20 happen by the ignorance of attorneys," the Society of Gentlemen Practisers voted to deny him briefs until he apologized in writing.[11] He was quick-witted, self-confident, and cocky, with a ready sense of humor, and no fear of Lord Mansfield.[12]

When the Chief Justice interrupted Davy in the middle of one argument by interjecting, "If this be the law I must burn all my books, I see," Davy replied, "Your Lordship had better read them first." And when Mansfield announced he intended to hear cases one Good Friday, Davy angrily replied, "Your Lordship will be the first judge to have done so since Pontius Pilate."[13] He was famous for his ability to cross-examine. In one seemingly hopeless case, Davy, bent on proving an election had been won through bribery, managed through grit and competence to force a reluctant witness to concede he had been part of a conspiracy to bribe.[14] But there would be no cross-examination in Somerset's habeas corpus case, and Davy was neither a civil libertarian nor was he known for his legal acumen.

We know Dunning did not draft the writ. He hadn't done a bad job as Lewis's counsel and, with the exception of Dunning's reticence to attack the legality of English slavery in his closing to the jury, Sharp had no reason to be displeased with him. But Steuart had pounced on Dunning first, probably to pre-empt Sharp.[15] And Dunning had accepted, to Sharp's disgust. In the margin of the page that records how Dunning told the Stapylton jury he reserved the right to insist that slavery could not exist in England, Sharp would scrawl, first along the bottom, then straight up the right margin,

> When Mr. Dunning spoke these words he held in his hand G. Sharp's Book on the illegality of tolerating slavery in England (printed in 1769), having one finger in the book to hold open a particular part: and after so solemn a declaration he appeared on the opposite side of the question against James Somerset the very next year. This is an abominable & insufferable practice of lawyers to undertake causes diametrically opposite to their own decided opinions of Law and Common Justice!!!

Sharp complained to Serjeant Davy about what Dunning had done: "In the [Stapylton] trial [Dunning said], I will maintain in any place, and in any Court in this Kingdom reserving to myself a right to insist that our laws admit no property [in a slave]. Thus Mr. Dunning had publickly pledged himself to maintain not only that our Laws admit no such property but also that no such property can exist, which is certainly true."[16]

A nineteenth-century serjeant argued that Sharp, untrained in the law, failed to appreciate a barrister's solemn duty to accept any case brought him, "based upon constitutional liberty, for every subject in the realm has a right to avail himself of the services of any lawyer, unless he be otherwise retained, or unless in office under the Crown."[17] Senator Sumner would acknowledge that Westminster Hall barristers acted this way, but believed it "the lawyer's duty to uphold *human rights* . . . and when he undertakes to uphold a wrong outrageous as slavery, his proper function is so far reversed that he can aptly be described . . . [as] the Devil's Advocate."[18]

The problem was Dunning's "audacious assertion . . . of the maxim, that a new brief will absolve an advocate from the disgrace of publicly retracting any avowal however solemn, of any principle however sacred."[19] It was not that he was representing one man's claim to the right to sell another—many distinguished lawyers would argue slavery's legality and suffer no diminishment of their reputations—but that he had so stoutly and sincerely claimed that English slavery could not legally exist then, a few months later, stoutly and sincerely claimed not only that it did but that it always had. Britons would have been reminded of Jonathan Swift's description of lawyers in *Gulliver's Travels* as having been "bred up from their youth in the art of proving by words multiplied for the purpose, that white is black and black is white, according as they are paid."[20] It didn't help that lawyers and judges had been under assault for decades, charged with exacting exorbitant fees, with speaking and writing incomprehensibly, single-mindedly catering to wealth, and unreasonably delaying litigation, which partly explained such a steep decline in Westminster Hall suits that only about a sixth of the number of suits heard in 1670 were being heard in 1770.[21]

One historian jeered that Dunning "never allowed his liberalism and high moral principles to interfere with his pocket."[22] In this his sixteenth year of barristering, Dunning was at the height of his earning power, having amassed the breathtaking barrister's income of 8,535 pounds in 1771 and 8,015 pounds in 1770; he acted as leading counsel for the Crown in the Court of King's Bench more than seventy times and earned about twenty times the income of a middle-class Englishman, 50 percent more than the next highest-earning barrister.[23] He had outlasted hard times, having made less than 300 pounds in the first four years of practice combined. Adam Smith would claim that twenty barristers failed for each who succeeded; even Blackstone had thrown in the towel after seven bleak years.[24] Having scrabbled to the pinnacle, Dunning knew he had just a few years to make his fortune before he fell from favor, and the West Indies interests paid handsomely. But he was not just a greedy lawyer, for he had, on principle, resigned as Solicitor General, an office that brought high fees, knowing it would almost certainly cost him the opportunity of attaining high judicial office, the Chief Justiceship of the Court of King's Bench or Court of Common Pleas, or the Lord Chancellorship; any of these positions would have led to greater, and more permanent, income.[25] That he was a man torn became obvious during the case, for he would not be his usual self. So "dull and languid" did Steuart believe Dunning that he would write to a Boston friend near the end of the case that Dunning "would have made a much better figure on [Somerset's] side."[26] On the other hand, none of Somerset's five lawyers asked for, or received, a penny for their services.

Dunning was not the only spur to Sharp's anger. He was choleric over Mansfield's having exacted promises, apparently from the three godparents, to pay heavy penalties of 140 pounds if James Somerset failed to appear in court: "[H]is Lordship (instead of binding the defendant [Steuart] to answer for his notorious outrage) advised the widow, who had been at the expense of the writ, to purchase the Plaintiff [Somerset] of the Defendant [Steuart], but he was answered very properly by the widow, that the same would be an acknowledgment that the Defendant had a right to assault and imprison a poor innocent man, and that she would never be guilty of setting an example."[27]

Sharp should not have been upset. Although he had thoroughly prepared the *Representation,* he remained a layman with extremely limited court experience, and he misunderstood the nature of habeas corpus. After the treachery of Mansfield in Stapylton's case, then Dunning in

Somerset's, Sharp's dislike of lawyers and judges flared. So many lawyers appeared mesmerized by Talbot and Yorke, Blackstone and Dunning (as Solicitor General) being the most prominent, and in recent years, Sharp had become used to instructing lawyers, rather than being instructed, about the law of English slavery.

It has been charged that Sharp was misled by the young reporter of decisions, Capel Lofft, who "committed an unforgivable sin for a barrister of entitling the case, *Somerset v. Stewart*."[28] It is true Somerset's case is entitled either *England, the King v. James Somersett, a Negro* or *England* ex parte *James Summersett* in the *Rule Book of the Court of the King's Bench from Trinity 1768 to Hilary 1774*, and that *The Compleat Guide* repeatedly refers to a habeas corpus petitioner as the defendant or prisoner.[29] But, in the latter half of the eighteenth century, Court of King's Bench habeas corpus reports used an array of habeas corpus case names that might easily have confused both Lofft and Sharp.[30]

Mansfield acted correctly in ordering a bond to secure James Somerset's appearance. It would have been irrational to place Charles Steuart under bond, for the worst thing that could have happened to him was an order to release James Somerset. Better for Somerset if Steuart failed to defend, as Stapylton had, and conceded Somerset's freedom. On the other hand, a bond was meant to encourage Somerset to return for the hearings on the legality of his detention, for the worse thing that could have happened to him would have been shipment to Jamaica. Mansfield could have remanded him into custody, but chose not to do so.

The amount of bail Mansfield imposed is another story, for 140 pounds was more than the average unskilled London laborer earned in four years.[31] The usual bail imposed was high enough, 20 pounds for the defendant, and two others had to guarantee 10 pounds apiece.[32] At one hearing, John Dunning, emphasizing how much money was tied up in the bodies of England's estimated 15,000 English slaves, would place the worth of each slave at 50 pounds. One hundred and forty pounds therefore amounted to almost three times Somerset's value as a slave on the open market and more than three times the usual bail amount imposed. Sharp had plenty to grouse about here.

James Somerset's knock on Sharp's Old Jewry door on January 13, 1772, forced Sharp into a critical decision. He quickly ascertained that Lord Mansfield, guilty he believed of moral cowardice and gross dereliction of judicial duty toward Thomas Lewis, was to preside over Somerset's trial and that it was scheduled to begin in just a few weeks. Should he pass Somerset by and wait for another test case, perhaps in the Court of Common Pleas, even the Chancery? As he recorded in his diary, "I gave the best advice I could."[33] We have no idea what that was, but do know the following day a Mr. Cade, who lived at 7 Cumberland Street, Drury Lane, and may have been related to the godparent Elizabeth Cade, called on Sharp, who had already swung into action.

Two days later, Sharp privately published the cutting memorandum he had written after Stapylton's trial. He immediately placed this *Appendix to the Representation Against Slavery* in Serjeant Davy's hands, with a note saying it was "merely intended to prevent this trial from being quoted as a precedent, and not to injure the character of the Judge." He asked Davy not to mention it or show it to anyone "not immediately concerned" in Somerset's cause, unless it was unavoidable: "[A]s the point in question is a public cause, the author would be extremely sorry that there should be the least appearance of private resentment, by making these remarks more public than is absolutely necessary for the purpose intended."[34] Before the *Somerset* case ended, Sharp would send the *Appendix* to each of the judges.[35]

Nine days later, on January 24, 1772, the second day of Hilary Term, Somerset appeared again before Lord Mansfield. Taking shorthand, at the cost of a pound and a shilling, was Sharp's stenographer, William Blanchard, who had taken down the *Lewis* proceedings. The hearing was brief.[36] After Captain Knowles's return to the writ of habeas corpus was read aloud, Serjeant Davy asked that the case be put over to Easter Term, which followed Hilary, to allow the lawyers adequate time to prepare such an important matter. Mansfield agreed to continue the case just a fortnight, to February 7, and set it down for the first full day of argument. However, Mansfield said that "if it should come fairly to the general question, whatever the opinion of the court might be, even if they were all agreed on one side or the other, the subject was of so general and extensive concern, that, from the nature of the question, he should certainly take the opinion of all the [twelve] judges on it."[37] The following day, the *General Evening Post* reported that "[t]he cause of the trial was, to know how far a black servant was the property of the purchasers by the laws of England, as the black refused going back with his master to Jamaica. But as it was thought by the Court a very important decision, it was postponed till towards the end of the term, when his Lordship said he would take the opinion of the rest of his brother judges."[38]

The next Saturday, Sharp heard again from Francis Hargrave, now thirty-one years old, with whom he had corresponded about slavery while in the throes of the Lisle lawsuit. A friend, Hargrave wrote, had just informed him of the previous day's argument before the Court of Kings Bench. He figured Sharp's work in the Jonathan Strong case made it likely he would know what was going on. If so, "I am very ready to communicate any arguments that occur to me on the subject," Hargrave wrote, "with as much pleasure, as if I had been retained as one of the Counsel in the Cause."

Three years before, Hargrave had sent Sharp some rough thoughts, "too loose and inaccurate to bear a critical examination," and asked that Sharp not allow anyone to see them. In the interim, Hargrave believed he had more capably "thought upon the subject" and desired to forward Sharp the fruits of his thinking.[39] Sharp had greatly influenced him. At page 412 of his copy of the first edition of Blackstone's *Commentaries*, where Hargrave disputes that a slave could ever enter into a valid contract with his master, is the inscription: "See Sharp's Representation on the Injustice of Tolerating Slavery in England."[40] James Somerset delivered Sharp's reply the following day, along with a copy of the newly minted *Appendix*. Sharp noted that no one but Lord Mansfield would fully understand it, but he explained that it had resulted from the injustice Mansfield had perpetrated in Stapylton's case. He said he had been happy to learn from Blanchard's transcript of Friday's hearing that Mansfield now appeared to be backing away from the doubts he had expressed in Stapylton's case "and even went so far as to drop some hints of favourable wishes for the cause of the Negro."

The bearer, James Somerset, is the unfortunate Negro whose cause is now before the Court; and in whatever manner you can best serve him, either as one of his counsel, to assist Serjeant Davy, or as his advocate in print (I mean in respect to the *general question*), you will certainly do a great act of private charity, as well as a public good. The hint, which I have already given you about Lord Mansfield's behaviour on Friday, will convince you, that arguments on this point cannot be produced at a more critical or more favourable time than the present.

Sharp tucked in a copy of an opinion by Lord De Grey, then Chief Justice of the Court of Common Pleas, written when he was Attorney General, that a master might have a contractual interest in the services of a female slave, but "no property in her person by the Laws of this Country."[41] De Grey had forbidden Sharp from publishing the opinion because it was a private case, and it was not usual to make such matters public, but he had been of the same opinion in 1769. Sharp offered Hargrave a transcript of Friday's hearing, as well as the transcripts of proceedings "on similar cases."[42]

On Wednesday, January 29, Sharp handed Mr. Hughes, clerk to his solicitor, Mr. Priddle, six pounds, six shillings, to retain two counsel in Somerset's case. Two days later, Hargrave told Sharp that he had received the retainer and that Sharp might "be assured, that no application shall be wanting" on Hargrave's part "to conduce to that great end" to which Sharp aspired. He was convinced "that the state of Slavery, in which a Negro may be before his arrival in England, gives no title whatever to Service here, either on the ground of property, or on presumption of a Contract."

However eager he was to assist in the great cause, this was still Hargrave's first case as a barrister, and he was worried.

[N]ever having yet argued any Case publickly, I distrust my ability to acquit myself, as such a cause requires. On that account my situation will be painfull, tho' I hope, that the Expectation of that Indulgence of the Court, usually given to persons under my circumstances, and the assurance that others who shall hear me will make the due allowances, will so far operate on my mind, as to give me the Opportunity of urging all the arguments which shall occur to me.[43]

That Hargrave proved himself would be demonstrated by Justice MacLean's 1856 dissent in the *Dred Scott* case, in which he mentioned that *Somerset* "was argued at great length, and with great ability, by Hargrave and others, who stood among the most eminent counsel in England."[44]

As the next hearing was just nine days off, Sharp instructed Priddle to hasten his briefs, which summarized the evidence and case, to Hargrave and the other barristers, who now numbered three. Priddle's clerk promised Sharp the briefs would be delivered by Monday. To Sharp's delight, he now received a note from the prominent Quaker physician, John Fothergill, with whom he had been corresponding for almost three years, with a copy of his own *Representation*, as abridged by the Pennsylvania Quaker, Anthony Benezet, without this knowledge, for distribution in America. It was the same man whose work, *A Short Account of That Part of Africa Inhabited by the Negroes*, Sharp had abridged and distributed in London without Benezet's knowledge in 1767. James Somerset delivered Sharp's reply to Dr. Fothergill, in which he wrote that Benezet had "very judiciously extracted the very marrow of my book." He went on: "The bearer, James Somerset, is the Negro whose cause comes on next Friday." Sharp asked Fothergill to give Somerset any copies of Benezet's abridgment that he might spare, so that he could provide them to Somerset's counsel and the judges.[45] Fothergill sent Sharp five more copies. Sharp immediately dispensed one to each of Somerset's four barristers and one to the prime minister, Lord North. The sixth he had James Somerset deliver directly to Lord Mansfield.[46]

On the Tuesday before the hearing, solicitor Priddle promised Sharp that the briefs would be delivered to counsel by Wednesday, just two days before the hearing. The next day, Sharp delivered an iron muzzle used on black slaves to Serjeant Davy:

It is, indeed *an Iron Argument*, which must at once convince all those whose hearts are not of a harder metal, that men are not to be entrusted with an absolute authority over their brethren. The instrument is called a *Mouth Piece* and many wholesale ironmongers in town keep quantities of them ready in order to supply the merchants and planters orders for the West Indian Islands. They are used on various occasions, sometimes for punishment, when Negroes are what they call *Sulky* (and who would not be *Sulky* under arbitrary power), and sometimes to prevent the poor wretches from gnawing the sugar canes. And sometimes they are used to prevent the poor despairing wretches in slavery from *eating dirt* (in order to commit suicide)."[47]

The day before the hearing, Sharp wrote Hargrave of his disappointment that solicitor Priddle, as late as the evening before, had still not sent the briefs to Hargrave "nor to any of the other gentlemen. To what his behaviour is to be attributed I don't know, but I make no doubt that you and the other gentlemen will be sufficiently aware to prevent his negligence (wilful or otherwise) from injuring the poor man's cause."[48]

CHAPTER 11

Lord Mansfield Is Deceived

My Lord, this is as great a question and perhaps a question of as
much consequence as can come before this or any court of justice.

Serjeant Davy to the Court of King's Bench, February 7, 1772

O N FRIDAY, FEBRUARY 7, 1772, three puisne, or associate,
judges—Richard Aston, Edward Willes, and William Henry
Ashurst—took their seats to hear the *Somerset* case, alongside Lord
Mansfield. They had sat as the Court of King's Bench since June 1770,
and would continue sitting together until 1778, when Aston died.[1]
Heavily bewigged, the four judges were in their winter robes, dressed
according to rules handed down on June 4, 1635. Westminster judges in
term were to wear gowns of either black or velvet with matching hood,
over which they were to wear a mantle, the end of the hood hanging
over behind, velvet caps, lawn coifs, cornered caps, and, in winter, robes
faced with white furs of miniver.

William Blackstone had very nearly sat in place of Ashurst. In 1770,
Blackstone had been appointed to the Court of Common Pleas, then
switched places with Justice Yates, of the Court of King's Bench. When
Yates died, Blackstone returned to the Court of Common Pleas,
Ashurst taking his place. One can only speculate what Blackstone

might have said and done, in light of his *Commentaries'* varying opinions on the legality of English slavery and his belief that villeinage and slavery were different, and how he might have affected the Mansfield Judgment had he remained on the Court of King's Bench. Perhaps he might have broken with Lord Mansfield, as Mansfield would break with Lord Hardwicke. As it was, none of the puisne judges took a large public role in the *Somerset* case.

Aston, who said little during the *Somerset* hearings, had come to the Court of King's Bench in 1765 by way of the Irish Court of Common Pleas, where he had been Chief Justice. He was a solid journeyman judge, undistinguished in legal ability or learning, and was said to be rough-mannered. He lived almost next door to his Chief in Bloomsbury Square, obviously respected Mansfield, and was the closest of the judges to him. Willes, whose ascent to the bench had opened the way for John Dunning to become Attorney General four years before, was suffering the sustained, sometimes withering, contempt of Lord Mansfield. Son of the unpopular, indolent, and biased former Chief Justice of the Court of Common Pleas, Sir John Willes, Edward Willes's nineteen years as Court of King's Bench justice were marked mostly by "a certain flippancy of manner and a neglect of costume."[2] Willes resented Mansfield's disrespect. To Willes's chagrin and occasional fury, Mansfield sometimes publicly displayed his scorn by turning away from Willes in open court, instead of soliciting his opinion, as he did with other justices. Finally, Willes could bear no more. "I have not been consulted," he shrieked, "and I will be heard!" Young Jeremy Bentham, then a student at Lincoln's Inn, like other legal beginners, often attended hearings at which Mansfield presided. Bentham was sitting in Westminster Hall that day, and Willes's outburst became etched so deeply in his mind that decades later he recalled that "the feminine scream issuing out of [Willes's] manly frame" was still tingling in his ears.[3] He dissented three times, once insisting that juries had the right to give a general verdict in libel cases.[4]

The *London Evening Post* of February 8 reported that the previous day's habeas corpus hearing had been brought "with a view of trying the point how far a negro, or other black, is a slave in England, and consequently entirely at his master's disposal."[5] In the audience sat the thirty-year-old Attorney General of Rhode Island, Henry Marchant, future Continental Congressman and federal judge, who had stayed in London for several months during a tour of England. He, too, recorded that the case had been brought "with a view of trying the point how far a negro or other black, is a slave in England, and consequently entirely at his master's disposal."[6] That was certainly Sharp's intention, but had someone actually said so at the hearing?

According to Steuart's answer to the petition for a writ of habeas corpus, or return, at the time "James Sommersett" was taken from Africa, and for a long time before, Englishmen had been trading for the large numbers of negro slaves who, by local law, were chattels and goods, needed to supply Jamaica, Virginia, and other British colonies. "Sommersett" had been a slave in Africa before being shipped to Virginia for sale on March 10, 1749. He remained a slave when Charles Steuart, a Virginia inhabitant, purchased him in Virginia on August 1, 1749, and had not been set free. On October 1, 1769, Steuart left America for England on business, intending to return when his business was transacted. He brought "Sommersett" to England as "his slave and property" to attend and serve him. They had arrived in London in the parish of St. Mary-Le-Bow in the ward of Cheap on November 10, 1769. When Steuart's business was finished, he intended to bring Sommersett back to America with him. Sommersett served Steuart until October 1, 1771, when he left, without Steuart's consent and against his will, "and without any lawful authority." When Somerset "absolutely refused" to return to his service, on November 27, 1771, Steuart delivered him to Captain Knowles, master and commander of the *Ann and Mary*, a ship then lying in the Thames. There he was being "safely and securely kept" until Captain Knowles could transport him to Jamaica "to be there sold as the slave and property of the said Charles Steuart."[7]

The return was deceptive. In an age in which common lawyers omitted nothing material from their filings, at peril of suffering dismissal, one vital fact was missing: Steuart and Somerset had lived in Massachusetts for the four years before they sailed for England. A fair reading of the return leaves the strong impression that Virginia was the place of every significant American event and that Virginia law applied. For nearly a hundred years, every newspaper, magazine, book, and monograph report stated, or strongly implied, that the pair had come to England from Virginia. The return never actually stated that Virginia law determined Somerset's slave status at any time, except the date of his 1749 sale, or that Steuart and Somerset had lived in Virginia continuously since 1749, or that the two had embarked for England from Virginia, or that they intended to return to Virginia. Listening to the return read in open court, Henry Marchant recorded that Steuart was "the proprietor of a negro slave in Virginia," that "Steuart then purchased him as a slave [in Virginia], and from hence brought him to England," and that Steuart had been "about to return to Virginia," when Somerset escaped. None of it was true, but it was in Steuart's interest for everyone to believe it was.

If the return had mentioned that Steuart and Somerset had lived in Massachusetts the four years before they sailed for England, Somerset's status, slave or free, might have been determined by the law of Massachusetts, not of Virginia. To a certainty, Somerset would have been counted a slave in Virginia. For most of the eighteenth century, the only slavery debate in that colony had been whether blacks should be classified as real property, along with land, or grouped with cows as personal property.[8] That was not the story in Massachusetts. Its legislature had never explicitly approved slavery and, along with public opinion and the judges, had been uncertainly groping toward liberty for all.[9] The governors were the exceptions; as late as 1771, Thomas Hutchinson vetoed a bill to prohibit the importation of slaves into Massachusetts. At the beginning of the Revolution, the military governor, Thomas Gage, showed no more sympathy. That changed after the British were evicted from Boston.[10]

In 1795, Dr. Jeremy Belknap, the abolitionist founder of the Massachusetts Historical Society, responded to queries on the history of Massachusetts slavery from Virginia Judge St. George Tucker. In response to one that asked "to what causes [slavery's] abolition is to be ascribed," Belknap replied, "[T]he principal cause was publick opinion." To another that sought the mode of Massachusetts abolition, Belknap responded, "[S]lavery had been abolished [in Massachusetts] by publick opinion; which began to be established about 30 years ago."[11] That would have been around 1765, as Somerset and Steuart were settling into Boston.

A series of cases had "resulted in something of a Massachusetts 'common law' of abolition"; many were filed while Steuart and Somerset were living there.[12] In the 1766 case of *Slew v. Whipple,* a woman born of a white mother and black father sued for trespass after being kept four years as a slave. The case was brought by Jeremiah Gridley, one of Massachusetts's most prominent lawyers and a hero to John Adams. Adams was in the courtroom when judgment was announced and recorded Justice Oliver, of the Essex Superior Court of Judicature, declaring: "This is a contest between liberty and property—both of great consequence, but liberty of most importance of the two."[13] In *Margaret v. Muzzy,* which began in 1768, a black sued to possess herself and the jury awarded her to herself.[14] A 1774 Essex County jury freed Caleb Dodge finding "no law of the province [held] a man to serve for life"[15]; the Quock Walker cases of 1781–1783 definitively ended Massachusetts slavery.

Belknap wrote to Judge Tucker that several suits were instituted by blacks before the Revolution "and the juries invariably gave their verdict in favour of liberty." A Boston publisher would be the first colonist to reprint Francis Hargrave's written version of his *Somerset* argument.[16] Looking back from Washington, D.C., the same year Belknap answered Tucker's queries, Vice President John Adams recalled his own participation "in several causes in which negroes sued for their freedom" before the Revolution: "The arguments in favor of their liberty were much the same as have been urged since in debates in Parliament &c arising from the rights of mankind."[17] Adams claimed that he "never knew a Jury by a verdict to determine a negro to be a slave—and they always found them free."[18]

Adams's memory had failed him. In 1768, the jury in *Newport v. Billing* not only determined the plaintiff was a slave, but Adams was the master's counsel![19] From Adams's Delphic trial notes it appears he argued that a negro was presumed enslaved, yet James Putnam, Adams's first legal mentor, now counsel for the black, repeated Montesquieu's satire that negros were "all over black, and with such a flat nose, that they can scarcely be pitied [and so] [I]t is hardly to be believed that God . . . should place a soul, especially a good soul, in such a black ugly body," and cited Lord Holt's antislavery opinions in *Smith v. Gould, Smith v. Brown and Cooper,* and *Chamberline v. Harvey.*[20] The year *Somerset* was decided, 1772, in *Caesar v. Taylor,* another master, again represented by Adams, was convicted of false imprisonment, though he claimed he owned the plaintiff, and Adams argued that Massachusetts courts presumed all blacks to be slaves.[21]

Serjeant Davy assumed Virginia's was the applicable colonial law. At the February 7 hearing, referring to the laws of Virginia, he would tell the judges that a "new species of tyranny" was gripping America, "created entirely by Colony government," and that Davy was "afraid of fighting the air not knowing precisely upon what ground . . . they [would] insist upon the prevalence of the Colony laws in this country . . . [for] all the people that come into this country immediately become subject to the laws of this country." "[E]ither this man remains upon his arrival in England in the condition he was abroad in Virginia or he does not. . . . If he does . . . the master's power remain as before. [But] either all the laws of Virginia . . . attach to him here or none, for where will they draw the line?"

The return, Davy said, stated: "[I]n Africa there are slaves and that this man was . . . brought from Africa being a slave and sold in Virginia. Now my Lord these are two distinct matters, his being a slave in Africa and his being a slave in Virginia, for by the laws of Virginia his having been a slave in Africa does not at all affect the question here . . . I have looked in the Virginia laws." Davy had located two relevant Virginia statutes, the second repealing the first and making slaves of "[a]ll negros and others that cannot make due proof of being free in England or in any other Christian country . . . notwithstanding their being converted to Christianity afterwards." He then asked two questions: "[W]ith regard to the laws of Virginia, do they bind here? Have the laws of Virginia any more influence, power, or authority in this country than the laws of Japan?" The king could make whatever laws he pleased for Virginia, but he could not make laws in England "without the consent and authority of parliament." He would refer to Virginia slave law more than two dozen times, and never once mentioned Massachusetts.

Neither of Steuart's lawyers ever corrected Serjeant Davy's misunderstanding, nor the misapprehensions of Somerset's other barristers. In 1864, Emory Washburn noted the discrepancy in an address to the Massachusetts Historical Society, yet detected nothing untoward in the mix-up, "Virginia and America, probably being, in an Englishman's mind, synonymous terms."[22] The members of the Massachusetts Historical Society would not have understood England and Europe as synonymous, nor Middlesex County and England. Charles Steuart, John Dunning, and James Wallace were capable of differentiating England from France, and Lord Mansfield easily distinguished Massachusetts from Virginia.

The deceit began with the return. But who drafted it? John Dunning was not yet Steuart's lawyer, and duping a court would have been unlike him. Captain Knowles had too slight an interest in Somerset's fate to risk such a deception. The West India slave interests, whose control over tens of thousands of Caribbean slaves and hundreds of thousands of pounds, could turn on the outcome, might have been willing to try, but they were not yet involved the case. That leaves Charles Steuart. Although Robert Stapylton had been willing to forfeit his claim to Thomas Lewis, Charles Steuart had decided to fight for Somerset. In December 1771, when the return was drafted, his anger over Somerset's betrayal was whitest, and lawyers' fees and costs had not yet begun to build.

Lord Mansfield observed that the return claimed Somerset as Steuart's property. "My Lord," Serjeant Davy began, "this is as great a question and perhaps a question of as much consequence as can come before this or any court of justice."

CHAPTER 12

Upon What Principle Is It That a Man Can Become a Dog for Another Man?

It has been established for over 200 years that people cannot, at common law, own people, *Somerset v. Stewart.*

J. Binney, dissenting[1]

IN HIS OPENING argument, Serjeant Davy vowed to persuade the judges that "no man at this day is, or can be, a slave in England," emphasizing "at this day," for, he acknowledged, "there had been a time when slavery was understood to exist in this kingdom. But that was a great while ago indeed."[2] Roman, Danish, or Christian, "whatever was its origin, at whatever time it commenced, [slavery was] tyranny and oppression . . . a usurpation upon the natural rights of mankind," though villeinage had never been as terrible as black chattel slavery: "No lord of a villein could dare to say what this honest gentleman says here by this return. It would not have been endured that he was his property—his slave—that he was going to transport him and sell him abroad."

Villeinage's potential for mischief weighed Davy's mind, as it burdened Sharp's. That it had never been abolished opened the way for the argument not just that "as villeinage was allowed by the common law, it cannot be argued that a state of servitude is absolutely unknown to and inconsistent therewith," as Blackstone had written Sharp, but that English common law recognized, to that day, a status arguably akin to chattel slavery, and perhaps to slavery outright. That no one had occupied that position for almost two centuries didn't mean it didn't exist. This argument Serjeant Davy meant to preempt and, according to Henry Marchant, he "very forcibly argued."

Villeinage ended because "the people themselves and the interpreters and oracles of the law who were the judges—they in all ages seem[ed] to have revolted against villeinage," Davy said.

> [B]y every subterfuge, by every art and chican and by every possible contrivance, though they were never able to contradict the laws . . . I consider the commencement of villeinage to be entirely an oppression and I consider the extinction of it to be nothing more than a general assertion of the natural rights of mankind, according to the temper, disposition, and spirit of the people of this country, its climate, the genius of the people and the soil all which I look upon to be the ingredients to make up the English constitution.

Suppose that a man for half a crown, Davy proposed, agreed to confess that he was a villein in open court and found a barrister willing to act the accomplice,

> I should be glad to know what the Court would say of it—if a learned counsel or serjeant very gravely and sagaciously—[here Davy's wit emerged]—as in the Common Pleas it must be a grave serjeant with a grave, that is to say, a sad countenance, was to move the Court that [the man's confession] might be admitted upon record, My Lord, I don't know what the judges of the Court of Common Pleas would say, but I am sure they would stare at it. I do believe it is impossible for a serjeant to be found to make such a move. If they did they must do it with a very sad countenance indeed. But I am sure it would be a very sad effect, for it is impossible [that] any judge would hear more of it. They would be told

that all England would revolt at it, that the genius of the people would nor suffer it, that there could not be any man that would dare to introduce such a record in any court. But yet there is no law against it, no Act of Parliament against it. Why? Why not? Why should not a man be a villein? Where is the law? Where the statute? Where the distinction? Where is the common law? Show the book if you can that forbids it! No such book can be found, but there is the law written in the hearts of men of this country. That is the law. It is the constitution. For the constitution of this country requires it when that is not found in particular books it is growing out of the hearts of men.

What if Somerset were a slave "at Virginia," Henry Marchant recorded Serjeant Davy's argument. "If the laws of Virginia reach here, and continue him a slave, all the laws of Virginia may as well reach here and so we are governed by the laws of Virginia, and not our own, at least all the laws affecting his state as a slave." What if a Christian slave brought from Turkey or a Bashaw arrived in England "with half a score Circassian women slaves for his amusement? I believe he would make but a miserable figure at the bar of the Old Bailey upon an indictment for rape." The relationship between master and slave, Davy insisted, was either "totally affected" or it was affected not at all.

Davy called the judges' attention to the ancient *Mirror of Justice*'s claim that baptism enfranchised slaves, though not villeins, and argued that it was probably correct with respect to enslaved non-Christians, because they were infidels and subjects of an infidel prince. "[I]f there was such a sort of people as these, the instant they were baptized they ceased to be infidels and were then out of the state and condition from whence their slavery accrued." It was only logical that "if the right of slavery attached upon them merely upon account of their being infidels—if slavery was the effect of their being infidels—if removed by baptism he ceases to be a slave." Davy's source wasn't reliable, though it would be fifteen years before a writer would express skepticism.[3] The *Mirror of Justice* was written about 1290 by Andrew Horn, a chamberlain of London, and is such a chimera of sober legal chronicling and laughable falsifications that some suspect it was a huge joke. It wasn't even discovered until the sixteenth century, but was then received as gospel.

Why was Davy attempting to resurrect the ghost of the "baptism brings freedom" argument, when the Joint Opinion appeared to have nailed that coffin? Perhaps he was testing whether the Court of King's Bench might have opened to the argument. Its 1677 *Butts v. Penny* decision had justified slavery alternatively on the infidelity of blacks. James Somerset was no infidel; that Davy could prove. He must have scrutinized the faces of the four judges to detect even a flicker of interest. Apparently he saw nothing, for he immediately abandoned the attempt: "I don't pretend that baptism makes any alteration, for I am afraid that idea has hindered many of those poor men from being instructed in the religion of this country, so I renounce the idea of baptism making any alteration in slavery in this country." Baptism didn't matter. A slave might arrive from Poland and, if his owner "should ask what is their enfranchisement, I answer, the soil and the air is their enfranchisement and their arrival here sets them free."

Davy's version of Sharp's heroic tale of how the determined common lawyers and judges of England had vanquished villeinage implicitly suggested to the judges of the Court of the King's Bench how they should treat black slavery today. When a man's villein status was disputed, Davy said, up to the time of the eleventh year of the reign of Queen Elizabeth I, when the last case involving a villein was reported, "the judges by some device or other freed the men. In every one of these accounts, I don't find a man ever came into court and went out a villein in any case for these two or three hundred years past. In the instance I alluded to the man did not go out again a villein."

This last case was Cartright's Case, in which a Russian slave had been brought to England in the sixteenth century. Then, Davy said, "it was resolved that England was too pure an air for slaves to breathe in," a sentiment expressed not in the enlightened eighteenth century, but in the gloomier day of Queen Elizabeth, when the English people were treated by the House of Commons "in a very different manner to what the Crown would presume or dare to treat them now. And when Monarchy held its head so very high in this country, as it did in the reign of Queen Elizabeth, it was resolved that England was too pure an air for slaves to breathe in." Davy paused. "I hope, my Lord, the air does not blow worse since. I hope it is not, but unless there is a change of air I hope they will never breathe here. For that is my assertion. The moment they put their feet upon English ground, that moment they become free." Henry Marchant was impressed: "That any slave being once in England, the very air he breathed made him a free man" went into his diary.

Davy conjured the England that might evolve should the judges fail James Somerset; in that England, nothing would stop the West Indian owner of an English estate from "stocking his farm with negroes . . . instead of the farmers who now drive his plough, he would say call out a hundred of my fellows and set them to the plough, and go to the ironmongers for half a score of tortures to make them do it the better. I have one at home [this was the iron muzzle Sharp had given him two days before] tho' I did not think it proper to bring it down to show your Lordship." Perhaps another West Indian might come to England "with half a million in his pocket, build a fine house, but is served entirely by negroes, here is one upon his coach box, and half a dozen behind, some at the plough, some at the carts, some a serving, others reaping and so on." Such men might become grandfathers to ten slaves, which "would occasion a great deal of heartburn." In this England, a master could inflict the "moderate punishment" (for Virginia) of slicing off half a man's foot with an axe had he the temerity to attempt escape, or even kill him during correction. This also impressed Marchant, who recorded that planters might "yoke them in his ploughs, or carts, instead of horses."

To Davy's repetition of Montesquieu's ironic arguments—"[S]ugar would be dearer, therefore for God's sake let these men be slaves. What a ridiculous argument [and] suppose these men cannot have souls . . . at least these are not men that they are divested of all rank of humanity"— Mansfield dryly inquired, "Have you any account how many planters were persuaded to that by Montesquieu?" "Oh, planters," Davy replied; was it with disdain? Then he moved on.

Davy summarized the major slavery cases. Reaching *Smith v. Brown and Cooper,* he said Lord Holt had correctly instructed the plaintiff to amend his complaint to allege that, though sold in London, the slave had never left Virginia. Lord Mansfield objected: "In truth and in fact the slave was sold in London, was not he?"

Davy became flustered. "Yes. But the slave himself was in London and sold in London." This was a serious blunder that could harm Somerset's case; Davy's co-counsel must have stiffened. "The slave himself was in London and sold in London," Justice Willes repeated, as if to give Davy the opportunity to recant. But Davy said nothing. Justice Ashurst leaped to make it plain what Davy was conceding: "So it was as a fiction . . . to have effect to the sale that the slave was in Virginia, when in London at the same time." Lord Holt's strong opinions against English slavery could be cast in an entirely different light if the judges believed that what Holt had actually been doing was bending the law nearly to breaking to legitimate the sale of a slave, to the extent of directing the plaintiff to pretend the man had been in Virginia, when he had actually been in London.

"Nothing else," Davy said. He had plainly become befuddled. Someone handed him a note or whispered in his ear, because he finally snapped to. "Oh! I beg pardon. It was not a fiction. The truth of the case was that he was in Virginia (I see now). If he was in England he dare not be sold. No more than me or you or any man, he could not be sold in England, not being the subject of private property . . . but if he was in Virginia, there he might be the subject of property . . . they might be slaves abroad, but not here." After a brief discussion of some minor cases, Davy sat down. He had spoken for two and a half hours.

Serjeant John Glynn rose and apologized that he "was not better informed than I am, having been applied to but two hours before [coming] into Court."[4] Thin-lipped, beetle-browed, Roman-nosed, Serjeant Glynn was fifty years old; he had been a barrister for twenty-three years, a serjeant for nearly eight. He was a tireless, educated, and talented Enlightenment civil libertarian. The most learned serjeant of the age, Serjeant Hill, thought "every thing which Dunning knew, he knew accurately; but Glynn knew a great deal more."[5] He was a founder of the Society for the Supporters of the Bill of Rights and such a thorn in the government's side that an irritated King George III had not elevated him to the rank of King's Serjeant.[6]

Much of Glynn's most important work had been done on behalf of John Wilkes, the civil liberties cause célèbre for nearly the entire previous decade of the 1760s. Wilkes specialized in attacking detested public figures and claiming that England was governed wholly in the interest of the Scots. When he went to the Tower for seditious libel, Serjeant Glynn won his release through a writ of habeus corpus granted by the Court of Common Pleas. Then he sued the Under-Secretary of State for illegally seizing Wilkes's papers and won the substantial sum of 1,000 pounds. Next he unsuccessfully prosecuted Philip Webb, Solicitor of the Treasury, on behalf of Wilkes, for committing perjury during one of Wilkes's trials.[7]

Fleeing to France, Wilkes missed his seditious libel trials. Despite Glynn's vigorous defense, Wilkes was convicted in absentia of two counts, then outlawed and sentenced to death by Lord Mansfield. John Dunning successfully argued that a general warrant to arrest unnamed and undescribed persons alleged to have published the *North Briton,* number 45, was illegal, and when a pamphlet appeared claiming Mansfield had illegally altered the record in the Wilkes case, Serjeant Glynn teamed with Dunning to defend its author.[8] When the House of Commons refused to seat Wilkes, who had returned from France and successfully stood for election, Serjeant Glynn had himself carried into the House of Commons to vote against the motion to seat the man's opponent.

On April 20 and 27, 1768, Wilkes appeared before Mansfield to challenge the legality of his death sentence. After ferocious argument, Serjeant Glynn obtained a reversal. In later years, Wilkes returned to the king's favor and was asked by George III about Wilkes's old friend, Serjeant Glynn. "My friend, Sir. He is no friend of mine; he was a Wilkite, Sir, which I never was."[9] Glynn was indeed the Wilkite Wilkes never was.

Glynn had dueled with Mansfield throughout the 1760s, before the Court of King's Bench and in Parliament, over whether the judge or jury in seditious libel cases was more appropriate in determining whether a libel had been published with the necessary criminal intent. Wielding the special verdict, Mansfield usually limited the jury to determining merely whether the libel had been published; if so, as far as he was concerned, guilt automatically followed. Glynn repeatedly argued this was both wrong-headed and dangerous.[10] In one 1764 confrontation, Mansfield threatened to take the opinion of all twelve royal judges on the issue if Glynn raised it again. Not doubting Mansfield's domination of the other eleven judges, Glynn muzzled himself and when that jury found the defendant guilty of publishing the libeleous material, Mansfield took it as a verdict of guilt on the charge of seditious libel.[11]

In June 1770, Glynn unsuccessfully defended publisher John Almon against the seditious libel charge of publishing personal attacks by the anonymous "Junius" against Mansfield himelf, who then conducted the trial. When in November 1770, Mansfield called Almon for judgment, Glynn had had enough. In December, he moved in the House of Commons "that a committee be appointed to enquire into the administration of criminal justice and the proceedings of the judges in Westminster Hall, particularly in cases relating to the liberty of the press and the constitutional power and duty of juries."

Now, little more than year later, he was before that very same man, his political enemy, on the most important case of his professional life. Apparently, he had had just two hours to think about what he would say. But that was long enough for Serjeant Glynn.

> [L]ittle preparation will be necessary to support any man whatsoever to gain a good and sufficient judgment against a return of this sort. . . . Whatever might have been the ancient laws of this kingdom, whatever the degree of slavery might have been tolerated in it and whatever barbarous customs in remote ages have prevailed . . . no such return as this was ever admitted by the court [for Steuart] claims as goods and chattels . . . a man breathing the air of England.

The issue was of "the utmost consequence," for James Somerset and English liberty. As had Sharp and Davy, Glynn emphasized that "the judges who were the most enlightened part of those ancient times" thought villeinage violated English law and engaged in "all sorts of subterfuges . . . in favor of emancipation." When the law tolerated villeinage, it was only with "great reluctance," for the judges had "checked it in its progress and opened every door for escape . . . and shut every door from coming into it." At least with a villein, everyone clearly understood "how he came into it and how he came out of it and we have the comfort to know he can never enter it again." This was not true for slavery. "Is it confined to complexion? Is it confined to a particular quarter of the world? *Upon what principle is it that a man can become a dog for another man?*"[12]

If Charles Steuart was to abridge James Somerset's liberty, the African's situation would have to be chiseled to fit some category that English law recognized. Villeinage was the most likely. Let Steuart try to prove Somerset was a villein and, if he could not, Somerset's would be no different that the case of the Russian slave two hundred years before, "when it was resolved that England was too pure an air for slaves to breathe in." Whatever a man's legal status in Africa or Virginia, "as soon as he arrives here [he] ceases to be a slave." Whatever might be their laws, "they cannot come to England."

Next, Glynn overplayed the strength of the cases. "Your Lordship perceives that there has been, by great authorities, determinations that trover or trespass does not lie for a negro." These would have been the two decisions by Lord Holt, *Smith v. Gould* and *Smith v. Brown and Cooper*, in which he said the determination in *Butts v. Penny* that trover would lie for negros had been "reprobated and otherthrown," and "trodden down as not law"; it "was not law" and "a man cannot be a slave in England upon any authority whatsoever." Holt's new "determination has been adhered to ever since and there has been no contradictory determination." Maybe not by the Court of King's Bench, but Yorke and Talbot had famously disputed it in 1729 and Yorke, as Lord Chancellor Hardwicke, had contradicted it squarely in *Pearne v. Lisle* in 1749.

After more than an hour, Serjeant Glynn concluded. Henry Marchant thought Glynn had "argued very strongly" and "upon every ground entered upon by Serjeant Davy, and gave much force to the arguments.

He was very sensible, solemn, and affecting." But something was bothering Lord Mansfield. "Is there any traces there ever existed such a case as that of the Russian slave?" he asked. "I know nothing more than I told your lordship," Davy replied.

"This thing seems by the argument probable to go to a great length and it is the end of the term, so it will be hardly possible to go through it without stopping it," said Mansfield who, according to Henry Marchant, thought the case "could not be properly attended to without too much interfering with the ordinary business of court." Mansfield announced he would "let it stand till next term." They would not assemble again until May 9.

CHAPTER 13

Fluorishing Away on the Side of Liberty

I felt myself over-powered by the weight of the question.

Francis Hargrave to the Court of King's Bench in Somerset v. Stewart

T HE RHODE ISLANDER, Henry Marchant, smelled hypocrisy. "I could wish Americans had never fallen into so disagreeable and baneful a trade as that of buying and selling a part of the human race," he wrote in his diary. But they "borrowed the idea from Europe and never could have supported themselves in the trade had not Great Britain found her advantage and interest in supporting it." Britain had built castles along the African coast and used its ships to protect the slave traders and transport Africans. "Where is the difference between subjugating these unhappy people to slavery and selling them and bringing home the profits . . . and employing the persons they make slaves in their own businesses? . . . Let Britains then be consistent and discourage slavery entirely" or abandon their "pretense to more noble ideas of liberty than their neighbors" and the claim that their air and soil differ from the air and soil of America and thereby "cheat an honest American of his slave."

On February 14, a writer calling himself "A Friend of Mankind" entered the public debate on the pages of the *Gazetter:* "Every person in

England, and every person in a civilized state, has a claim to the protection of its laws, as he is subject to them, without regard to the place of his nativity, or from whence he came last: and it is absurd to suppose that the complexion of a man can make any alteration." The paper's "legal correspondent" replied three days later that appeals to humanity and justice were fine, but went only so far: "The discussion of this very important and hitherto undecided point depends upon other, and far more remote principles," and he listed seven. On February 20, "A Friend of Mankind" scoffed at this pettifogging and demanded that judges decide "in favour of liberty, that chief, common, indefeasible right of mankind."[1]

On the day the *Gazeteer's* legal correspondent published his views, "A Man" echoed Shylock ("Hath not a Jew eyes? Hath not a Jew hands, organs, dimensions, senses, affections, passions?") in the *London Chronicle:* "How disgraceful to those who profess Christianity, and whose pride it is to be called civilized nations, is it, to carry on a traffic in the human species, to buy and sell their fellow creatures, to make slaves of those whom heaven made of the same flesh and blood, implanted in them the same appetites, passions, and desires, and who are equally with us the sons of God." No less than England, he argued, the African countries are "certainly the property of the Almighty, therefore what earthly power can authorize their subjects . . . to treat them as the brute creation, to buy or sell them and their descendants as slaves for ever, to separate them from all they hold dear, to lay them in chains, carry them to a distant country, and use them even worse than their hounds."

Unperturbed, Mansfield went about his business. On February 10 and 11, he sent two cases to arbitration. On February 22, one hosier who claimed he had been libeled by another was awarded a shilling's damages. That day, the *London Evening Post* identified the Chief Justice as the principal draftsman of the recent Royal Marriage Bill, which was intended to prevent the descendants of King George II from marrying without the permission of his son, the present king. Three days later, he presided over a life insurance claim stemming from the recent death of Lord Halifax. On March 3, he sent a case for work and labor to arbitration. On March 4, he began the first of Henry Capel's two trials for forestalling and engrossing, unlawfully buying large amounts of butter.[2] On March 19, the *London Evening Post* printed a letter from "Tribunus" charging that Mansfield "sedulously sought, and carefully improved, every opportunity of extending prerogatives, and making the King absolute."

Whether Sharp initially believed Somerset's was the right case at the right time before the right judge, he was now fully committed to assisting in every way he could. Even if Somerset was freed, it would be just one skirmish in the war that was building to end English, then colonial, slavery, and finally the entire African slave trade. "Because the subject (being at present before the judges) is now become a public topic; and admitting if it, or otherwise, is certainly a point of considerable consequence to this kingdom," Sharp set about educating the highest policy-makers. On February 18, he was bold enough to send his *Representation*, marked at its most important pages, Benezet's book, and a manuscript about Maryland slavery, to Lord North, a prime minister unused to receiving suggestions on altering important colonial policy from unknown clerks. But Lord North knew Sharp from his music.

"G#," as Granville occasionally signed his name, sang, wrote music, and played the English flute, clarinet, oboe, double-flute, hautboy, traverse harp, and kettle drums, and his brothers and sisters sang and played the cello, jointed serpent, organ, piano, and french horn. The year he met Jonathan Strong, Sharp published *A Short Introduction to Vocal Music* for children. The Sharp Family Orchestra presented musical concerts every other weekend for years, featuring the work of Handel. Throughout the 1750s and 1760s, they delighted the glitterati of London society, including Lord North and David Garrick, in William's small surgery on Mincing Lane. By the beginning of Somerset's trial, the Sharps had floated a huge barge, the *Apollo*, which horses towed up the Thames, on which they presented concerts so well played and popular that they sometimes attracted the attention of the king as they passed Windsor Castle or moored nearby for the night. In 1778, Lord North would ask the Sharps to entertain a bevy of foreign ambassadors and foreign ministers aboard ship.

With the books and manuscripts, Sharp sent a letter to Lord North: "English law is sufficiently clear with respect to slavery in this island

[and] if the judges do their duty, by determining according to the laws already in force . . . there will be no necessity for the Parliament to interfere." Colonial slavery, he wrote, was a different matter. Parliament lacked the power to legislate against it, though the King and Privy Council did not.

On Wednesday, May 13, the *Gazetter and New Daily Advertiser* reported: "[L]ast Saturday came on in the King's Bench, before Lord Mansfield, and the rest of the Judges of the Court, the much talked cause of Somerset the black, against Stewart, Esq. his master which was by mutual consent, put off from the last term . . . Counsel for the plaintiff went very spiritedly into the natural rights and privileges of mankind."[3] This referred to Somerset's third lawyer, James Mansfield (no relation to the Lord Chief Justice). Not yet forty years old, he possessed an excellent reputation. Called to the Middle Temple bar in 1758, he advised John Wilkes upon his return to England from France ten years later, then failed to convince Lord Mansfield to allow Wilkes on bail, while Serjeant Glynn was successfully attacking Wilkes's conviction for outlawry.

Four days earlier James Mansfield had argued that Somerset's natural right to liberty precluded the possibility that he could be a slave in England, for a claim by one man to the perpetual service of another was unheard of in English law. Somerset's American bondage had nothing whatsoever to do with whether he could be a slave in England. Indeed, went Mansfield's argument, he could give an answer such as

> [I]t is true, I was a slave; kept as a slave in Africa. I was first put in chains on board a British ship, and carried from Africa to America: I there lived under a master, from whose tyranny I could not escape: if I had attempted it, I should have been exposed to the severest punishment: and never, from the first moment of my life to the present time, have I been in a country where I had the power to assert the common rights of mankind. I am now in a country where the laws of liberty are known and regarded; and can you tell me the reason why I am not to be protected by these laws, but to be carried away again to be sold?

Had Somerset been an escaped galley slave, no English judge would have thrust the oar back into his hands. Somerset would be "as fully and clearly entitled to the protection of [English] laws, as is every one who now hears me." "Where then is the mighty magic air of the West Indies that by transplanting [slaves] for a while there, they should become our absolute property here?" Steuart's claim necessitated a new species of English slavery, a change in English law so vast that it could only be enacted by Parliament. James Mansfield concluded his argument: "I hope that such a kind of slavery will never find its way into England; and I apprehend that, by your Lordship's decision, this man will receive his liberty."[4]

Because one of Somerset's counsel, probably Francis Hargrave, was sick, Lord Mansfield put the case over for five more days. Meanwhile, word of the importance of the case was circulating in London, and crowds were forming before each session. John Baker, a barrister in London, the Solicitor General on St. Kitts, and friend of Hogarth's and Garrick's, tried to attend. In his diary for May 14, he recorded that, with two others, he went to Westminster Hall "to hear Negro Cause" but, arriving at eight o'clock, found he had arrived far too early. The gentlemen breakfasted, then Baker and another left to view an exhibition of pictures. Joined by a gentlewoman who had lived in the West Indies, they returned to the Westminster Hall, "but too late—one Hargrave speaking for the Negro but could hear nothing thro' the crowd."[5]

The visit to the picture gallery cost Baker the chance to listen to one of the most famous arguments ever given in an English-speaking courtroom, a speech the next day's *Morning Chronicle* called "[o]ne of the most learned and elaborate" ever heard. The report went on: "[I]t is almost impossible to imagine what a number of precedents, apposite to the case in point, this gentleman had, with uncommon pains, gleaned from the law books and historical tracts of the ablest and most approved writers."[6] Nearly a century later, Senator Sumner called the written version "one of the masterpieces of the bar."[7] As a result, "[o]vernight [Hargrave] acquired fame and reputation as one of the most learned of English lawyers of his or any time."[8] In the audience sat a London agent for Barbados, Samuel Estwick, who glumly recognized

Hargrave's argument for what it was, not merely a plea for James Somerset, but "a course of reasoning upon the general question of the state and condition of negroes."[9]

Young Hargrave, recovered from the previous Saturday's illness, was making his first appearance as a barrister. He must have deeply contrasted with those who had gone before, especially Davy and Glynn. The serjeants were seasoned, self-assured, experienced at oratory, long-faced, and lanky. Hargrave was babyfaced, fat-cheeked, inexperienced, unskilled at oration, younger-appearing than his thirty-one years, and smelling more of the lamp than the public house. He gave an earnest and untheatrical presentation, profound in its analysis, and forceful on the side of liberty.

We have no exact record of what he said, but we know he had been studying the slavery problem for at least the three years of his sporadic discussions with Granville Sharp. He would polish and publish an extended version of his oral argument soon after the *Somerset* trial ended and would republish it several years later in an appendix to a volume of his *Collection of State Trials*, prefacing it with this disclaimer: "The following argument, on the behalf of the negro, is not to be considered as a speech actually delivered: for though the author of it, who was one of the counsel for the negro, did deliver one part of his argument in court without the assistance of notes; yet his argument, as here published, is entirely a written composition. This circumstance is mentioned, lest the author should be thought to claim a merit, to which he has not the least title."[10] It takes up most of the standard report of the *Somerset* case found in *Howell's State Trials*, in which Hargrave's disclaimer has been relegated to a footnote often missed. By the time Capel Lofft published his report of the May 14 hearing four years later, Hargrave's written supplement was, he wrote, "at large," and, he presumed, "ha[d] been read by most of the profession." He went on: "I hope this summary note, which I took at the time, will not be thought impertinent; as it is not easy for a cause in which that gentleman has appeared, not to be materially injured by a total omission of his share in it."[11]

Lofft reported that Hargrave, like the others, began by noting "[t]he importance of the question." It "will I hope justify to your

Lordships the solicitude with which I rise to defend it; and however unequal I feel myself, will command attention. I trust, indeed, this is a cause sufficient to support my own unworthiness by its single intrinsic merit." The question was "not whether slavery is lawful in the colonies . . . but whether in England? Not whether it ever has existed in England; but whether it be not now abolished?" In the written version, Hargrave would emphasize that Steuart's "return fairly admits slavery to be the sole foundation of Mr. Steuart's claim; and this brings the question, as to the present lawfulness of slavery in England, directly before the Court."

Hargrave needled the return's draftsman:

> It would have been more artful to have asserted Mr. Steuart's claim in terms less explicit, and to have stated the slavery of the negro before his coming into England merely as a ground for claiming him here, in the relation of a servant bound to follow wherever his master should require his service. The case represented in this disguised way, though in substance the same, would have been less alarming in its first appearance, and might have afforded a better chance of evading the true question between the parties. But this artifice, however convenient Mr. Steuart's counsel may find it in argument, has not been adopted in the return; the case being there stated as it really is, without any suppression of facts to conceal the great extent of Mr. Steuart's claim, or any colouring of language to hide the odious features of slavery in the feigned relation of an ordinary servant.[12]

Hargrave sketched a history of slavery, noted its harsh consequences for both master and slave, then got to the point: "There is now at last an attempt, and the first yet known, to introduce it into England; long and uninterrupted usage from the origin of the common law, stands to oppose its revival. All kinds of domestic slavery were prohibited, except villenage." He broke with Sharp, Davy, and Glynn, not claiming that villeinage had always been illegal and that it just took a while for the common law to stamp it out, but conceding "the condition of a villein had most of the incidents" of slavery, including being the subject of property, but that it was the only kind of slavery—if that's what villeinage was—that English law had tolerated since the Conquest. He insisted the common law courts' discouragement of villeinage had "greatly contributed" to its extinction in the sixteenth century, not least by making the status of villein exceedingly hard to prove, applying it only to men and women whose ancestors had been villeins in an unbroken chain from time out of mind. It could not be applied to James Somerset, who had not been born in England.

Twice Hargrave mentioned that England's air was too pure for slavery, once while discussing the case of the Russian slave. He had plainly been listening when Lord Mansfield had asked whether, really, there ever had been such a case. "If the account of it is true," Hargrave would write, "the plain inference from it is, that the slave was become free by his arrival in England." Nearly unheard of for an English barrister, he began to discuss the law of a foreign nation, France, by mentioning the case of condemned criminals who had fled Spain, only to be set free in France. "Rightly," interjected Lord Mansfield. "For the laws of one country not whereby to condemn offences supposedly to be committed against those of another."

Parliament's support for colonial slavery was irrelevant when transplanted to English soil, Hargrave argued, for "the utmost which can be said of these statutes is, that they impliedly authorize the slavery of negroes in America; and it would be a strange thing to say, that permitting slavery there, includes a permission of slavery here." But wasn't it the general rule that the law of the place where the slavery commenced should prevail, even when the slave had been removed to a place where human bondage is not recognized? The answer was no; the general rule was that the law of the place should not have effect "if great inconveniences would ensue from giving effect to it. Now I apprehend, that no instance can be mentioned, in which an application of [this rule] would be more inconvenient, than in the case of slavery . . . [for] [o]ur law prohibits the commencement of slavery in England; because it disapproves of slavery, and considers its operation dangerous and destructive to the whole community."

Hargrave was nearly ready to sit. "[H]ow opposite to natural justice Mr. Stewart's claim is, in firm persuasion of its inconsistence with the laws of England [and hoped] as much honour to your Lordships from the exclusion of this new slavery, as our ancestors obtained by the abolition of the old." He would end his written version in a similar way: "[T]his court, by effectually obstructing the admission of the new slavery of negroes into England, will in these times reflect as much honour on themselves, as the great judges, their predecessors, formerly acquired, by contributing so uniformly and successfully to the suppression of the old slavery of villeinage." His argument had been punctuated by applause. Now he received a standing ovation.[13]

A fifth had joined Somerset's legal team, even more inexperienced than Hargrave. Mr. J. Alleyne had been a barrister just since the previous Friday. He was so new that the following day's *Morning Chronicle* would misspell his name as "Allen," though calling his speech equal to Hargarve's, "but on very different principles; his speech was graceful eloquent oration, delivered with perfect ease, and replete with elegant language, classical expression, and pertinent observation."[14]

"Though it may seem presumption in me to offer any remarks," Alleyne began, "after the elaborate discourse just now delivered, yet I hope the indulgence of the Court: and shall confine my observations to some few points, not included by Mr. Hargrave." His most powerful argument extended Hargrave's: the law of the place where the slavery commenced should usually prevail, except when great inconvenience would ensue. "[S]lavery is not a natural, it is a municipal relation; an institution therefore confined to certain places, and necessarily dropt by passage into a country where such municipal regulations do not subsist." Because slavery violated natural law and was merely a municipal relation, as soon as a slave passed from the jurisdiction that had authorized his enslavement, that law vanished.

When Alleyne referred to the case of the French setting the condemned Spanish criminals free, Lord Mansfield was ready. "Note the distinction in the case: in this case, France was not bound to judge by the municipal laws of Spain; nor was to take cognizance of the offences supposed against that law." But Alleyne was ready for Mansfield:

Ought we not, on our part, to guard and preserve that liberty by which we are distinguished by all the earth! To be jealous of whatever measure has a tendency to diminish the veneration due to the first of blessings? The horrid cruelties, scarce credible in recital, perpetrated in America, might, by the allowance of slaves amongst us, be introduced here. Could your Lordship, could any liberal and ingenuous temper endure, in the fields bordering on this city, to see a wretch bound for some trivial offence to a tree, torn and agonizing beneath the scourge? Such objects might by time become familiar, become unheeded by this nation; exercised, as they are now, to far different sentiments, may those sentiments never be extinct! the feelings of humanity! the generous sallies of free minds! May such principles never be corrupted by the mixture of slavish customs! Nor can I believe, we shall suffer any individual living here to want that liberty, whose effects are glory and happiness to the public and every individual.

At that, Alleyne sat. Somerset's case was made. So were the reputations of the two young barristers, Hargrave and Alleyne. The following month, Charles Steuart would write to his Boston friend, James Murray: "[S]ome young Council fluorished away on the side of liberty and acquired great honour."[15] Now it was the turn of Charles Steuart's barristers to try to convince the judges that nothing in English law prohibited the owning of slaves, and it was therefore allowed.

CHAPTER 14

The Death of the Joint Opinion

The case alluded to was upon a petition in Lincoln's Inn Hall,
after dinner; probably, therefore, might not . . .
be taken with much accuracy.

Lord Mansfield to barrister James Wallace in Somerset v. Stewart

IN HIS HISTORY of English law, William Holdsworth singled out
three lawyers as being the most distinguished of the latter half of
the eighteenth century.[1] Two of them represented Charles Steuart,
Dunning, and James Wallace. But, at some point, perhaps fearing a re-
peat of Stapylton's habeas corpus capitulation, the West Indies
slaveocrats had contacted Steuart and offered to pay his costs. We
don't know when this occurred, but at the May 21, 1772, hearing, Wallace admitted to Lord Mansfield, in response to a question, that the
West Indies interests were indeed backing Steuart.[2] On June 15,
Steuart would tell his Boston friend, James Murray, what had been the
quid pro quo: "The West-India planters and merchants have taken it
off my hands; and I shall be entirely directed by them in the further
defence of it."[3] Lord Mansfield liked Wallace, once comparing him favorably to Dunning, whom he thought "too minute and refined in his
arguments and he laboured before special juries," and at a disadvantage

when opposing a more straight-talking lawyer, such as Wallace, who radiated bluff good sense.[4]

Wallace argued history. Steuart's claim was no moral or legal oddity, Somerset's was. Slavery "is found in three quarters of the globe, and part of the fourth. In Asia the whole people; in Africa and America far the greater part; in Europe great numbers of the Russians and Polanders." England had never been exempt; for centuries, and in great numbers, "slaves could breathe in England." They just weren't called slaves, but "villeins." Whatever their name, they were "mere slaves."[5] Parliament had been hip-deep in the support of human bondage for a very long time. By divesting the African Company of its slaves and vesting them in the West India Company, by making slaves subject to the payment of debts, Parliament had approved at least "the trade in slaves and the transferring of slavery." Wallace argued policy. Steuart rightfully owned Somerset under Virginia law, and it would be absurd and unjust to divest him of his property merely because he had brought that property to England.[6]

He argued precedent, both mercantile and legal. He knew Mansfield often tried to harmonize law with the manner in which the merchants actually carried on their business. It was "a known and allowed practice in mercantile transactions if a cause arises abroad, to lay it within the kingdom; therefore the contract in Virginia might be laid to be in London" and could not be denied. This argument so fascinated the *Scot's Magazine* that it claimed Wallace had thrown "new and interesting light" on the entire matter. The problem was that the "contract" to which Wallace was referring was the one supposedly entered into between Somerset and Steuart in which the black sold himself into perpetual bondage for absolutely nothing, with Steuart able to exercise life-and-death power over Somerset. It was involuntary and so could not be a contract, as Granville Sharp never tired of pointing out. Dunning must have had something to do with this argument, for he had made it to Sharp during their 1768 conference about the Lisle suit in the Solicitor General's office with Sir James Eyre and Dr. Blackstone. Now he heard Lord Mansfield take Sharp's side. According to *Scot's Magazine*, Mansfield said that he seriously doubted a slave and master

could ever be analogized to a servant contracted to work for some specified time.[7]

Then Wallace argued that *Butts v. Penney* and *Gelly v. Cleve*, both
decisions of the Court of King's Bench, "directly affirm an action of trover." Trover, as everyone knew, applied to chattels, which the judges in
those cases must have thought blacks were. Lord Holt's subsequent
claim that slavery could not exist in England was "mere dictum," Wallace said, a judicial side musing, that had not directly overruled either
case, and besides, even Holt had referred to the black as a "slavish servant." But Mansfield was not going to allow the hands of judges long
turned to dust, even the dead hand of such a figure as Lord Holt, to
force his decision on this monumental question.

Wallace did not understand this. He began to administer what he
probably believed was the coup de grace, the 1729 Joint Opinion, which
had "pronounced a slave not free by coming into England." Oddly, Justice Aston interjected that the Bishop of London agreed that baptism
did not change a black's legal status.[8] Not only had the Attorney General, Philip Yorke, and the Solicitor General, Charles Talbot, offered
legal opinions on this issue forty-three years before, but so had the present Bishop of London. Where were the judges?

Sharp had learned, to his chagrin, that the Joint Opinion was accepted as law by London's most prominent lawyers and judges. Philip
Yorke never softened. Twenty years later, as Lord Chancellor Hardwicke, he refused to order a defendant to return fourteen rented baptized
negroes in Antigua to the plaintiff, having "no doubt" they were slaves
and "as much property as any other thing."[9] That the blacks had been
baptized did not change their slave status, and for that proposition he relied upon unimpeachable authority, the younger Attorney General,
Philip Yorke. "There was once a doubt, whether, if they were christened,
they would not become free by that act . . . till the opinion of Lord Talbot and myself," he wrote, confusing judicial decisions with after-dinner
speeches. He refused to redeliver the slaves, but only because they were
not irreplaceable, the way a plot of land was, or a finely engraved cherry
stone, or an extraordinarily well-wrought plate, each of which was
unique. Black slaves were fungible. And the slaves couldn't possibly be

returned in the condition in which they had been rented, for they had been leased two years before, and negroes "wear out with labour, as cattle or other things; nor could they be delivered on demand, for they are like stock on a farm, the occupier could not do without them, but would be obliged, in case of a sudden delivery to quit the plantation."

Wallace had every reason to believe he could rely on the Joint Opinion. Philip Yorke had been one of that century's most distinguished judges and lawyers, serving as Solicitor General, Attorney General, Chief Justice of the Court of King's Bench, and Lord Chancellor, and sitting alongside Lord Mansfield in the House of Lords. The two had formed long, intimate, and diverse connections. Hardwicke had become Mansfield's mentor and teacher, friend and neighbor, the model of a fair-minded judge. Both Yorke and Talbot had helped young Mansfield obtain scarce briefs during his lean years as a new barrister. Mansfield spent a large part of his private law practice years arguing before Hardwicke in the Chancery Court, where he had so thoroughly absorbed Hardwicke's judicial philosophy that the Chancellor's twentieth-century descendant and biographer, Philip C. Yorke, would remark that "[i]t was on Lord Mansfield that fell Lord Hardwicke's mantle. He followed in his footsteps. He had the same wide outlook, and the same knowledge of Roman law. He handed on Lord Hardwicke's doctrines and judicial methods, and he inherited Lord Hardwicke's great traditions of the grandeur and dignity of the law."[10] The two lived as next-door neighbors in Bloomsbury Square for years until the older man's death in 1764. Mansfield effusively and admiringly praised Hardwicke at his 1756 retirement: "If I have had in any measure success in my profession, it is owing to this great man . . . it was impossible to attend him, to sit under him every day, without catching some beams from his light."[11] In his *Somerset* judgment, Mansfield would refer to Yorke and Talbot as "two of the greatest men of their own or any times."

So Wallace must have been stunned to hear Mansfield's first public utterance on the validity of the Joint Opinion. A veteran of many long, wine-soaked evenings in the Inns of Court, the Chief Justice thought that "[t]he case alluded to was upon a petition in Lincoln's Inn Hall, after dinner; probably, therefore, might not, as he believes the contrary is not unusual at that hour, be taken with much accuracy." This was a bomb-shell! But Mansfield wasn't finished: He had a line to draw. "[T]he principal matter was then, on the earnest solicitation of many merchants, to know whether a slave was freed by being made a Christian? And it was resolved, not." Until then, English slave-owners "took infinite pains . . . to prevent their slaves being made Christians," and the French suggested they should bring their slaves into France "to make them Christians . . . the distinction was difficult as to slavery, which could not be resumed after emancipation, and yet the condition of slavery, in its full extent, would not be tolerated here. Much consideration was necessary, to define how far the point should be carried." However far that was, slavery, "in its full extent," could not exist in England.

Alleyne, a barrister for less than a week, failed to grasp the significance of what Mansfield said because, four days later, he conveyed his alarm to Granville Sharp at Wallace's "having insisted on Lord Hardwicke's opinion as represented in Mr. Sharp's Book." He begged Sharp to send him a copy of the opinion that Lord Chief Justice De Grey had given when he was Attorney General, that one man could not have a property interest in another, so that it "might be thrown in to the opposite scale" when the proper moment arose; basic De Grey to neutralize the acid Hardwicke.[12] Alleyne promised to return Sharp's copy when he had finished with it. But his fears were unfounded.

Wallace understood right away that the Joint Opinion was dead and promptly returned to policy. There was, he said, a lot of money at stake: "The Court must consider the great detriment to proprietors; there being so great a number in the ports of this kingdom, that many thousands of pounds would be lost to the owners by setting them free." A gentleman called from the audience that this was no great danger, "for in a whole fleet, usually, there would not be six slaves." Wallace soldiered on. If Somerset, a slave in Virginia, could be made free by breathing English air, wouldn't any slave become equally free merely "by going out of Virginia to the adjacent country, where there are no slaves, if change to a place of contrary custom was sufficient?"

Dunning rose to close for Charles Steuart. But Mansfield noted the hour was late and ordered the case to stand in recess for another week.

Before he left the bench, he signaled the seriousness of Alleyne's argument. It had been "very material for the consideration of the Court and that is, whether the law of a foreign country is or is not to be adopted in this."

Whether one country's law governs in another country is the legal problem called "choice of law," and it is not always easy to resolve. Each state generally governs itself under whatever law it sees fit. But chaos would ensue if one's basic legal status changed at every border. For example, Mansfield said a marriage, properly solemnized under the law where it occurred, was valid wherever the couple went. Yet no one believed he would have recognized exceptions for marriages that were polygamous or incestuous, or otherwise severely contravened public policy.[13]

A variant of this problem would arise in the United States. In one case, J. P. Bell, a white man, married a black woman in nineteenth-century Mississippi, where interracial marriages were legal. But when the couple moved to Tennessee, where miscegenation was illegal, Bell was indicted. "Each State is sovereign," said the Supreme Court of Tennessee, "and cannot be subjected to the recognition of a fact or act contravening its public policy and against good morals, as lawful, because it was made or existed in a state having no prohibition against it or even permitting it." If Bell escaped punishment because he was lawfully married under Mississippi law, "we might have here in Tennessee the father living with his daughter, the son with the mother, the brother with the sister, in lawful wedlock, because they had formed such relations in a State or country where they were not prohibited. The Turk or Mohammeden, with his numerous wives, may establish his harem at the doors of the capitol, and we are without remedy. Yet none of these are more revolting, more to be avoided, or more unnatural than the case before us."[14]

Two centuries later, slave historian David Brion Davis would observe that, in Somerset's case, Lord Mansfield had been faced with the question of whether human slavery should be analogized to polygamy, which was assumed to be illegal everywhere local law did not sanction it, or to the possession of cats or horses, which was presumed to be legal wherever it wasn't prohibited.[15] If Virginia slave law followed a Virginia master and slave to London, then Russian and Polish slave law would follow Russian and Polish masters and slaves. "If a Pole should come here with one of those slaves," Mansfield said, "whether in any question between them, they should or should not adopt the law of their own country . . . that, I think, is very well worth considering."

Mansfield must not have understood the true rigors of American colonial slavery; if he had, he would not have compared them so favorably to those of Russian and Polish slavery. In 1829, the North Carolina Supreme Court made them clear: slavery's end is "the profit of the master, his security and the public safety; the subject, one doomed in his own person and his posterity, to live without knowledge and without the capacity to make anything his own, and to toil that another may reap the fruits . . . The power of the master must be absolute to render the submission of the slave perfect."[16] That James Somerset had not been ill-used over a long period was entirely due to the admirable benevolence of Charles Steuart. However, that an aroused Steuart had decided to punish James Somerset severely should have made the reality clear. A second time, Mansfield implied that homegrown English slavery was not legal: "[I]f that law is not to be adopted here, then the other consequence will follow, because there is no other means of introducing it." Alleyne's distinction, he warned, between local and natural law was "very material."[17]

The Chief Justice was not deaf to arguments about public policy and consequences and was always attuned to the needs of commerce. Before he closed court for the day, Mansfield added that "[i]f the merchants think the question of great consequence to trade and commerce, and the public should think so too, they had better think of an application to those that will make a law. We must find the law: we cannot make it."[18] West Indies slaveocrats, he was announcing, if you wish to bring your slaves to England, go to Parliament, for if the judges of the Court of King's Bench believe Virginia slavery is fundamentally immoral, your man, Charles Steuart, is going to lose.

Lord Mansfield had just done John Dunning the enormous favor of openly saying how impressed he was with Alleyne's choice of law argument. Now he had given the barrister a full week to figure out how to neutralize it. But, if his pathetic performance in Stapylton's case on the issue of whether Thomas Lewis could prove he was free by his own testimony was any indication, it seemed likely that Dunning might not seize the advantage.

Failure could be as fatal to Steuart as it had been to Thomas Lewis, for momentum was flowing toward James Somerset. The day before John Dunning would have his say, a letter signed "Vindex" appeared in the *Gazetter:* Somerset's case, the writer argued,

> [is the] disgrace of our age and country, that reason should be so far perverted as to endeavor the vindication of bigotted prejudice . . . were the toleration of slavery which is now contended for, to take place among us, we should insensibly become callous to every humane feeling, and be as little shocked to see a fellow-creature flea'd alive, as if he were viewing a beast's carcase hanging in a butcher's shop. I am further persuaded that such a toleration would by degrees introduce a system of slavery into our constitution, and our posterity would justly undergo that yoke which we only piously intended for others.[19]

At about eleven o'clock on the morning of his argument, an obviously unhappy John Dunning rose to speak. He was not his usual self, and he believed he was on enemy ground. "It is my misfortune to address an audience, the greater part of which, I fear, are prejudiced the other way. But wishes, I am well convinced, will never enter into your lordships' minds, to influence the determination of the point: this cause must be what in fact and law it is; its fate, I trust, therefore, depends on fixt invariable rules, resulting by law from the nature of the case."

There followed the extraordinary public spectacle of a barrister's pushing his client away,

> The gentlemen on the other side, to whom I impute no blame, but on the other hand much commendation, have advanced many ingenious propositions; part of which are undeniably true, and a part (as is usual in compositions of ingenuity) very disputable. For myself, I would not be understood to intimate a wish in favor of slavery, by any means; nor on the other side to be supposed the maintainer of an opinion contrary to

my own judgment. I am bound by duty to maintain those arguments which are most useful to Captain Knowles, as far as is consistent with truth; and if his conduct has been agreeable to the laws throughout, I am under a further indispensible duty to support it.

He requested that attention be paid suitable to "the importance of the question." This he received. He concluded in the fruitless hope that he had "not transgressed [hisl duty to humanity" and would not "suffer in the opinion of those whose honest passions are fired at the name of slavery." An albatross hung about the neck of John Dunning as a result of his fiery summation in Stapylton's case. Thomas Lewis could not be Stapylton's property, he had thundered just the year before, in the same place and to the same man: "[N]o such property can exist . . . in any place and in any court in this kingdom . . . our laws admit of no such property!"

Thankfully for Dunning, Charles Steuart was not present, but he received a full report. Three weeks later, he would write to the Bostonian James Murray: "Dunning was dull and languid, and would have made a better figure on [Somerset's] side."[20] Dunning emphasized the importance of the case, but in a way entirely different from that of Somerset's lawyers. They had trumpeted enduring and historic principles and rhapsodized on the endless struggle between liberty and slavery. Dunning merely expanded on Wallace's claim that there was a lot of money at stake. "About 14,000 slaves, from the most exact intelligence I am able to procure, are at present here; and some little time past, 166,914 in Jamaica; there are, besides, a number of wild negroes in the woods."

He didn't bother to mention the Joint Opinion. Though only a week had passed since Lord Mansfield had dismissed it, it must have felt like ancient history. Instead, as James Wallace had done, Dunning went straight to policy, listing the parade of horribles that a decision in favor of Somerset would produce. Leading off was financial ruin for thousands of English masters: "The computed value of a negro in those parts 50 pounds a head. In the other islands I cannot state with the same accuracy, but on the whole they are about as many."

Dunning didn't do the math; he didn't have to. The total was almost three-quarters of a million pounds worth of English slaves, and another 17 million pounds worth of West Indian slaves, a staggering economic loss at a time when the average annual wage of a journeyman printer was not much more than 50 pounds. That would have given a commercially sympathetic judge such as Lord Mansfield a lot to think about, had it anything to do with the case. But it did not, for however the Court of King's Bench disposed of James Somerset, the Caribbean slave trade would remain unaffected. Only those slaves who managed to make it to England would be free. Serjeant Davy had tried to minimize the risk: "[T]here are sufficient laws in all the plantations to prevent slaves being brought over—there can be no danger of a man's escaping and so coming into this country."

Now Dunning tried to make it appear as if England's being overrun by hundreds of thousands of Carribean slaves were a clear and present danger. "Most negros who have money (and that description I believe will include nearly all) make interest with the common sailors to be carried hither." But the idea that slaves had money for passage to England was laughable. Of course, their masters could voluntarily bring them to England. "The means of conveyance, I am told," Dunning said, "are manifold, every family almost brings over a great number, and will, be the decision on which side it may." Yet few West Indies planters were likely to be so stupid if Mansfield ruled for James Somerset.

Moreover, Dunning declared, slavery wasn't so bad. The relationship between Somerset and Steuart was nothing like that of the fabled Russian slave and his English master. "Russian slavery, and even the subordination amongst themselves, in the degree they use it, is not here to be tolerated." And the sad truth was that serious deprivations of liberty were terribly common, for "there is perhaps no branch of this right, but in some at all times, and all places at different times, has been restrained: nor could society otherwise be conceived to exist. For the great benefit of the public and individuals, natural liberty, which consists in doing what one likes, is altered to the doing what one ought." The relationship between Somerset and Steuart was actually akin to the relationship Dunning had with his footman, or that of a master and his apprentice, or of a soldier who had enlisted in the army whom Parliament was requiring to continue serving in a public emergency even after his enlistment was up.

He did not go so far as Sir William Daines who, in a 1792 House of Lords debate on the abolition of the slave trade, would declare that the slaves he had seen appeared so happy that he often wished he himself could be a slave![21] But Dunning was traveling that road:

> Slavery, say the gentlemen, is an odious thing, the name is: and the reality; if it were as one has defined, and the rest supposed it. If it were necessary to the idea and the existence of James Sommersett, that his master, even here, might kill, nay, might eat him, might sell living or dead, might make him and his descendents property alienable, and thus transmissible to posterity; this, how high soever my ideas may be of the duty of my profession, is what I should decline pretty much to defend or assert, for any purpose, seriously; I should only speak of it to testify my contempt and abhorrence.

The idea of eating one's slaves was not as fanciful as Dunning would have it. As the French trader, Jean Barbot, slaving the Guinea Coast at the end of the eighteenth century, would point out: "[A]ll the slaves . . . believe that we buy them to eat them."[22] One catalyst for the famous 1839 *Amistad* mutiny, in which African slaves seized control of a Cuban coastal vessel, would be the Africans' leader, Cinque, who had been signing to the ship's cook about what their captors intended to do with them. The man pointed to some barrels of beef and signed that they intended to cut the Africans' throats, chop them into pieces, and salt and eat them.[23]

Dunning argued that the relationship between master and slave was like that of any other master and servant:

> It would be a great surprise, and some inconvenience, if a foreigner bringing over a servant, as soon as he got hither, must take care of his carriage, his horse, and himself, in whatever method he might have the luck to invent. He must find his way to London on foot. He tells his

servant, Do this; the servant replies, Before I do it, I think fit to inform you, sir, the first step on this happy land sets all men on a perfect level; you are just as much obliged to obey my commands.

But Dunning knew that Somerset's case was not about a claim for perfect equality among men, but whether one man could own another in the despotic manner in which he owned his horse or dog.

He insisted that England had been caught in the vise of slavery for a very long time, in the form of villeinage, and still was. "Let me take notice, neither the air of England is too pure for a slave to breathe in, nor the laws of England have rejected servitude. Villenage in this country is said to be worn out. . . . Are the laws not existing by which it was created? . . . the gentlemen are right to say the subject of those laws is gone, but not the law; if the subject revives, the law will lead the subject." To prove his point, Dunning challenged Serjeants Davy and Glynn solemnly to declare themselves villeins, in the proper form that English law had for centuries prescribed. Once they had done that, Dunning declared, he would "claim them" as his property: "I won't, I assure them, make a rigorous use of my power; I will neither sell them, eat them, nor part with them," he promised. Dunning's little joke implied a deeper problem for his argument; it implied that Steuart *could* kill and eat poor Somerset, but had never chosen to do it. To argue that Steuart couldn't sell Somerset or possess his descendants was ludicrous.

Dunning was also beginning to realize that Mansfield was not going to accept that Somerset was Steuart's chattel and, being the competent barrister, switched gears. Though it was very late in the game, Dunning now ventured that Steuart really wasn't claiming a right to Somerset in either trover or trespass, but was merely seeking confirmation of his right to the services of his servant, James Somerset, the way any master might claim the services of his apprentice: "As to the purpose of Mr. Stewart and Captain Knowles, my argument does not require trover should lie, as for recovering of property, nor trespass: a form of action there is, the writ *per quod servitium amisit,* for loss of service." In the abstract, this might have seemed a pretty good argument in light of Lord Holt's similar suggestion in *Chamberline v. Harvey.* But, as Francis

Hargrave had pointed out, Captain Knowles had not asserted this in his return to the habeas corpus because it wouldn't have advanced Steuart's claim that James Somerset was his slave. The West Indies representatives who were paying Dunning's substantial fees to have him legitimate English slavery must have choked on their sugar cane.

Perhaps in desperation, Dunning descended into the ooze.

> The gentlemen who have spoke with so much zeal have supposed different ways by which slavery commences; but have omitted one, and rightly, for it would have given a more favourable idea of the nature of that power against which they combat. . . . There are slaves in Africa by captivity in war, but the number far from great, the country is divided into many small, some great territories, who do, in their wars with one another, use this custom. There are of these people, men who have a sense of the right and value of freedom, but who imagine that offences against society are punishable justly by the severe law of servitude. For crimes against property, a considerable addition is made to the number of slaves. They have a process by which the quantity of the debt is ascertained, and if all the property of the debtor in goods and chattels is insufficient, he who has thus dissipated all he has besides, is deemed property himself; the proper officer (sheriff we may call him) seizes the insolvent, and disposes of him as a slave. We don't contend under which of these the unfortunate man in question is, but his condition was that of servitude in Africa; the law of the land of that country disposed of him as property, with all the consequences of transmission and alienation; the statutes of the British Legislature confirm this condition, and thus he was a slave both in law and fact. I do not aim at proving these points; not because they want evidence, but because they have not been controverted, to my recollection, and are, I think, incapable of denial.

Did Dunning really think eight-year-old James Somerset had committed a property crime in Africa and, when couldn't repay his debt, the African equivalent of an English sheriff had toted up the value of everything he owned, found it wanting, reluctantly declared him insolvent, and seized him as a slave?

Worse for Steuart, Dunning had wasted the entire week Mansfield had given him to think of ways to counter Alleyne's argument that Somerset could be a slave only because of Virginia's municipal law, that this law was repugnant to natural law and public morality, and therefore he was free the moment he entered England. Now all he could do was admit that "Mr. Alleyne justly observes, the municipal regulations of one country are not binding on another. . . . I understand the municipal relations differ in different colonies, according to humanity, and otherwise." Inexcusably, he merely compared the relationship of master and slave to that of husband and wife: As the one remains unchanged wherever one ventures, so should the other.

Even that was untrue and he knew it. Everyone understood that Lord Mansfield would never recognize an incestuous or polygamous marriage solemnized in some heathen clime. Serjeant Davy had framed the problem correctly: "Upon what principle is it that a man can become a dog for another man?" Dunning had had months to figure out how to answer that question and failed. If the judges of the Court of King's Bench believed that human slavery was immoral, in a class with polygamy and incest, Charles Steuart was lost. Dunning's job was to argue not that slavery was good for England, but that it was right in England.

His was a simple argument. Steuart owned Somerset the way he owned his dog and horse. But there was nothing wrong with that. In the coming decades, American southerners and West Indians never shrank from making it. Ten-year-old Frederick Douglass would be just another item in the 1828 estate sale of his deceased master, including, he would write, "horses and men, cattle and women, pigs and children, all holding the same rank in the scale of being."[24] This argument probably would have failed. But it was the only one he had, and either Dunning's nerve failed him, his logic, or his conscience.

CHAPTER 15

All We Can Do Is Declare the Law

There is no possibility of modifying our decision, so as
to mitigate the inconveniences on either hand.

Lord Mansfield during the hearing in Somerset v. Stewart, *May 21, 1772*

O N MAY 22, the *General Evening Post* reported that, in rebuttal,
Serjeant Davy claimed the first slave he read about had been
mentioned in an old book of reports by a reliable reporter named
Moses. It related the story of one Joseph, whose nefarious brothers had
sold him into slavery. Lord Mansfield asked Davy if he was certain that
Joseph had been the first slave mentioned in that old book of reports.
Hadn't Serjeant Davy heard of a bondswoman named Hagar, mentioned earlier? Davy was unsure. But the two slave cases were found in
the same reporter, Mansfield insisted: "[Y]ou, brother Davy, have not
gone so far into the book." Davy replied, "[T]rue, my Lord, I do recollect the case, but that is mentioned subsequent to my precedent, consequently I cannot conceive Hagar to be the first slave, unless your
Lordship supposes that I read the Bible backward." Lord Mansfield, of
course, was correct. Hagar had been Abraham's concubine.[1]

Most of Serjeant Davy's rebuttal was occupied by more serious argument. "My learned friend has thought proper to consider the question

in the beginning of his speech, as of great importance: it is indeed so; but not for those reasons principally assigned by him. I apprehend, my Lord, the honour of England, the honour of the laws of every English-man, here or abroad, is now concerned." Not just the English law, he might have added, but English morality for, if slavery was immoral in England, Virginia slave law should not apply.

> To punish not even a criminal for offences against the laws of another country; to set free a galley-slave, who is a slave by his crime; and make a slave of a negro, who is one, by his complexion; is a cruelty and absurdity that I trust will never take place here . . . [for] [i]t would make England a disgrace to all the nations under earth: for the reducing a man, guiltless of any offence against the laws, to the condition of slavery, the worst and most abject state. . . . For the air of England; I think, however, it has been gradually purifying ever since the reign of Elizabeth . . . it has been asserted, and is now repeated by me, this air is too pure for a slave to breathe in: I trust, I shall not quit this court without certain conviction of the truth of that assertion."

The case went into in the hands of the judges. Everyone in West-minster Hall must have assumed they would decide in the usual way, immediately, orally, and unanimously. Lord Mansfield quickly dis-abused them of that thought. "We are neither inclined nor prepared to decide on the present question; the matter will require some delibera-tion before we can venture an opinion on it," the *Gazetter* reported. Im-mediately, Mansfield launched into an extraordinary preview of what that decision might be, and it became clear that certain policy consider-ations were troubling him deeply, and that they might spell trouble for James Somerset.

"The question is, if the owner had a right to detain the slave, for the sending of him over to be sold in Jamaica," Capel Lofft recorded Mans-field saying. According to the *Gazetter*, "The prime, nay the only ques-tion properly before us, is whether the colony slave-laws be binding here, or if there be established usage or positive law in this country" that would allow Steuart to send Somerset to Jamaica. This decision would require some "delicacy":

[N]ot that I believe that the difficulty will so much lie in the question it-self, as in the probable consequences resulting from it. On the one hand, we are assured, that there are no less than 15,000 slaves now in England, who will procure their liberty, should the law declare in their favor, and whose loss to the proprietary, estimated at a moderate sum of more than 700,000 pounds. On the other, should the coercion of the colony slave-laws be found binding to the extent argued, it must imply consequences [that would reverberate far beyond English slavery].

According to Lofft, Mansfield expressed these thoughts:

The setting 14,000 or 15,000 men at once loose by a solemn opinion is very disagreeable in the effects it threatens . . . 50 pounds a head may not be a high price; then a loss follows to the proprietors of above 700,000 pounds sterling. How would the law stand with respect to their settlement; their wages? How many actions for any slight coercion by the master? These are the obstructions that militate against immediate decision.[2]

It might be a just and simple thing to free James Somerset. But what Pandora's box might the justices thereby open?

Quoting Mansfield, the *Gazetter* reported that the quality of argument had been high, especially among the legal novices: "[M]emory does not furnish me with an instance in which a matter of such difficulty has been more clearly and satisfactorily explained . . . and it gives me great pleasure to see youth [presumably Hargrave and Alleyne], talents, and great industry unite in the present occasion." In Lofft's version, Mansfield was "greatly obliged to the gentlemen of the Bar who have spoke on the subject; and by whose care and abilities so much has been effected, that the rule of decision will be reduced to a very easy compass. . . . I can not omit to express particular happiness in seeing young men, just called to the Bar, have been able so much to profit by their reading."[3]

Mansfield began by beginning to shred Steuart's defenses. Neither villeinage nor contract justified Steuart's actions. "I think them clearly out of the present question, it is impossible that the former [villeinage] can apply, and as for the latter," in light of the naked coercion inherent in the master/slave relationship, "every idea of a contract ceases."[4] Any doubt that chattel slavery was legal under English common law had also vanished. He agreed with Francis Hargrave that "[t]o bring about the intended effects, the affair could have been conducted with more dexterity," for "contract for sale of a slave is good here; the sale is a matter to which the law properly and readily attaches, and will maintain the price according to the agreement."[5] He stood with Lord Holt on the question of whether a contract for the sale of a slave made in England was good, though the slave was actually in Viriginia. However, "Mr. Stewart advances no claims on contract; he rests his whole demand on a right to the negro as slave, and mentions the purpose of detainure to be the sending of him over to be sold in Jamaica."

Thanks to Steuart's kidnapping of Somerset, "here the person of the slave himself is immediately the object of enquiry; which makes a very material difference. The now question is, whether any dominion, authority or coercion can be exercised in this country, on a slave according to the American laws?" The consequence of John Dunning's having wasted the week Mansfield had given him now became unmistakable: "The difficulty of adopting the relation, without adopting it in all its consequences, is indeed extreme; and yet, many of those consequences are absolutely contrary to the municipal law of England."

In Stapylton's case, Mansfield would have had "all masters think they were free and all negroes think they were not, because then they would both behave better." Again he spoke of compromise, for, he said, the judges could "by no means draw a discretionary line" if they were required to rule: "[T]here is no possibility of modifying our decision, so as to mitigate the inconveniences on either hand. We cannot say the law is rigidly so, but such and such consequences must be carefully avoided. No, the legislature may do this. We are circumscribed: all we can do is declare the law."[6] He invited the slave interests to avoid the judicial arena altogether. "An application to Parliament, if the merchants think the question of great commercial concern, is the best, and perhaps the only method of settling the point for the future."[7]

"I remember five or six cases similar to this . . . but they were either compromised, amicably adjusted, or given up by one or the other parties: perhaps the present may end in like manner."[8] On the *Somerset* cases' "first coming before me, I strongly recommended it here."[9] This hope was vain, for each party saw in the case an opportunity for a definitive ruling. Yet Mansfield continued to prod: "It is not improbable that Mr. Stewart may decline insisting on a decision in the present instance. I shall wait for his result," reported the *Gazetter*. "Mr. Stewart may end the question, by discharging or giving freedom to the slave," Lofft wrote. Or the parties could "choose to refer [the case] to the [court of] Common Pleas, they can give them that satisfaction whenever they think fit." If that happened, the opinion of the twelve judges would be required, the *Gazetter* added.

"But if the parties will have it decided, we must give our opinion," Mansfield warned. "Compassion will not, on the one hand, nor inconvenience on the other, be to decide; but the law: in which the difficulty will be principally from the inconvenience on both sides . . . [i]f the parties will have judgment, '*fiat justitia, ruat cœlum*' [let justice be done though the heavens may fall]."[10]

This was the Mansfield Sharp had been hoping for. Serjeant Glynn's heart would have leaped, for this was the second time he had heard Mansfield speak of justice like this. The first had been four years before, as Glynn was trying to persuade the Chief Justice to overturn John Wilkes's death sentence for outlawry. Then Mansfield had taken "some notice" of the "numerous crowds" attending the proceedings in Westminster Hall, "the tumults" occurring elsewhere, the vociferous "addresses in print," and pleas to overturn the conviction for "[r]easons of policy, from danger to the kingdom, by commotions and general confusion." But even "if rebellion was the certain consequence," Mansfield had declared, we are bound to say, "*fiat justicia, ruat coelum.*" And of the threats and denouncement:

[If] they have any effect, it would be contrary to their intent: leaning against their impression, might give a bias the other way. But I hope, and I know, that I have fortitude enough to resist even that weakness. No libels, no threats, nothing that has happened, nothing that can happen, will weigh a feather against allowing the defendant, upon this and every other question, not only the whole advantage he is entitled to from substantial law and justice, but every benefit any defendant could claim, but every benefit from the most critical nicety of form, which any other defendant could claim under the like objection. The only effect I feel, is an anxiety to be able to explain the grounds upon which we proceed, so as to satisfy all mankind, that a law of form, given way to in this case, could not have been got over in any other.

Then he reversed Wilkes's conviction.[11]

Mansfield might find it disagreeable that such a large number of English slaves, perhaps 15,000, could be set at large by his ruling, might find it irritating that so many masters would lose so much money, might find it horrifying that England could become a destination for every slave in the world. But *fiat justicia*. "If Mr. Stewart consents to emancipate the slave," Mansfield concluded, "there is an end of the matter, if, on the contrary, he shall insist on demanding a final judgment, we shall not fail to give it faithfully, however irksome and inconvenient."[12] It was two o'clock, and court adjourned. The *Gazetter* reported that "[i]t is now said that the cause between Somersett . . . and his master, will be compromised."

But Granville Sharp and Somerset's barristers would have been in no mood to compromise; victory seemed within their grasp. Sharp may have "persuaded Somerset to refuse any compromise offer of manumission," as David Brion Davis claims.[13] But it is unlikely that such an "offer" was extended, for it was one Somerset could not have refused. Manumission was the right of an owner to disclaim his ownership, unless legally restrained from doing so. That sometimes happened when a slave was very young, very old, or very crazy, but none of those fit James Somerset.[14] If such an offer was in fact made and Sharp persuaded Somerset to refuse it, and somehow he could legally have done so, it would have occurred in the four weeks between the final hearing and the June 22 decision. Even though the case seemed to be going Somerset's way, it is hard to imagine Sharp, pious, sensitive, self-reflective, still overwhelmed with guilt for having cost Mrs. Banks so much money in the Stapylton prosecution, advising Somerset, unlettered, vulnerable, a stranger in a strange land, to risk premature death in a West Indies cane field, if they guessed wrong. He did not know that, on June 12, Steuart's friend, James Parker, had written to Steuart to tell him that the "ungratefull Villain Somerset," if he was decreed Steuart's, "should be sent where he will be at hard Labour during life," but he might have guessed.[15]

If he received an offer of manumission, James Somerset would have been a brave man indeed, having decided to risk his freedom in order to lead thousands of other slaves to freedom. Neither Sharp nor Steuart would have seen profit in taking their dispute to the Court of Common Pleas, and ultimately the Twelve Judges, who were dominated anyway by the personality of Lord Mansfield.

On June 9, Serjeant Glynn chose an unfortunate time to antagonize Lord Mansfield when he stirred up old animosities from the Wilkes case by arguing in another case that a statute was invalid because it had been enacted by a House of Commons infected with the presence of Colonel Luttrell, who had illegally taken Wilkes's seat. Impatient, Mansfield instructed the jury to find against Glynn's client. The clerk didn't even bother to wait for the verdict. He was announcing "not guilty" when one juror piped his disagreement. Mansfield sternly told the jurors that they had better do as he said, and they did.[16]

Meanwhile, the battle of the letters to the editor escalated. A Thursday, June 4, *Gazetter* letter, signed "Negro," was so filled with legal knowledge and so well written that one suspects it might have flowed from Sharp's quill, or at least from the pen of someone who had studied his *Appendix*. Outraged at Mansfield's "long disagreeable catalogue of apologies," it addressed the judge directly: "The difference, Sir, between you or any other Englishman, and a negro is only in colour, and why that distinction should unfortunately exempt him from the blessings of liberty, I own I am at a loss to determine. The same God who created you, gave him life, and endowed him with the like powers of reasons and reflections." "Negro" reminded Mansfield of his acts and words in the Wilkes cause: "[T]he Judges were bound by their oaths, and in their consciences, to give such a judgment as the law would warrant. . . . If insurrection and rebellion were to follow their determination, they had not to answer for the consequences, through they should be the innocent cause. They could only say, *fiat justicia ruat coelum.*" "Negro" was disgusted that Mansfield's would have the least concern over the consequences of a decision in Somerset's favor:

> A Judge has nothing to do with consequences; his business is to determine the law . . . surely the number of negroes now in England has no more to do with the merits of the question, that the inquiry about who is to pay for the expenses of the litigation . . . was I Judge, so far from wishing to have the matter compromised, I would not hesitate a moment to pronounce judgment of law, and let the world know if it delights in cruelty and slavery, or takes pleasure in universal liberty.

In the Monday, June 15, *Gazetter,* "No Party Man" charged "Negro" with aligning himself with "the degenerate part of mankind" and insisted that Lord Mansfield had "pledged himself to the public, that if a final judgment shall be insisted on, he shall be solely guided in it by principles of law and of the constitution." On Saturday, June 20, the *Gazetter*'s legal correspondent, "Attorney General," replied that Mansfield's "business on the Bench is not to talk of inconveniences, but to interpret the laws, either as to the letter of as to the spirit of them." Then he lambasted the Chief Justice for delaying the decision. These and similar arguments would rage even after judgment was handed down. On June 26, four days after the case ended, "No Party Man" expressed his disgust with "Attorney General's" "gross and severe attack upon the noble Judge," which drove "Attorney General" to riposte at length the following week.

After listening to Francis Hargrave, being unimpressed with Dunning's and Wallace's efforts, that glum London agent for the Barbados, Samuel Estwick, had been waiting in vain for "some much abler pen than mine engaged in the discussion of so important a question."[17]

When none appeared, he went to work. Sometime in June, able to give the matter "a few days attention only," he completed his *Considerations of the Negroe Cause Commonly So Called, Addressed to the Right Honourable Lord Mansfield, Lord Chief Justice of the Court of King's Bench,* and rushed it into print. Though it was, he would confess in the second edition, "written with haste, and published in a hurry," he intended it to be a legal arrow aimed directly at Lord Mansfield.[18]

He conceded that neither Parliament nor the common law supported English slavery and that there was a great difference between villeinage and slavery; he didn't even see how pressing seamen could be supported. But he admired the Joint Opinion, for "no opinion was ever given in any case whatever with greater solemnity, or more deliberation," an unbelievable claim considering the circumstances in which it had been delivered. He had a problem with the word "slavery"; it was "odious" and he preferred "property" that had lawfully vested. "Instead of slaves, let the [blacks] be called ASSISTANT PLANTERS," a correspondent to *Gentleman's Magazine* would recommend.[19] It was ridiculous to think that "property" became free upon arrival in England or could ever be the subject of a writ of habeas corpus, and he chastized Hargrave for his "horrid and frightful picture of the barbarity, and cruelties, that were exercised on these beings in the colonies"; these were necessary for keeping discipline and order and more humane than the punishments transgressing soldiers and sailors received.[20]

The world received notice that the *Somerset* decision would be announced, in open court, on the morning of Monday, June 22. Because Estwick had believed a report saying that the decision would not issue until the end of the next term, his "publication was not forwarded with that dispatch that a contrary expectation would have occasioned. As it is, they have lost their object, and I, in some measure, am foiled in my purpose."[21]

CHAPTER 16

The Mansfield Judgment

Exactly what Lord Mansfield said . . . has been
the subject of microscopic examination.

James Oldham,
"New Light on Mansfield and Slavery," Journal of British Studies *27 (1988):45, 54*

T HE MANSFIELD JUDGMENT was delivered at about ten o'clock
in the morning. The courtroom was packed and unusually tense,
for not only was a momentous decision on human liberty expected, but
a financial panic was sweeping the nearby City. Sharp nervously waited
at Old Jewry, fearing his presence in Westminster Hall might unhappily control the outcome. Steuart, at home in Holborn's Baldwin's Gardens, less than a kilometer from Sharp, gloomily awaited the end he
was expecting, having written to his friend, James Murray, the week before: "Upon the whole," he said, "every body seems to think it will go in
favour of the negroe."[1]

Even Serjeants Glynn and Davy, James Mansfield, and Wallace, old
hands at winning and losing, were probably jittery, for they were used to
hearing judgment pronounced immediately at close of argument, before
one could get really nervous, not waiting a full month. John Dunning
probably just wanted the ordeal to be over. He had done his duty and,
as Steuart had written Murray, "come in for pretty good share for taking

the wrong side."[2] An anxious James Somerset must have scanned the face of each judge as he ascended the bench in the hope that a set of eyes would light on his, a smile would flicker, that something would tell him that his life was to be the harsh one of a free black in London and that he would not have to endure the clamping of irons, weeks in a swaying putrid ship's hold, a short back-breaking life, and a lonely death.

Lord Mansfield began to speak. If his barristers had explained to Somerset what to listen for, this is what they might have said. It would be bad if Mansfield analogized black slavery to villeinage, or claimed, as Blackstone had told Granville Sharp, that villeinage was proof that England could embrace unfreedom. It would be bad if he approved the statements in *Butts v. Penny* or *Gelly v. Cleve* that black slaves were things recoverable in trover or trespass, or endorsed the Joint Opinion, or referred sympathetically to the large number of slaves who might be affected by a decision in Somerset's favor or to the large sums that such a decision would cost English masters. Reliance upon *Butts* or *Gelly* for the proposition that blacks were chattel because they were heathens, however, might be very good indeed for a man who had gotten himself baptized, as would a positive reference to the nearly mythical Russian slave case, the free air of England, or the ancient English presumption in favor of liberty.

Anything Mansfield said about English choice of law would reveal his view of black chattel slavery: Was it akin to owning cats and horses and to a marriage properly solemnized, or was it more like an incestuous or polygamous marriage? If the former, he would probably allow Virginia law to reach from the James to the Thames to fetter James Somerset. If the latter, he would likely deem black slavery so deeply immoral, such a violation of fundamental English public policy, that he would refuse to recognize Virginia slave law in England and free James Somerset. Mansfield might conceivably find that Somerset remained a slave in England, but that Steuart could not take him out of England against his will, and thereby place both parties in a permanently uncomfortable position.

Because of the period's primitive court reporting, we don't know Lord Mansfield's exact words. It would have helped had a written decision been prepared; one newspaper reported that he did indeed read from a prepared text. But no such text has been found. Eight years later, the anti-Catholic

Gordon rioters—"[t]he lawless herd, with fury blind, / Have done him cruel wrong," Cowper would write—burned Mansfield's Bloomsbury Square house to the ground, destroying his library.[3] The loss was so terrible that, in *Barnaby Rudge,* Charles Dickens would memorialize the destruction of "the rarest collection of manuscripts ever possessed by any one private person in the world, and worse than all, because nothing could replace this loss, the great Law Library, on every page of which were notes in the Judge's own hand, of inestimable value being the results of the study and experience of his whole life."[4] If a hand-written copy of the judgment was in that library, it rose as ash in the June dawn, with all the other ash.

However, it seems unlikely Mansfield read from a prepared text. The judgment was not lengthy, he was used to ruling extemporaneously, and he had an extraordinary memory. It was not uncommon then for judges to scribble the oral opinions of the other judges on the backs of pleadings. Recently found among Justice Ashurst's papers at Lincoln's Inn Library were the judge's hurried and incomplete jottings of what Mansfield said, scrawled on the back of Somerset's pleadings. Why would Ashurst, who didn't know shorthand, have scratched the words as fast as he could if Mansfield was reading from a prepared text that he could have later read?[5] It was left to Capel Lofft to record the entire decision. Just twenty-one when he listened to *Somerset,* Lofft would report decisions for fewer than three years, become a member of the bar in 1775, and in 1776 publish all his reports simultaneously. He would become an ardent abolitionist and eager correspondent of Granville Sharp's and maintained that he always tried to make his reporting as inclusive as possible. He took shorthand and understood that if he erred: "The cases are too recent to pass unobserved or uncondemned."[6]

Mansfield spoke for a unanimous Court: "We are so well agreed, that we think there is no occasion of having it argued, as I intimated an intention at first, before all the judges, as is usual . . . on a return to a habeas corpus." After summarizing Captain Knowles's answer to the writ of habeus corpus, Mansfield went right to the Joint Opinion. Yorke, as Lord Hardwicke, had confirmed it in his 1749 decision of *Pearne v. Lisle,* stating that trover lay for the return of a black slave, baptism did not emancipate a negro, and a man could, even in the eighteenth century, confess himself a villein in gross, that is, a villein attached not to the land but to the person of his lord. To all these the Chief Justice promised the Court of King's Bench would give "all due attention." Mansfield made it clear how much attention the Joint Opinion was due; he never mentioned it again. He said, "[T]he only question before us is, whether the cause on the return is sufficient? If it is, the negro must be remanded; if it is not he must be discharged." The Joint Opinion was now officially dead.

As recorded by Lofft, the heart of the Judgment took just 144 words, less than a minute to pronounce. "Accordingly, the return states that the slave departed and refused to serve, whereupon he was kept to be sold abroad. So high an act of dominion must be recognized by the law of the country where it is used." A master could remove his slave from England only if English law permitted it:

> The power of a master over his slave has been different in different countries. The state of slavery is of such a nature that it is incapable of being introduced on any reasons, moral or political, but only positive law, which preserves its force long after the reasons, occasion, and time itself from which it was created, is erased from memory. It is so odious that nothing can be suffered to support it but positive law. Whatever inconveniences, therefore, may follow from a decision, I cannot say this case is allowed or approved by the law of England, and therefore the black must be discharged.

The completeness of Somerset's victory was stunning. Black chattel slavery was "of such a nature . . . so odious" that English common law would never accept it. The decision implied that slavery resembled an incestuous or polygamous marriage, not the ownership of dogs or horses. Virginia slave law would not control an English court. Sharp wrote to Dr. Findlay: "[The decision] operate[d] just as I could wish, being for the most part agreeable to the doctrine I down in my own Tract."[7] Only such positive law as an act of Parliament, expressly intended to abrogate the common law, could permit slavery in England. Until, and unless, the West Indies interests could persuade Parliament to enact such a statute, English slavery would remain illegal.

The brief decision was silent about *Butts v. Penny, Gelly v. Cleve*, all of Lord Holt's decisions, the Russian slave case, free English soil or air, a presumption in favor of liberty, or baptism. It implied that certain new "inconveniences" would follow: Between 14,000 and 15,000 English blacks were to be freed, three quarters of a million pounds of property lost, 166,000 Jamaican slaves would permanently fix their eyes on England, and the prudent West Indian master would henceforth leave his slaves dockside when sailing for England. The judge who had twice allowed justice to be done at the risk of the heavens falling, who had proclaimed to the House of Lords that "[t]here is no custom or usage, independent of positive law, which makes (religious) nonconformity a crime," concluded that, whatever these inconveniences were, "the black must be discharged." If English slavery was to exist, it would have to be legislated.

What had inspired him? Cicero's injunction that "we ought to aim at nothing other than what is right" is one candidate, so, if slavery was wrong, it could not be English common law, though it might be Virginia's; other possibilities are Montesquieu's and Blackstone's arguments that slavery could neither be rationally nor historically justified, Granville Sharp's legal and political history lessons, set out in such detail in his *Representation,* and the ancient common law presumption in favor of liberty, about which Englishmen were so justifiably proud.

Perhaps he was swayed by his affection for his mulatto niece, Dido Belle. Some speculated that Dido had even badgered him into it, though it is hard to believe a child could accomplish that.[8] Yet he did adore her. By 1785, aged twenty-two, she was receiving an annual allowance greater than 30 pounds, twice the salary of Mansfield's first coachman, and nearly four times that of a kitchen maid, though substantially less than the 100 pounds her cousin, Lady Elizabeth, was receiving, though that could have been because Dido was illegitimate, not because she was a mulatto. Perhaps anticipating what Lord Stowell would do to the Antiguan slave, Grace, in 1827—decree her freedom dissolved upon leaving England and her slave status re-attached upon returning to Antigua—Mansfield took pains to ensure that no one could ever claim Dido a slave. On April 17, 1782, his first will generously "confirm[ed] to Dido Elizabeth Belle her freedom and after the

Decease of my Dear Wife I give her one hundred pounds a year during her life."[9] The following year he left Dido another 500 pounds. That Mansfield "confirmed" Dido's freedom implied he had already freed her. Despite the Mansfield Judgment and his prior manumission, he did not leave her freedom to chance.

One critic thought the decision so un-Mansfieldian that he charged Capel Lofft with placing Francis Hargrave's words into Mansfield's mouth, for no reason other than Lofft's admiration for the scholarly young barrister, and another declared Lofft's report "notoriously untrustworthy."[10] Yet it appears unlikely that Lofft could have made such a mistake. Hargrave had argued on May 14; the Mansfield Judgment was given on June 22. Lofft could not easily have confused the argument of the one with the judgment of the other six weeks apart. It seems very unlikely that Lofft falsified Mansfield's words; the participants, the spectators, the press, and the judges would have noticed.

Lord Mansfield never quarreled with it. If he thought Lofft wrong, he had numerous opportunities, over decades, to expose any error. In 1785, hearing arguments in a case involving an alleged slave, Mansfield groused that *Somerset,* already passing into legend on both sides of the Atlantic, was being roundly misinterpreted. But he never accused Capel Lofft of getting any of his words wrong. He knew what had been published, because the *Somerset* case report had been percolating through the bar for almost ten years. If Mansfield thought the world erroneously believed that Francis Hargrave was his ventriloquist, and he Hargrave's dummy, in one of the most famous and important English cases ever decided, he could have said something, and it is hard to believe he would not have.

Francis Hargrave, listening that June morning to his first Court of King's Bench decision, the most important of his life, plainly believed that Capel Lofft had gotten the Mansfield Judgment right. After he became a noted reporter of decisions, he set out "The Case of James Sommersett, a Negro, on a Habeas Corpus, King's Bench, 1771 and 1772" in volume 11 of his *Collection of State Trials:* "In Mr. Lofft's Reports there is a note of the arguments of all the counsel, and the judgment of the court as delivered by Lord Mansfield, to which the editor begs leave to refer the Reader."[11]

CHAPTER 17

Versions of the Mansfield Judgment

Mansfield Judgment, 1772—Granville Sharp, a clergyman's son, fought a successful test case for James Somerset, a slave from Virginia, to establish the principle that "as soon as any slave sets foot on English ground, he becomes free." The judgment, delivered by Lord Mansfield in 1772, set free between 10,000 and 14,000 negro slaves then held in England.

Geoffrey Treasure[1]

T HE LEGEND OF the Mansfield Judgment has a *Rashomon*–like quality. It turns out that the New-York Historical Society possesses a second version of what Mansfield said. Captioned "Trinity Term 1772 on Monday 22 June 1772 in Banco Regis," it is unsigned and bears no other indication of what it purports to be, what it's doing there, or who wrote it. Perhaps it is the work of the stenographer Granville Sharp retained to record the proceedings.

This version notes Mansfield's promise to "pay due attention" to the Joint Opinion, as emphasized twenty years later by Lord Hardwicke. "We have likewise paid due regard to the many arguments urged at the bar of inconveniencies, but we are all so clearly of one opinion upon the question before us that there is not necessity to refer it to the 12 judges."

According to the answer to the writ of habeas corpus, Steuart wished to send Somerset "abroad to Jamaica, there to be sold." It continued:

> So high an act of dominion must derive its force from the laws of the country and, if justified here, must be justified by the laws of England . . . no foreigner can in England claim a right over a man: such a claim is not known to the laws of England . . . tracing the subject to natural principles, the claim of slavery never can be supported. The power claimed was never in force here, or acknowledged by the law . . . the man must be discharged.

A third version appeared in the *Scots Magazine* shortly after the Mansfield Judgment, and in several newspapers.[2] Sharp inserted it as an appendix to a short book he published on slavery four years later, with additions he had snipped from the notes of an anonymous lawyer who claimed to have been present that morning in Westminster Hall.[3] In it, Mansfield promised to "pay due attention" to the Joint Opinion, repeated by Lord Hardwicke in 1749. He added: "We feel the force of the inconveniences and consequences that will follow the decision of this question: yet all of us are so clearly of one opinion upon the only question before us, that we think we ought to give judgment without adjourning the matter to be argued before all the judges." As to the kidnapping of James Somerset:

> So high an act of dominion must derive its authority, if any such it has, from the law of the kingdom where executed. A foreigner cannot be imprisoned here on the authority of any law existing in his own country. . . . The state of slavery is of such a nature that it is incapable of being now introduced by courts of justice upon mere reasoning, or inferences from any principles natural or political; it must take its rise from positive law . . . and in a case so odious as the condition of slaves must be taken strictly. Tracing the subject to natural principles, the claim of slavery can never be supported. The power claimed by this return was never in use here: or acknowledged by law. No master was ever allowed here to take a slave by force to be sold abroad because he deserted from his service, or

for any reason whatever; we cannot say, the cause set forth by this return is allowed or approved by the laws of this kingdom, and therefore the man must be discharged.

The existence of several more versions of this historic decision outdoes even *Rashomon*. A fourth version was found among the manuscripts of perhaps the smartest, and certainly the oldest, of the serjeants practicing in late eighteenth-century London. Serjeant George Hill, fifty-six years old, was so phenomenally erudite that his wits became tangled and he often had serious trouble explaining anything. So frequently lost his way in the mazes of his own convoluted arguments, he became known as "Sergeant Labyrinth." Over the years, he constructed a private system for tracking how judges decided cases. Atop that, his memory for precedent was phenomenal, and his reputation for accuracy, on that score, great.

Hill claimed that Mansfield had said that a master's power over a slave "must be regulated according to the law of the place it is exercised":

> So high an act of dominion must derive its authority from the law of the country. A foreigner can't be imprisoned here on any law of his own country . . . [slavery] must be from positive law. . . . Slavery is so odious that it must be construed strictly. . . . Slavery is of such a nature as not to be introduced by inference from principles either natural or political. . . . No master was ever allowed here to send his servant abroad because he absent himself from his service or for any other cause. No authority can be found for it in the laws of this country.[4]

There are fifth, sixth, and seventh versions. Justice Ashurst's jottings on the back of the pleadings are marred by omissions that might be explained by the fact that, unlike Capel Lofft, he didn't take shorthand.[5] What he managed to get down included these remarks:

> So high an act of dominion must derive its authority from the law of the country where exerted. A foreigner can't be imprisoned here under any authority of the law of his own country. . . [The power of a master] is to

be exercised according to the l[aw] of the country where [they] inhabit. Slavery can't be traced back to any other source but positive l[aw] . . . the power claim[ed] by this return never was in use here—to be sent abroad and sold—for any cause. The cause set forth by the return is not allowed by the law of this country.[6]

The sixth version was printed in a June 1772 edition of the *Gentleman's Magazine.* However, it is usually said not to be the work of an observer but a compilation of reports found elsewhere.[7]

If we ignore the *Gentleman's Magazine*'s compilation and the seventh version, which we'll get to shortly, we are left with four versions other than Lofft's, the unsigned document in the Granville Sharp papers at the New York Historical Society, the *Scots Magazine*'s, Sergeant Hill's, and Justice Ashurst's, and they do not differ in the most important ways. They agree, even if they don't use exactly the same words, that "so high an act of dominion" must be recognized or justified or authorized by the country in which it is exercised and the law of the home country of the master and slave need not be recognized. All but the New-York Historical Society's version and Justice Ashurst's agree that Mansfield used the word "odious" to describe black chattel slavery and that it could therefore be authorized only by positive law, strictly construed, and not upon any principle, variously called natural, moral, and political. By "positive law," Mansfield probably meant statutory law and not merely a practice that has been widely accepted for a long time.[8]

The seventh version is found in Lord Campbell's *Lives of the Chief Justices of England,* published seventy-seven years after the Mansfield Judgment. It is the maverick, differing significantly from the six other versions:

[W]hat ground is there for saying that the status of slavery is now recognized by the law of England? That trover will lie for a slave? That a slave-market may be established in Smithfield? I care not for the supposed dicta of judges, however eminent, if they be contrary to all principle. . . . Villeinage, when it did exist in this country, differed in many particulars from West India slavery. The lord could never have thrown his villein . . .

into chains, sent him to the West Indies, and sold him there to work in a mine or in a cane-field. At any rate, villeinage has ceased in England, and it cannot be revived. The air of England has long been too pure for a slave, and every man is free who breathes it. Every man who comes into England is entitled to the protection of English law, whatever oppression he may heretofore have suffered, and whatever may be the color of his skin. . . . Let the negro be discharged.[9]

Like Lord Mansfield, John Campbell served as Solicitor General, Attorney General, Chief Justice of the Queen's Bench, and as a member of the Houses of Commons and Lords. Like Mansfield, he was made a baron. Mansfield rebuffed every attempt to make him Lord Chancellor, but Campbell accepted that post. He reported jury cases for almost ten years and completed two monumental historical studies, one on the lives of the Chief Justices, the other on the lives of the Lord Chancellors of England, each beginning at the time of the Norman Conquest. His life of Mansfield alone runs nearly three hundred pages.

The quality of Campbell's writing and his grasp of history has been fiercely attacked, though the Mansfield scholar James Oldham finds Campbell's study of Mansfield "generally reliable," and William Holdsworth labeled it "one of Lord Campbell's most successful biographies."[10] Oldham, however, ignores Lord Campbell's version of the Mansfield Judgment. The historian F. O. Shyllon tut-tuts that "Lord Campbell's account of the Somerset case is a fabrication and tells us what the Somerset case was not about."[11] Professor William Wiecek has pronounced Lord Campbell's version "undocumented" and "so widely variant from all other versions, and so much at variance with Mansfield's ascertainable sentiments on the subject of slavery, that it must be viewed as spurious."[12]

In 1858, the Georgian slavery apologist, T.R.R. Cobb, a decent, if deeply racist, legal historian, flatly rejected Lord Campbell's version.[13] "[N]ot one word," he said, could be found in the *Howell State Trials* version. Yet other versions are also undocumented, because we don't know who wrote them or that the authors were even present in Westminster Hall. Before he brings himself to imply that Lord Campbell had fabricated the whole thing, Cobb says he wrote to Lord Campbell and asked for his sources. He claims that, "in a courteous note" dated August 27, 1855, Lord Campbell replied, "I am not able to refer you to any printed authority for the words of the judgment of Lord Mansfield, in Somersett's case, as I have given it. It agrees, in substance, with the printed reports, and I have every reason to believe that it is quite correct."[14] Because Lord Campbell was born seven years after the *Somerset* trial, he almost certainly did not obtain his information from an eyewitness. If Cobb accurately reported Lord Campbell's response, it is extraordinary.

On the other hand, Lord Campbell's version has its defenders. In deciding the *Dred Scott* case, the Supreme Court of Missouri was clearly referring to *Somerset* when it noted that, in England, "it is said her air is too pure for a slave to breathe in, and that no sooner does he touch her soil than his shackles fall from him."[15] An 1883 compilation of "Great Opinions by Great Judges" presents Lord Campbell's version as the Mansfield Judgment.[16] A justice of the New York Supreme Court wrote in 1941 that "[t]o this day, students of the law thrill over the eloquence of the opinion," that is, Lord Campbell's version.[17] It was reported in the *City Press* article about the 1972 *Somerset* bicentennial dinner that Lord Mansfield had "reiterated the declaration made by Lord Justice Holt in the seventeenth century: 'That England was too pure an air for slaves to breathe in'" and that the Mansfield judgment had "established for all time the axiom 'As soon as any slave sets foot on English ground he becomes free,'" an obvious reference to Lord Campbell's version.[18] According to the 1998 *New Encyclopedia Britannica*, *Somerset* said that "as soon as any slave sets foot upon English territory, he becomes free," meaning Lord Campbell's version.[19]

The evening of the Mansfield Judgment, the *London Chronicle* reported that, as the words "the man must be discharged," settled over the cramped courtroom, the blacks in the audience rose and "bowed with profound respect to the Judges, and shaking each other by the hand, congratulated themselves upon their recovery of the rights of human nature, and their happy lot that permitted them to breathe the free air of England."[20] "Breathe the free air of England." This remnant of the Russian slave case was repeatedly invoked by Somerset's lawyers, the last time in May. It is also what Lord Campbell, and only he, reports

Lord Mansfield actually said. If the newspaper report is accurate, it is plausible that the blacks were paraphrasing what Mansfield had just finished saying: "[T]he air of England has long been too pure for a slave, and every man is free who breathes it." Five days after the judgment, the following appeared in the *Morning Chronicle* and *London Advertiser:*

> Tyrants, no more the servile yoke prepare,
> For breath of Slaves too pure in British air.[21]

It may have been what William Cowper, trained as a lawyer, was referring to in his famous 1785 poem, *The Task:*

> *Slaves cannot breathe in England; if their lungs*
> *Receive our air, that moment they are free:*
> *They touch our country, and their shackles fall.*[22]

In 1832, the editor of the eighteenth English and first American edition of Blackstone's *Commentaries* wrote that, after *Somerset,* slavery "exists not in the contemplation of the common law," and "what was said even in the time of Queen Elizabeth, is now substantially true, that the air of England is too pure for a slave to breathe in."[23]

Lord Campbell's version is mysterious. Though it significantly departs from most of the other versions, the suggestion that a legal historian, former court reporter, prominent Crown official, member of both houses of Parliament, Chief Justice of the Queen's Bench, and Lord Chancellor would openly fabricate a new Mansfield Judgment is hard to swallow. It would be as if William Howard Taft, former President of the United States and former Chief Justice of the United States, had decided to write a history of the lives of the presidents of the United States from George Washington on and, upon reaching Abraham Lincoln, inserted a wholly fictional version of his Gettysburg Address. Lord Campbell was either correct or daft.

CHAPTER 18

Ripples of Liberty

It is a matter of pride to me to recollect that, while economists
and politicians were commending to the Legislature the protection of this traffic, and senators were framing statutes for its
promotion, and declaring it a benefit to the country, the Judges
of the land, above the age in which they lived, standing upon
the high ground of natural right, and disdaining to bend to the
lower doctrine of expediency, declared that slavery was inconsistent with the genius of the English constitution, and that
human beings could not be the subject of property.

Forbes v. Cochran[1]

THE MANSFIELD JUDGMENT overjoyed London's blacks. A
few nights later, nearly two hundred gathered for a ball at a public
house near Westminster Hall—five shillings a head and no whites allowed—at which they toasted Lord Mansfield's health. Whether he
had intended it or not, Lord Mansfield had struck off an abolitionist
spark. Fanned by the British press, England became convinced that
Mansfield had abolished slavery in the mother country. Then it lighted
Scotland, America, finally even the West Indies.

Scrutiny commenced immediately. Although the Anglican minister Thomas Thompson found "something very affecting, and disagreeable, in the appearance and the notion of human creatures, even the lowest of such, being treated as mere beasts and cattle," slavery, he argued, remained vital to the British economy of 1772.[2] The August 1772 *Gentleman's Magazine* proclaimed the nearly simultaneous publication of two anonymous frontal attacks on the Mansfield Judgment, Samuel Estwick's forty-six-page *Considerations on the Negroe Cause,* and the seventy-six-page *Candid Reflections Upon the Judgment Lately Awarded by the Court of King's Bench in Westminster Hall on What Is Commonly Called the Negroe Cause,* written anonymously by "A Planter," actually Edward Long, a former Vice Admiralty judge, long-time resident, and brother-in-law to that island's Lieutenant-Governor.[3]

The invention of printing "has been ascribed to a soldier, of gunpowder to a priest," Long began. "[P]erhaps the longitude may be discovered by a taylor; but the art of washing the Black-a-moor white was happily reserved for a lawyer: the thing that Solomon thought impossible when he said, 'Can the Aethiop change his skin?'"[4] Lest confusion break out, Long would "not be misunderstood to stand forth a champion of slavery"; it was just that Jamaican "Negroes do not feel . . . hardships." It would also be "presumption in an obscure writer, to deny [the *Somerset* decision] is built on sound law." Instead, Long desired merely to "point out some of the many inconveniences" for masters that it would produce. "[T]hough the judgment may have been consistent with the spirit of English law, I will not take upon me to determine, sure I am, that it cannot be made compatible with the spirit of English commerce."[5]

West Indian planters, steeped in English history and parliamentary law, had been shocked by *Somerset*'s outcome, Long said. The consequences were sure to be profound: None but negroes could work the plantations, and escaped slaves would inevitably swarm England, to be embraced by "the lower class of women . . . [who] are remarkably fond of blacks, for reasons too brutal to mention, they would connect themselves with horses and asses, if the laws permitted them." This would so thoroughly contaminate English blood that, only a few generations on, everyone in England would come to resemble the Portuguese "in complexion of skin and baseness of mind."[6]

On Christmas Eve, 1772, Granville Sharp delivered a copy of Long's philippic to Francis Hargarve, who replied on January 12, 1773. He had already purchased the pamphlet: "In my opinion it contains no arguments deserving of an answer, and therefore it is most probable that it will not receive any Notice from me."[7] But a more dangerous publication was circulating:

> A new edition of another Pamphlet has been lately advertised, which is more speciously and candidly written as I found on purchasing the first Edition. The author seems to rely wholly on the operation of the Statutes which have been made concerning Negroes and though I think the inference he draws from the statutes is already sufficiently answered in one part of the Argument I lately published. Yet, as the statutes are so much relied on, it is my design in case of a New Edition to consider them in a more formal and minute manner.[8]

This was Samuel Estwick's revised edition of his *Considerations on the Negroe Cause*.

As in the first edition, Estwick tried to contain the Mansfield Judgment in the narrowest of channels: "[T]he determination rested on this particular case *only*, from circumstances of insufficiency arising out of the return made to the writ of habeas corpus." In this second expanded edition, Estwick claimed to have "fully refuted" each of Hargrave's arguments, though he did not know "which most to admire, the labour of this gentleman's researches, or the ingenuity with which his collected materials are systematized and disposed." Steuart's fundamental mistake, in Estwick's opinion, had been his failure to claim that James Somerset had been "bought . . . out of a ship's cargoe from Africa, together with some elephants teeth, wax, leather, and other commodities of that country . . . [and] that a writ of *Habeas Corpus* might as well issue on account of his elephant teeth, his wax, his leather, and his other commodities of that country, as on account of the Negroe."[9]

Estwick introduced a chilling argument. The numerous statutes that regulated colonial slavery and the African slave trade reflected Parliament's decision "that negroes under the law should not be considered as human beings. . . . Human nature is a class, comprehending an order of beings, of which man is the genus, divided into distinct and separate species of men."[10] John Locke had signaled reason to be "the characteristic difference man and beasts." Estwick argued that men and beasts shared reason; it was "the exertion in degree of that faculty (particularly in obtaining abstract ideas) that creates the great difference between man and beast." Similarly, moral sense had raised man "from the tenth to the ten thousandth link of the chain." This "power of exercising that faculty, and the compound ratio of its exercise . . . makes the grand difference and distinction between man and man," and in it negroes were greatly defective.[11] To consider whites and blacks the same species would "break in upon and unlink the great chain of [being]."[12]

On May 11, 1773, the Prerogative Court in London decided otherwise in *Cay v. Crighton:* A certain A. B., dying in 1769, "among other effects, left behind him a Negro Servant."[13] When Cay demanded an inventory of A. B.'s "goods and chattels," the executor Crichton "omitted the Negro" and defended by claiming "that, by a very late case in the King's Bench of *Stewart and Somerset,* negroes were declared to be free in England, consequently they could not be the subjects of property, or considered to be any part of a personal estate." Cay insisted that *Somerset* "was determined only in 1772, that A. B. died in 1769, at which time negroes were, in some respects, considered as property, and therefore he ought to have been included in the account." The judge, Dr. Hay, declared that the Prerogative Court had "no right to try any Question relating to freedom or slavery, but as negroes had been declared free by the Court which had the proper jurisdiction," and sided with the executor. The following year, John Wilkes, out of jail and a London alderman sitting as a lay magistrate, relied on *Somerset* to discharge a slave from his master, and even advised the man to sue for fourteen years of back pay.[14]

Learning of *Somerset* from a newspaper, young Joseph Knight, a slave prompted perhaps by some Scottish Granville Sharp, quit his master and declared his freedom.[15] John Wedderburn had purchased Knight in Jamaica and brought him to Scotland. After the justices of the peace had returned Knight to him, Wedderburn began threatening to send him to the West Indies. Knight petitioned the sheriff of Perthshire. "[S]lavery is not recognized by the laws of this kingdom," the sheriff found, "and is inconsistent with the principles thereof . . . the regulations in Jamaica, concerning slaves, do not extend to this kingdom . . . perpetual service, without wages, is slavery." It was 1776 and Wedderburn appealed to Scotland's high court, the Court of Sessions.

As in *Somerset*, eminent counsel appeared for both sides. Their legal arguments were *Somerset* redux. African slaves had cultivated West Indian soil from its settlement, argued counsel for Wedderburn, and the slave trade was extensive and sanctioned by a Parliament that recognized a master's property in his slaves that could not be lost "by a mere change of place. Equity demanded that rights acquired under the laws of foreign countries are . . . enforced by the courts of law here." *Butts v. Penny* and *Gelly v. Cleve* supported him, Wedderburn added, as did the Joint Opinion. Then he added the wrinkle that John Dunning had tried to import at the eleventh hour in *Somerset;* he was demanding only Knight's lifelong service, in Scotland, not title to his person. This was, he argued, neither immoral, unjust, nor unusual, though it was difficult to square with his original demand to remove Knight to Jamaica.

Knight's barristers insisted that "service for life, without wages, is, in fact slavery." Jamaican slave law was municipal, therefore not binding in Scotland, and it was "repugnant to the first principles of morality and justice." As he had been enslaved when a child, Knight could not even legally contract. Whatever advantages Wedderburn obtained from Knight were irrelevant: "Oppression and iniquity are not palliated by the gain and advantage acquired to the authors of them." Knight emphasized Lord Holt's opinions and *Shanley v. Harvey:* "But the late case of Sommersett, the negro, decided in the King's-bench, in the year 1772, was chiefly relied on, and said to be on point; at least upon the question, 'Whether the negro could be sent out of England.'" On January

15, 1778, the judges ruled, over four dissents, that "the dominion assumed over this negro, under the law of Jamaica, being unjust, could not be supported in this county to any extent; that therefore [Wedderburn] had no right to the negro's service for any space of time, nor to send him out of the country against his consent."

British masters hit back, often forcing slaves to sign documents in which they appeared to contract to become indentured servants. These indentures should have been easily invalidated, but sometimes weren't.[16] Such setbacks at the hands of reactionary, possibly racist, judges certainly undercut *Somerset*'s spirit. But even phony black "apprentices" and counterfeit "indentured servants" had more rights than did slaves, for their terms of service were limited, they could own property, they possessed other civil rights, and their slave status did not pass to their children.[17]

In *Williams v. Brown*,[18] one of at least fifteen cases in which English judges sided with blacks after *Somerset*, a slave, having escaped his master in Grenada, made his way to London (as Dunning claimed slaves could) and foolishly agreed to serve as a seaman on a merchant ship sailing back to, of all places, Grenada. Unsurprisingly, upon landing, his former master reclaimed him, and he escaped only because he, his former master, and his ship's captain agreed that, upon the captain's payment of a sum to the master, the black would serve the captain aboard ship for three years at a specified wage. When the ship reached London, the black had the temerity to sue for higher wages in the Court of Common Pleas. Though he failed to win those wages, the Lord Chief Justice declared that he was "as free as any one of us while in England" and "by the law of England slavery be prohibited in this country."

Seven years later, when the captain of a Portuguese vessel jailed his black crewmen for debt to keep them available to man his ship upon departure, a Liverpool magistrate "restored the poor blacks to their newly acquired liberty."[19] In 1824, the Court of King's Bench heard the demand of a Florida master for the thirty-eight slaves who had taken up a squadron commander's invitation to escape onto British warships during the War of 1812. Both sides agreed that slavery did not exist in England; the defendant specifically claimed the benefit of *Somerset*. According to one judge: "The moment [a slave] puts his foot on the shores of this country, his slavery is at an end." And another: "Slavery is a local law, and therefore, if a man wishes to preserve his slaves, let him attach them to him by affection, or make fast the bars of their prison, or rivet well their chains, for the instant they get beyond the limits where slavery is recognized by the local law, they have broken their chains, they have escaped from their prison, and are free."

Three years later, Admiralty judge Lord Stowell, sitting in Antigua, examined "a new question, namely—whether the emancipation of a slave, brought to England, insured a complete emancipation to him upon his return to [Antigua], or whether it only operated as a suspension of slavery in [Antigua], and his original character devolved upon him again, upon his return to his native island. This question had never been examined since an end was put to slavery in England, fifty years ago."[20] Eighty-two years old, crotchety, conservative, hostile to *Somerset*, Stowell was so infirm and visually impaired that one of the barristers had to read his judgment in *The Slave Grace*. While dripping sarcasm ("even since slavery became odious in England, it has been fully supported by the authority of many statutes for the purpose of carrying it into full effect in the colonies"), Stowell never doubted not only that Lord Mansfield, and every succeeding judge, had "determined . . . that slaves coming into England are free there, and they cannot be sent out of the country," but that Mansfield had "reversed" Lord Hardwicke's attempt in *Pearne v. Lisle* to etch the Joint Opinion into law.[21]

If anything, the Mansfield Judgment was even more influential in America. American periodicals, especially the colonial Tory press, covered *Somerset*, though the salacious details of the Danish Queen's affair with her court physician, and the subsequent attempt of this sister of King George III to unseat her cuckolded husband, were given greater prominence. As the New York *Journal* reported:

The late decision with regard to Somerset the Negro a correspondent assures us, will occasion as greater ferment (particularly in the islands) than the Stamp Act itself; for slaves constituting the great values of (West Indian property especially) and appeals from America in all cases of a civil process to the mother country, every pettifogger will have his neighbor entirely at his mercy, and by applying to the King's Bench at Westminster leave the subject at Jamaica or Barbados wholly without a hand to cultivate his plantations.[22]

In 1774, a Bostonian would reprint Hargrave's written *Somerset* argument in its entirety. Twenty years later, Jeremy Belknap would attribute a slew of antislavery legal challenges to its influence.[23]

Some American slaves believed that Mansfield had abolished slavery in England.[24] In the fall of 1773, nineteen-year-old Bacchus, a Virginia slave, would learn of *Somerset* and long for England, "a Notion," his master lamented, "now too prevalent among the Negroes."[25] The following spring Bacchus made for the coast, according to the *Virginia Gazette*, which had covered Somerset's case, "to get on Board some Vessel bound for *Great Britain*, from knowledge he ha[d] determined of *Somerset's* case."[26] It certainly made credible Lord Dunmore's November 1775 promise of freedom to any slave who quit his Virginia master and joined the British army.[27]

Before the Revolution, unless a contrary statute was enacted, colonial law simply absorbed the English common law. The new states continued to follow English common law, especially judgments entered before July 4, 1776, which is why Chief Justice Lemuel Shaw of the Massachusetts Supreme Judicial Court would speculate in 1836 that *Somerset* had abolished slavery in Massachusetts, and Justice John MacLean, relying on *Somerset* in his *Dred Scott* dissent, noted twice that it was a pre-Revolutionary decision.[28]

In his 1856 *Dred Scott* dissent, Justice MacLean wrote that "[n]o case in England appear[ed] to have been more thoroughly examined than that of Somersett."[29] It profoundly influenced American slave law. Its moral weight and the reputation of its author ensured that *Somerset* haters and lovers both would agree that it stood for three propositions: Natural law rejected slavery, English common law prohibited it, and only positive local law supported it. This was something for everyone. Although it pronounced English slavery illegal, it conceded its legality in Virginia, which, typically for the South, was awash in positive slave law. As a result, judges North and South absorbed *Somerset* into their common law and either freed slaves or didn't, depending on whether positive law creating slavery existed in their states.

At the time of *Somerset*, black slaves were real property, like land, by Virginia statute, and in this the Old Dominion was not alone. Before the Thirteenth Amendment to the United States Constitution was ratified in 1866, a third of the Southern states, by statute or judicial decision, defined slaves as real property or applied some form of real property law to them. The rest of the Southern states made them chattel.[30] "However deeply it may be regretted," a Kentucky court said in 1828, "and whether it be politic or impolitic, a slave by our code is not treated as a person, but as a thing, as he stood in the civil code of the Roman empire."[31] In 1799, the Maryland Court of Appeals, conceding *Somerset's* ruling that nothing could support slavery but positive law, dryly noted that "[b]y a positive law of this State in 1715, then the Province of Maryland, the relation of master and slave is recognized," and so the slave lost.[32] In 1807, a Michigan judge, faced with two slave cases, declared slavery unjust and in contravention of nature, and *Somerset* both just and in conformance with natural law. However, *Somerset* had said that positive law could "contravene . . . just and inalienable rights"; and the 1794 Jay-Grenville Treaty, which guaranteed that Michigan traders and settlers would "continue to enjoy unmolested all their property of every kind" actually did contravene these rights, and so the judge rejected the slaves' writs of habeas corpus. In the second case, however, the treaty didn't apply.[33]

Indirectly, the Mansfield Judgment led to the abolition of slavery in the United States. At the Constitutional Convention, James Madison argued that *Somerset* necessitated the U.S. Constitution's infamous Fugitive Slave Clause (Article IV, Section 2 [3]).[34] This clause allowed a series of Southern-dominated congresses to enact increasingly draconian Fugitive Slave Acts that finally forced Northerners—the vast majority of whom would have been content to leave Southern masters alone, if only those masters had left them alone—into becoming accomplices in what they believed to be the moral evil of returning fugitive slaves. The Confederate states, weary of this running sore, blackened their own constitution by nullifying *Somerset* and granting Southern owners the right "to transit and sojourn in any state of the Confederacy with their slaves."[35]

Somerset would occupy the thoughts of at least six of the U.S. Supreme Court's nine *Dred Scott* justices, those who would have freed him and those who kept him a slave.[36] MacLean of Ohio wrote that the "words of Lord Mansfield . . . were such as were fit to be used by a great judge, in a most important case." Concurring in the decision to keep Scott and his family slaves, Justice Daniels of Virginia sneered at *Somerset,* "so often vaunted as the proud evidence of devotion to freedom under a Government which has done as much perhaps to extend the reign of slavery as all the world besides." The decision, Daniels said,

> [went] no farther than to determine, that within the realm of England there was no authority to justify the detention of an individual in private bondage. If the decision in Somersett's case had gone beyond this point, it would have presented the anomaly of a repeal by laws enacted for and limited in their operation to the realm alone, of other laws and institutions established for places and subjects without the limits of the realm of England; laws and institutions at that very time, and long subsequently, sanctioned and maintained under the authority of the British Government, and which the full and combined action of the King and Parliament was required to abrogate.

Because so much positive slave law existed in the South, the major tests of *Somerset* in American law arrived when Southern slaves reached Northern soil. What was the effect of breathing free Northern air? Once a slave, always a slave? Or, if a slave was free for a minute, was he free forever? Or was such a slave free only while he breathed free air?[37] In the beginning, Northern and Southern courts reached a not uncomfortable accommodation; slaves who lived permanently in a free state were free, Northern judges declared, but slaves who lived temporarily in a free state remained slaves. In this spirit of comity, Southern judges permitted slaves who had domiciled

in a free state, but returned to a slave state, to remain free, while forcing slaves who had been taken only temporarily to the North, on a va-
cation or in transit, to remain slaves.

In 1836, Massachusetts abruptly ceased accommodating. After
Med, a six-year-old Louisiana girl born into slavery, was brought to
Boston from New Orleans by her vacationing mistress, a writ of
habeas corpus was lodged by several plaintiffs, principally the Boston
Female Anti-Slavery Society. Chief Justice Shaw brought *Somerset* to
Massachusetts, though it would still apply neither to fugitive slaves nor
to slaves who voluntarily returned to a slave state and freed Med.
Heaping Northern insult upon injury to her former mistress, Med was
adopted by Isaac Knapp, publisher of the radical abolitionist newspaper, the *Liberator*.[38] The following year, Connecticut freed a slave held
there for two years.[39] "Free for a minute, free forever" fever peaked in
1860 when, by writ of habeas corpus, the New York Court of Appeals
freed eight slaves in transit by ship from Virginia to Texas via New
York, though a prescient dissenting justice warned that such action
might be "just cause for war."[40]

Only a couple of Southern states tried to castrate *Somerset*. Louisiana
enacted a statute: "No slave shall be entitled to his or her freedom under
the pretence that he or she has been, with or without the consent of his
or her owner, in a country where slavery does not exist." The Missouri
Supreme Court, in the Missouri incarnation of the *Dred Scott* case, reversed course after decades and denied freedom to Scott, though he had
permanently resided in a free state:

> Times are not now as they were when the former decisions on this
> subject were made. Since then not only individuals, but States, have
> been possessed with a dark and fell spirit in relation to slavery, whose
> gratification is sought in the pursuit of measures, whose inevitable
> consequences must be the overthrow and destruction of our govern-
> ment. Under such circumstances it does not behoove the State of Mis-
> souri to show the least countenance to any measure which might
> gratify this spirit.[41]

But it was the ladies of the Boston Female Anti-Slavery Society who demonstrated most innocently, and therefore most convincingly, how deeply the Mansfield Judgment had taken root in the American imagination, for the ladies decided to bestow a proper name on the little Louisiana girl, now free: Henceforth she would be known as Med Maria Somersett.[42]

CHAPTER 19

Second Thoughts?

It is true that Mansfield was no noble humanitarian . . . [but] [n]o
judge in England left a more lasting or a more beneficent imprint
on the common law. No judge ever did more to demonstrate the
common law's capacity for growth, its power to meet the changing
needs of society, its continuity, its consistency and its supreme util-
ity in promoting justice and fair dealing between man and man.

Bernard L. Shientag[1]

MANSFIELD AND SHARP were not finished with each other on
slavery. In 1782, the Liverpool ship *Zong* approached Jamaica carrying 470, mostly ill, slaves.[2] Insurance law placed the loss caused by any of
their deaths in the purses of the ship's owners, with a notable exception.
The sacrifice of some to save the others would cause the loss to fall instead
on the insurer. After concocting a story that the *Zong* was low on water,
Captain Collingwood, who had a financial stake in the insurer bearing the
loss, ordered 133 slaves flung into the Caribbean, and the owners, including the Gregson family from Liverpool, later claimed damages. When the
insurer refused to pay, a Guildhall jury found for the owners.

The former slave, Olaudah Equiano, was alerted to the lawsuit by an
outraged letter to the *Morning Chronicle and London Advertiser* on

March 18, 1783. It began with the words of a recent sermon on the tribulations of the sugar plantation negroes, continued with news of the unbelievable jury verdict the author had witnessed at Guildhall twelve days before, and ended with the plaint that "our legislature can every session find time to enquire into and regulate the manner of killing a partridge, that no abuse should be committed, and that he should be fairly shot; and yet it has never thought proper to enquire into the manner of annually kidnapping about 50,000 poor wretches, who never injured us, by a set of the most cruel monsters, that this country can send out." The next day, Equiano went to Sharp and pleaded for help. Sharp promptly consulted a lawyer about the possibility of bringing murder prosecutions in the Admiralty Court.

The insurer applied for a new trial in the Court of King's Bench. Its barristers claimed to "appear as counsel for millions of mankind, and the cause of humanity in general," and argued that "the life of one man is like the life of another man, whatever the complexion is," their client having insured the slaves as any other property. The question was whether heaving the slaves overboard was "voluntary, or an act of necessity," as Solicitor General John Lee irritably insisted for the owners. "This is a case of goods and chattels. It is really so: it is the case of throwing over goods; for to this purpose and the purpose of the insurance, they are goods and property: whether right or wrong we have nothing to do with it."

Sharp, shorthand writer in tow, now conspicuous by fame, perched in the audience through all four days of hearings in *Gregson v. Gilbert*. Lee, whom Sharp would refer to as "the learned advocate for Liverpool iniquity," once turned toward Lord Mansfield and informed him that "a person was in Court who intended to bring on a criminal prosecution for murder . . . 'but it would be madness: the blacks were property . . . it would be folly and rashness to the point of madness.'"

Gregson was not to be the *Somerset* of the African slave trade. Lee had pinpointed the legal issue, and Mansfield ruled that the Guildhall jury had been required to decide whether the killing of the slaves was necessary: "[F]or they had no doubt (though it shocks one very much) that the case of slaves was the same as if horses had been thrown overboard. It is a very shocking case."[3] He then granted a new trial.

Sharp, determined to use *Zong* as a sword against the slave trade, wrote: "[T]here may not perhaps be ever so good an opportunity again of clear evidence to urge against that accursed branch of the African Trade & especially as those hardened dealers alledged a necessity to commit so horrible a cruelty, it must surely demonstrate an absolute necessity for the entire nation to put an entire stop to Slave-dealing."[4] Murder prosecutions might have become cause célèbres, but Sharp did not initiate them, probably because of the awesome expense. He was incapable of funding complex and serious court battles on his clerk's salary; he was already sporadically assisting as many as four hundred former slaves who had declared themselves free after the Mansfield Judgment, as well as former black American soldiers who had joined the British in the colonies after being promised their freedom.[5] Instead, he wrote to the Lords Commissioner of Admiralty and the Prime Minister, attached depositions, vouchers, and his own "Account of the Murder of One Hundred and Thirty-two Slaves on Board the Ship Zong," and demanded the government take the unusual step of prosecuting the killers. No one replied.[6]

After *Somerset,* Lord Mansfield would preside over a handful of slave cases. Five months before Governor Thomas Hutchinson, the royalist who had vetoed the Massachusetts General Court's 1771 prohibition on the importation of slaves, had visited Mansfield at Kenwood in August, 1779, Mansfield presided at the Guildhall trial of Amissa, a free African black, for assault and false imprisonment against a Liverpool ship's captain who had sold him in Jamaica, then spread the lie he had died. It took three years for the truth to emerge, but Amissa was finally redeemed and brought to London. Mansfield told the jury he thought such suits were humane and good policy and recommended they award punitive damages; Amissa was awarded the large sum of 300 pounds.[7] When nineteen slaves were killed in a mutiny, and thirty-six more died after leaping into the ocean, swallowing sea water, starving themselves, or succumbing to depression and despair, Mansfield gave the jury explicit instructions: "This was not like the case of throwing Negroes overboard to save the ship. Here there was a cargo of desperate Negroes refusing to go into slavery and dying of dispair." He charged them in accordance with standard insurance law of 1785; they were to award damages only for the slaves actually killed in the insurrection.[8] In the 1782 case of *Cook v. Kelly*, a jury awarded 59 pounds against a defendant who failed to pay for a slave delivered, but we know nothing about where or when the agreement was made, nor anything about the parties.[9]

At Kenwood, Thomas Hutchinson recorded more than his shock at the intimacy between Dido Belle and her great-uncle, William. Mansfield also chatted about two slave cases he had decided. The second was *Somerset*. The first involved two African princes of Calabar.[10] Little Ephraim Robin John and Ancona Robin Robin John were enslaved on the Guinea Coast's Bight of Biafra in 1767. Both were slavers themselves. The two offered ten slaves in exchange for their own freedom, and Little Ephraim returned to slaving after being freed. In August 1774, one brother wrote a benefactor: "[I]f we must not sell slaves I know not how we shall pay[,][that is, repay for his upkeep] which I have a great desire to doe." Calabar's Royal Houses would stubbornly oppose the abolition of the African slave trade and did everything they could to further slaving, even after it was finally made illegal.

After surviving a massacre aboard British ships anchored off Old Calabar, the princes were sold in Dominica. They managed to escape, but were re-enslaved and sold to a Virginian. After five years in the colonies, they convinced the captain of a Bristol ship to smuggle them home, but, after heading to Bristol, the captain there turned them over to an agent of their Virginia master. It was September 1773, fifteen months after the Mansfield Judgment.

The princes smuggled a letter to Thomas Jones, a Bristol slave trader whom they had known from Old Calabar, begging his assistance. He had not replied when their ship sailed for North America. Once again, the fates of men were determined by English breezes: "[T]he Lord as good [and] stayed the wind which prevented our sail then I write agin to Mr. Jones which moved him to pity."[11] Jones received a writ of habeas corpus from Lord Mansfield after filing an affidavit swearing that the princes were being detained "in order to be conveyed out of this Kingdom to Virginia against their consent and in order to be made Slaves."[12]

Once freed, the brothers left the ship, but were immediately re-arrested by the vessel's master on the spurious charge of failing to pay a debt, the price of passage from Virginia to Bristol. From Bristol's House of Correction, Little Ephraim again wrote Lord Mansfield, his deposition beginning, "Little Ephraim Robin-John and Ancona Robin Robin John, believing in One God, the Creator of the World, and that God is a rewarded of them that do well, and an avenger of those that do ill; do swear . . ." Mansfield "send to fetch us to London." That is what Mansfield told Governor Hutchinson: "[T]he Writ issued" and the princes "were brought up to London."

Mansfield thought the Robin Johns's case presented difficulties. Unlike James Somerset, the princes were not British subjects and had never lived in England: "[T]he whole transaction was beyond sea," Mansfield said, in Calabar, beyond the reach of English law. On the other hand, they claimed not to have been slaves under African law, but freemen. The defendants sought a delay in filing their answer to the writ of habeas corpus, then settled. Mansfield approved the settlement and the two were freed again. Hutchinson recorded that Mansfield "says he would have found a way to deliver them" and "seemed much pleased at having obtained their relief."

The year before, Mansfield had privately maintained that the abolitionist tales of *Somerset* were mistaken: "[N]othing more was then determined, than that there was no right in the master forcibly to take the slave and carry him abroad."[13] To Hutchinson, Mansfield again insisted that he had gone "no further than to determine the Master had no right to compel the slave to go into a foreign country, &c." Hutchinson was unimpressed: "[I] wished to have entered into a free colloquium," he wrote in his diary, "and to have discovered, if I am capable of it, the nice distinction [Lord Mansfield] must have had in his mind, and which would not make it equally reasonable to restrain the Master from exercising any power whatever, as the power of sending the servant abroad: but I imagined such an altercation would rather be disliked, and forebore."

In *Somerset,* Mansfield had worried aloud that "setting 14,000 or 15,000 men at once loose by a solemn opinion is very disagreeable in the effects it threatens. How . . . [would] the law stand with respect to their settlement; their wages?" Six years later, Mansfield faced one aspect in a case involving a former slave named Charlotte Howe and ended up repeating what he had told Hutchinson, this time in open court. Howe had been purchased in America and brought to London in 1781. She applied for relief under the poor laws in the two parishes in which she had lived, but neither parish conceded an obligation to support her, each claiming that poor laws applied only to hired servants. When Howe's lawyer argued that the master/slave relationship necessarily implied a hiring, Mansfield replied that "[t]he case of Somerset is the only one on the subject," that its "determination got no further than that the master cannot by force compel him to go out of the kingdom" and that "[w]here slaves have been brought here, and have commenced actions for their wages, I have always non-suited the plaintiff."[14]

Mansfield had long been torn by the odiousness and plain immorality of English slavery and the obvious fact that the slave trade enormously benefitted British merchants and planters as well as the Crown. His ambivalence was vividly demonstrated on November 28, 1771, when he outrageously rid himself of Stapylton's case early in the day, then saddled himself with Somerset's case that evening. The several thousand parish challenges to claims for poor relief that exist, one a fortnight from the sixteenth to the eighteenth centuries, demonstrate how determined parishes were to avoid claims for support, or settlement, if they could.[15] Children born of Catholic parents, for example, were considered illegitimate and were automatically entitled to support in the parishes of their birth, and the Irish poor flooding London could demand relief in the parishes in which they resided; the English poor had to return to their home parishes. When parish officers weren't litigating, they were seeking alternatives; these ranged from apprenticing poor children for unusually long periods to scheming to resettle the poor in work colonies, palming newborns off to cold parish nurses who slowly killed them, even dragging women about to break their water into other parishes.[16] Now Mansfield was faced with exposing overburdened parishes to claims from numerous former slaves for settlements if Charlotte Howe succeeded.

Declaring English slavery immoral, and therefore illegal, was one thing; requiring parishes to pay settlements to former slaves was a detail in which the devil dwelt. In his sixth debate in 1858 with Stephen Douglas, Abraham Lincoln would reveal a similar quandary: "I have no purpose to introduce political and social equality between the white and the black races . . . but . . . there is no reason in the world why the negro is not entitled to all the natural rights enumerated in the Declaration of Independence—the right to life, liberty, and the pursuit of happiness."[17] This has been called Lincoln's "minimum anti-slavery position," his "nub, the realizable minimum," that "[a]t the very least, it was wrong to treat human beings as property."[18]

Somerset was Mansfield's minimum antislavery position, his nub and, realizing the heavy economic burden that a decision for Charlotte Howe would place upon the parishes and that it might lead inexorably to other economic unpleasantries, Mansfield drew the line and construed the poor law narrowly: "The present case is very plain. For the pauper to bring herself under a positive law she must answer the description it requires. Now the statute says there must be a hiring, and here there was no hiring at all. She does not therefore come within the description." Blacks might no longer be slaves, but they had never been hired, and once free, they were not entitled to support.

Sharp, as always, was harsh, absolute, moralistic, and unforgiving. He received his first letter from the Pennsylvania Quaker Anthony Benezet the day of the Mansfield Judgment. On August 21, Sharp sent a copy of the judgment to Benezet with a letter: "[It] would have done Ld. Mansfield honor had he not all along seemed inclined to the other side of the Question."[19] Yes, Mansfield had given John Dunning a week to wriggle away. Yet Dunning had failed. Yes, he had advised the West India interests to take their concerns to Parliament, and they had tried. Four days after the final hearing in May, 1772, a member of the House of Commons brought a motion involving "certain Regulations relative to Blacks and other Slaves, who shall thereafter come or be brought into Great Britain or Ireland." It was defeated that day.[20] On October 10, 1772, Sharp would warn Dr. Fothergill: "The West India merchants, traders, and other interested persons, have formed a considerable association, to promote a Bill at the next meeting of Parliament for the toleration of slavery in this kingdom, in order to counteract the late clear decision of the Court of King's Bench in favour of James Somerset and of the [blacks] in general."[21] Nothing succeeded. The facts were that Lord Mansfield had issued Somerset's writ of habeas corpus when he didn't have to. He had freed James Somerset and, in a seismic judgment, condemned slavery as odious. His hemmings and hawings, tooings and froings, and open invitations to the slave interests to get what they needed from Parliament—and their stunning lack of success—ultimately heightened the significance of the only thing that counted, the judgment. Sharp wanted Jeremiah; what he got was Solomon, and still he wasn't satisfied.

Something else may have caused Lord Mansfield to reconsider the reach of the *Somerset* judgment. Perhaps he was influenced by the rising theory of polygeny, that human races are different species. The second edition of Samuel Estwick's *Considerations on the Negroe Cause* and Edward Long's *History of Jamaica,* published in 1774, two years after Long's broadside against the Mansfield Judgment, emphasized this scientific-sounding claim.[22] In some quarters it did catch on. The Philadelphia Abolition Convention of 1805 expressed concern that "many remain under the erroneous notion that the blacks are a class of beings not merely inferior to, but absolutely a species different from the whites."[23] Thomas Jefferson danced about this idea in his 1785 *Notes on the State of Virginia.*[24]

Perhaps it was providence that Estwick's polygenic arguments did not reach Mansfield before he decided *Somerset*; even Francis Hargrave failed to recognize the power of this new and dangerous plea to biology. Yet it would capture not just rabid racists, such as the South Carolina physician Josiah C. Nott, but respectable eighteenth- and nineteenth-century physicians, scientists, and philosophers, including Jefferson, David Hume—who not only compared a learned Jamaican black to a talking parrot, but claimed "there is but one genus or kind of man . . . subordinate to which there are several sorts of species of men"— British physician Charles White, a Royal Society member, and Swiss Harvard professor Louis Agassiz. Then there was Philadelphia physician Samuel Morton, at whose death the *New York Tribune* wrote that "probably no scientific man in America enjoyed a higher reputation among scholars throughout the world, than Dr. Morton."[25] His major accomplishment was spending decades collecting skulls that he insisted proved the human races had been created separately.

Polygeny was intimately related to the Great Chain of Being, one of the most powerful, persuasive, and pervasive explanations ever devised about how the universe ticked.[26] It incorporated three major ideas: All Creation existed in a hierarchy; every sort of being who could live did; and all species existed on a continuum with tiny gradations separating those species who stood above one from those who stood below. Its greatest eighteenth-century popularizer was none other than Lord Mansfield's boon friend, the classicist who had influenced the youthful Murray beyond all others, the famous poet who celebrated him in verse, Alexander Pope. Pope's first epistle of the *Essay on Man* is largely a paean to the Great Chain of Being. *Essay on Man* would become Pope's best-known poem, a huge seller in England, celebrated enough to be reprinted even in distant America sixty-eight times between 1747, three years after Pope's death, and 1809.[27]

> Far as creation's ample range extends, The scale of sensual, mental powers ascends. Mark how it mounts to man's imperial race. . . . Vast chain of being! which from God began; Nature's ethereal, human, angel, man, Beast, bird, fish, insect, what no eye can see, No glass can reach; from Infinite to thee; From thee to Nothing.

Though Pope did not mention polygeny, "[t]hen in the scale of reas'ning life 'tis plain. There must be, somewhere, such a rank as Man," implied that every sort of man must exist. With "[s]ome are, and must be, greater than the rest," he implied their inequality.

Estwick knew his Pope: His claim that moral sense raised man "from the tenth to the ten thousandth link of the chain" echoes Pope's "[f]rom nature's chain whatever link you strike, tenth or ten thousandth, breaks the chain alike."[28] Pope's ultimate morality? "One truth is clear, Whatever is, is right." Had Mansfield accepted the arguments of Estwick and Pope, *Somerset* might have gone the other way, for why would the superior's natural enslavement of the inferior be odious or immoral? Mansfield had transcended Lord Hardwicke, the mentor of his middle age. It might have been too much to expect him to disregard the hero of his young manhood.

Mansfield's subsequent attempts to compress *Somerset*, in Charlotte Howe's case and to Governor Hutchinson, who thought it ridiculous, were uncharacteristic. As Steuart had kidnapped Somerset and thrown him onto the Jamaica-bound *Ann and Mary*, *Somerset* could be read for the simple proposition that a master could not compel his slave to leave England. In that spirit, the decision could also be limited to slaves kidnapped as children, slaves brought from Africa to America to England, slaves owned by Crown officials, or slaves whose last name started with "S." If Mansfield really thought Steuart's sending Somerset from England was what *Somerset* was about, he could have said so at the time. But changing Somerset's country of residence was not what Mansfield proclaimed odious; his enslavement was.

History is filled with judges of two minds, judges who changed their minds, even judges who voted against their beliefs. In 1986, the U.S. Supreme Court, by a five to four vote, upheld a Georgia statute that criminalized homosexual sodomy. The swing vote came from Justice Lewis F. Powell, Jr., who filed a brief concurring opinion. The following year, Powell retired and, in 1990, conceded "I probably made a mistake in that one."[29] That reappraisal was not as dramatic as the 1937 "switch in time that saved nine," in which Supreme Court Justice Owen Roberts provided the fifth vote to uphold the constitutionality of a minimum wage statute nearly identical to the statute he had provided the fifth vote to strike down just the year before.[30] Then there is the case of Supreme Court Justice Stanley F. Reed and his vote to strike down racially segregated public schools in the landmark 1954 decision, *Brown v. Board of Education*.

Reed hailed from Kentucky, one of the handful of "border states" with a Southern culture that grudgingly remained in the Union during the American Civil War, essentially neutral during much of it.[31] In 1947, Reed refused to attend a Supreme Court party because its black messengers were invited. Months after *Brown* was argued, an amazed Reed returned from the conference at which the Court voted to declare that District of Columbia restaurants could not refuse service to blacks, saying, "Why, this means a nigra can walk into the restaurant at the Mayflower Hotel [where the Reeds regularly ate their meals] and sit down at the table right next to Mrs. Reed!" He thought racial segregation good social policy that benefited blacks, who had emerged from slavery just "a short time ago" and were making "great progress in the South."[32] Reed formulated a proposed *Brown* dissent, cast the sole dissenting vote at the Court's conference, and even stopped discussing *Brown* with his law clerks because they so strongly disagreed. Yet the Court soon afterward unanimously held segregated public schools to be unconstitutional, Reed having concluded that it would be best if the Court spoke with one voice, even if it were wrong.

Finally, Mansfield was concerned for his place in history; he wanted to be remembered as the great judge he was. Great judges defend freedom, not slavery. Great judges have appropriate monuments with suitable writings erected to their memory in hallowed places. Mansfield's bulky Westminster Abbey monument displays Pope's epigram, "Here Murray long enough his country's pride" and declares he passed to the other side "Full of Years & of Honours, As well the many he declined, As those he accepted." He desired, it says, private burial in the Abbey, "And would have forbid that idle instance of Human Vanity the erecting of a Monument to his memory," if, alas, one A. Bailey of Lyon's Inn had, unfortunately, not left money to erect the monument, of which Mansfield "had not previous knowledge or suspicion of, & had not power to prevent being executed." It would be sad to think the man who defined English law for decades was unable to prevent a gigantic florid monument in which his large marble likeness is seated in judgment from being installed in Westminster Abbey, if only Mansfield had not written the entire inscription himself.[33]

CHAPTER 20

The Beginning of the
End of Human Slavery

For those who feel that the incremental change allowed by the
Common Law is too slow compared to statute, we refer those
disbelievers to the holding in *Stewart v. Somerset*, which stands
as an eloquent monument to the fallacy of this view.

W. J. F. Realty Corp. v. State[1]

IN 1849, SIR James Stephens would write that *Somerset* was significant "[f]or the first introduction to Westminster Hall of Francis
Hargrave; for the audacious assertion then made by Dunning of the
maxim, that a new brief will absolve an advocate from the disgrace of
publicly retracting any avowal however solemn, of any principle, however sacred; for the reluctant abandonment by Lord Mansfield of a
long-cherished judicial error; and for the recognition of a rule of law of
such importance, as almost to justify the poets and rhetoricians in their
subsequent embellishments of it."[2]

He saved the most significant for last. *Somerset* was "above all memorable for the magnanimity of the prosecutor [Granville Sharp], who
though poor and dependent and immersed in the duties of a toilsome

calling, supplied money, the leisure, the perseverance, and the learning required for this great controversy."[3]

Sharp would continue his intense abolitionist activity for the rest of a long life. He would rescue more slaves, some in the nick of time. In 1786, Henry Demane was freed when Sharp's writ of habeas corpus reached the ship upon which he was being held captive, as "the anchor was getting up, the sails set, and the captain himself at the helm; so that a single minute more of delay would have lost the opportunity of recovery." Sharp reported he saved the African son of a Sierra Leone slaver "from on board a ship in the Downs, with nearly the same extraordinary circumstances as in the case of T. Lewis." He rescued two blacks, Antonio Barrat and Henry Martin Burrows, one a free negro from Antigua, who had escaped Cuban imprisonment only to be shipwrecked and rescued after drifting ten days without food or water. They had been rescued by the captain of a merchant ship who then concealed them when the ship anchored in the Thames, intending to sell them as slaves; one man's feet were so frozen his legs had to be amputated nearly to the knee.[4]

In the 1780s, Sharp helped form the Committee for the Black Poor, which entangled itself in a benighted Sierra Leone resettlement scheme. Sharp had dreamed of returning English slaves to Africa, and it seemed that any spot would do, though Africa was more that one hundred times as large as Britain, most English slaves, or their ancestors, had not come from Sierra Leone, and the slave trade flourished there. He believed wild tales of how mild and fertile the country was, and became so upset when English blacks wanted nothing to do with the scheme that he distributed handbills asking London's gentlemen to cease dispensing charity to poor blacks in order to nudge them toward Africa. The government stopped its daily welfare payments to hundreds.

Sharp blueprinted the new settlement's streets and churches and, after debating the matter with Benjamin Franklin, erected a system of frankpledge, the form of government he thought had been adopted by Moses and introduced to England by Alfred the Great, in which the population was divided into counties, parishes, hundreds, and tens, officials being elected to govern each group. Several hundred former slaves finally sailed in 1787 on this under-financed, under-provisioned, corruption-filled settlement attempt, with dozens of white prostitutes whom the English authorities, anxious to rid themselves of as many undesirables as possible, black and white, had married to the settlers while the women were drunk. On touching shore, the party named their settlement Granville Town.

Sharp gamely tried to provision the pestilential settlement and never believed that anything but rum and indolence were to blame for its ongoing chaos and failures. But two-thirds of the colonists were soon gone from disease, hunger, and desertion, some even becoming slave traders. Granville Town was burned to the ground by Africans, renamed Freetown, resettled by a thousand black colonists from Canada, and soon destroyed again, this time by the French, to be rebuilt.[5]

With William Wilberforce, Thomas Clarkson, and a handful of others, Sharp would form the Society for the Abolition of the Slave Trade. He would vehemently protest the society's limiting itself to the abolition of the slave trade, not slavery itself, which Sharp believed "was as much a crime against the Divine laws." He delivered this rebuke at a meeting "in the energetic manner usual to him when roused on the subject, with a loud voice, a powerful emphasis, and both hands lifted to heaven."[6] Outvoted, for the others unanimously believed that both could not be abolished, but one could, Sharp dutifully confined himself to attacking only the slave trade in that committee's name.[7]

But he worked with other antislavery committees, including one formed by Quakers, and the Clapham Sect, a small group of intensely religious, deeply committed philanthropists, again including Wilberforce, honored in 1919 by a plaque in the Clapham Parish Church. They "rested not," it said, "until the curse of slavery was swept away from all parts of the British Dominions."[8] Appalled that the new American Constitution permitted the slave trade for two more decades and expressly violated Deuteronomy's injunction, "Thou shalt not deliver unto his master the servant which is escaped from his master unto thee," with its Fugitive Slave Clause, Sharp would write to Benjamin Franklin that the two clauses were "so clearly null and void by their iniquity, that it would even be a *crime* to regard them as law."[9]

Sharp would strenuously oppose equal rights for Catholics all his life, though it was emphasized at his death that "he would not have hurt a hair of the head of any Roman Catholic." He would purport to demonstrate that Babylon and Rome were one and the popes were pretenders, and complain to the Bishop of London that men and women should not play each other's roles in the theatre because the Bible forbade it.[10] He would favor forbidding the guilty party in a divorce to remarry, decry encroachments made upon his beloved Thames, attack dueling, demand reforms in Parliament, attempt to establish an American Episcopacy (which he would discuss with both Franklin and John Adams), support a free English militia, discourse on Africa, Hebrew syntax and pronunciation, and the etymology of the word "Jerusalem," detail murder from manslaughter, expound on the profitable uses of oxen, rail against impressment, instruct foreigners on how to learn English, and use his knowledge of Greek to lay out six principles of syntax for interpreting the New Testament, which involved the use of the Greek article; his first principle is still widely known as "Granville Sharp's Rule."[11]

He would deplore the manner in which England treated its American colonies, and give 250 copies of a pamphlet to Benjamin Franklin, who forwarded them to America, where they were reprinted and widely distributed. On July 28, 1775, General Gage's report on the recent Battle of Bunker Hill arrived at the Ordnance Department where Sharp worked. Horrified, Sharp realized he had helped ship the bayonets that had torn through the colonist's lines; now Gage was demanding more ordnance. Sharp went to his supervisor and declared that he objected "to the being any way concerned in that unnatural business, and was advised . . . to ask leave of absence for two months." This he received. When that period expired, he wrote to his supervisor: "I cannot return to my ordnance duty whilst a bloody war is carried on, unjustly as I conceive, against my fellow-subjects; and yet to resign my place would be to give up a calling, which, by my close attendance to it for near eighteen years, and by my neglect of every other means of subsistence during so long a period, is now become my only profession and livelihood." A second unpaid leave of absence was granted.

His brother, James, wrote,

We very much approve *here,* of your asking for a farther leave of absence,
it may give some chance for a turn in public affairs . . . and if you think it
proper to give up your employment—I will now speak for my brother
William as well as myself—we are both ready and willing, and God be
thanked, at present *able,* to take care that the loss shall be none to you;
and all we have to ask in return is that you would continue to live
amongst us as you have hitherto done."[12]

William took Sharp into his home and, though a third leave was
granted in April 1777, it became clear the American war would be prolonged. Sharp resigned from the ordnance office, without any means of
support other than the generosity of his brothers. He would never work
for pay again.

He would receive honorary Doctor of Laws degrees from Brown,
Harvard, and the College of William and Mary, and die in his seventy-
eighth year, immersed in antislavery, prison, hospital, and other charita-
ble work, still determined to convert the Jews, the Catholics, too, and
propagate the Bible to the heathens, wherever they were, believing that
the Millenium was imminent, that the prophecies of the book of Revelation were soon to be fulfilled, and that there had been "nothing
doubtful or inexplicit in [the] judgment delivered by Lord Mansfield."
The father of the abolitionist movement by acclaim, Sharp was nearly
as famous as the Mansfield Judgment on both sides of the Atlantic.[13]
When, eleven years later, London's Court of Common Council voted
to install his bust in its Guildhall chamber, its resolution emphasized
how impressed the Council was with Sharp's "having most ardently
persevered and finally obtained the judgment of Lord Mansfield, which
established the great principle that every man, of whatever colour or
clime, is a free man as soon as he lands upon the British shore."[14]

In November 1772, John Glynn would be elected Recorder of London, the only judge who attended every session of the Old Bailey, by
just one vote. He would die in 1779, a stout defender of civil liberties
and an unrelenting opponent of royal prerogative, never having been

promoted to King's Serjeant. Bull Davy would die a King's Serjeant the following year. Soon after *Somerset*, James Mansfield would be appointed King's Counsel and would be elected to Parliament in 1779. After his defeat five years later, he would never re-enter the House of Commons, but would serve as Solicitor-General, then as Chief Justice of the Court of Common Pleas for the last decade of his life.

John Dunning would become a leader of the opposition to the British treatment of its American colonies. Spying a bill to punish the Massachusetts Colony by overhauling its government, Dunning would exclaim in the House of Commons, "Resist, and we will cut your throat; submit, and we will tax you: such is the reward of obedience."[15] He would dispute Lord North's claim that the colonies were in revolt in 1775, and vehemently oppose the suspension of the writ of habeas corpus for Americans in 1777 and the use of Hessian and Hanoverian mercenaries in the war. He would strongly support a 1778 bill for the relief of Roman Catholics—its passage would spark the Gordon Riots of 1780—and consistently fought to lessen the power of the monarch. He would finally marry in 1780 and father two sons, the older of whom would die, aged seventeen months, just four months before Dunning. In 1782, he would be named Baron, Lord Ashburton, and be given a cabinet seat, only to die the following year, as did his *Somerset* co-counsel, James Wallace. There is a story that these two barristers, knowing they were fatally ill, learned they were, by chance, occupying rooms in the same Bagshot inn in 1783. Arrayed onto facing couches, they spoke quietly for a long time, then were carried away, never to see each other again.[16]

Granville Sharpe never forgave Dunning for turning coat. His 1777 attempt to procure a writ of habeas corpus from Mansfield's puisne judge, Richard Aston, on behalf of Millichip, the Thames waterman repeatedly impressed into the Royal Navy, caught Sharp's interest. It is unsurprising that Sharp retained Serjeant Glynn on Millichip's behalf, so that when trial opened before Lord Mansfield, Glynn was in his place.

On January 13, 1773, Alleyne would write Sharp and beg him to "spare an hour . . . on the Old Subject of the Slavery of the Negroes. There is now a bill passing for the horrid purpose of legitimating the dire relationship of master and slave in England. It must and shall be opposed. I wish for the favour of your appointment, & will punctually wait on you where and when you please."[17] Francis Hargrave had written Granville Sharp the day before: "[T]he attention you shew to me, by communicating everything which occurs to you on the subject of the negro slavery, I consider as a very great favour." His *Somerset* argument propelled him to international fame, yet he would never formally involve himself in abolition again.[18] He received admiring letters on his performance from Lord Mansfield and Chief Baron MacDonald, demand for his legal services jumped, and he was quickly elevated to the rank of King's Counsel. Later, he would be appointed counsel to the Treasury, then removed by Prime Minister Pitt the Younger and elected Recorder of Liverpool in 1797. He became an esteemed legal historian, an avid collector of English law and legal history books, and a compiler of the records of British state trials. In 1813, he went insane. His extensive legal history collection—the index alone covers forty-nine pages—was purchased by the government for 8,000 pounds and placed in the British Library. He lived upon those proceeds until his death eight years later.

On July 10, 1772, less than three weeks after the Mansfield Judgment, Charles Steuart's friend, John Riddle, would lament to Charles Steuart from Bristol Wells that his slave, Mr. Dublin, had disappeared after receiving "a letter from his Uncle Sommerset acquainting him that Lord Mansfield had given them their freedom."[19] With that, James Somerset passed from history. He probably spent his life scrabbling to make a living in the burgeoning free black community of London, happy for it.

Slavery was not so quick to exit. Two centuries after the Mansfield Judgment, John T. Noonan, now a U.S. Circuit Court judge, would write that "[a] major function of Anglo-American law for three hundred years [was] the creation and maintenance of a system in which human beings were regularly sold, bred, and distributed like beasts."[20] *Somerset* delivered a wallop to the system from which it never recovered, though it had plenty of fight left. Granville Sharp lived to see Parliament prohibit the slave trade in 1807, though slavery would not be banished from the West Indies until the mid-1830s, after his death, and in British India not until 1862. It would die in America by constitutional amendment in 1865, by statute in the last European country, Portugal, in 1869, in Puerto Rico in 1873, the Portuguese empire in 1875, in Cuba in 1886, and the last South American holdout, Brazil, only in 1888, 116 years after the Mansfield Judgment.

After the League of Nations emerged from World War I, abolition-ists almost immediately turned their attention to the drafting of mulilateral antislavery treaties under the League's auspices. In 1926, the International Slavery Convention was signed, each signatory pledging to abolish slavery, in all its forms, and to suppress every remnant of the slave trade. It was entered into force within six months.[21] But that did not end human slavery. The Nazis industrialized it by shipping vast numbers of Jews and others to labor as slaves in war industries, simply replacing them as they fell. The Nuremberg Charter, under whose au-thority many Nazi leaders would be hanged, responded by authorizing the prosecution of slavery as one of those crimes, like genocide, that could be brought "whether or not in violation of the domestic law of the country where perpetrated." The Universal Declaration of Human Rights declared, "No one shall be held in slavery or servitude; slavery and the slave trade shall be prohibited in all its forms."[22]

Worldwide antislavery agitation continued after formation of the United Nations. In 1956, the Supplementary Convention on the Aboli-tion of Slavery, the Slave Trade, and Institutions and Practices Similar to Slavery declared that "freedom is the birthright of every human being" and took aim at practices similar to slavery, such as debt bondage, serf-dom, inheritance of women, and forced marriage. It required state par-ties to make all aspects of the slave trade crimes that carried "very severe penalties." It further stated: "Any slave who takes refuge on board any vessel (of any state party to the convention) shall *ipso facto* be free."[23] Meanwhile, regional conventions that included prohibitions on human slavery came into force. In 1950, the European Convention on Human Rights declared that "no one may be held in slavery or servitude," under any circumstances.[24] In 1969, the American Convention on Human Rights provided that "[n]o one shall be subject to slavery or to involun-tary servitude."[25] In 1981, the African Charter on Human and Peoples'

Rights prohibited "[a]ll forms of exploitation and degradation of man, particularly slavery [and the] slave trade."[26]

That black chattel slavery was so odious the common law would never support it was *Somerset*'s chief legacy. Yet Mansfield's proved just the opening salvo in a legal barrage that, within a century, splintered all of human slavery's bulwarks. No more are men and women legally treated as animals; just a scattered few are illegally enslaved. Human slavery, like murder, has not been stamped out, but it is a terrible crime everywhere. Meanwhile, *Somerset*'s principles have begun to radiate beyond humanity, as some lawyers are insisting today that at least the most cognitively complex nonhuman animals should no longer be treated as slaves.

NOTES

Prologue

1. James Walvin, *Black and White: The Negro and English Society 1555–1945* (Allen Lane/Penguin Press, 1975).

2. Details of the dinner can be found at Granville Sharp, *Abolition and Emancipation,* pt. 4, Granville Sharp Papers from Gloucestershire Record Office (reel 83), "Dinner to Celebrate the Bicentenary of the Prohibition of Slavery in Great Britain" (Adam Matthew Publications Ltd., 1996).

3. See the *Times* (London), July 15, 1972, 16.

4. "City's Radical Past Revived," *City Press* (London), July 20, 1972, 9.

5. Ibid.

6. Prince Hoare, *Memoirs of Granville Sharp, Esq. Composed from His Own Manuscripts* (Henry Colburn, 1828), 2:292 (emphasis in the original).

7. William Holdsworth, *History of English Law* (Metheun & Co., 1938; Sweet and Maxwell, 1956), 472.

Chapter 1   From Africa to Westminster Hall

1. Unless otherwise noted, all biographical data concerning James Somerset and Charles Steuart in this chapter come from the following sources: Ruth Paley, *New Dictionary of National Biography* (Oxford University Press, 2004); Mark S. Weiner, *Black Trials: Citizenship from the Beginnings of Slavery to the End of Caste* (Dutton, 2004); Mark S. Weiner, "New Biographical Evidence on Somerset's Case," *Slavery and Abolition* 23 (April 2002):121–136; Ruth Paley, "After Somerset: Mansfield, Slavery and the Law in England 1772–1830," in *Law, Crime and English Society 1660–1830,* ed. Norma Landau (Cambridge University Press, 2002), 165.

2. Olaudah Equiano, "The Interesting Narrative of the Life of Olaudah Equiano or Gustavus Vassa, the African 12" (James Nichols, 1814), in *The Classic Slave Narratives,* ed. Henry Louis Gates, Jr. (Mentor, 1987), 24–38. I acknowledge that some

scholars have recently doubted the truth of important segments of his claims; see, for example, Vincent Carretta, "Olaudah Equiano or Gustavus Vassa? New Light on an Eighteenth-Century Question of Identity," *Slavery and Abolition* 20 (December 1999):96; S. E. Ogude, "Facts into Fiction: Equiano's Narrative Reconsidered," *Research in African Literature* 13 (Spring 1982):31.

3. Linda Sturtz, *Within Her Power: Propertied Women in Colonial Virginia* (Routledge, 2002), 160, 191 n. 53, 244 n. 51.

4. Shyllon, *Black Slaves in Britain* (Oxford University Press 1974), 77. As did Shyllon, I use Granville Sharp's spelling.

5. Weiner, "New Biographical Evidence," 3.

6. Ibid., 7–8 (letter from Coffin to Steuart, October 12, 1770).

7. A. F. Steuart, "Letters from Virginia 1774–1781," *The Magazine of History* 3, no. 3 (March 1906):151; *Gentleman's Magazine* 68 (January–June 1798):442, 443.

8. Washburn, Emory, Proceedings of the Massachusetts Historical Society (February 1864), 307, 323.

9. Weiner, "New Biographical Evidence" (letter from Coffin to Steuart, October, 12, 1770), 4.

10. Francis Hargrave, *A Complete Collection of the State Trials*, #548, "The Case of James Sommersett, a Negro, on a Habeus Corpus, Kings Bench, 1771 and 1772": 12 George III, A.D. 1771–1772, 23.

11. Weiner, "New Biographical Evidence," 4.

12. *Gentleman's Magazine* 68 (January–June 1798):442, 443.

13. Shyllon, *Black Slaves in Britain,* 7–9.

14. Weiner, "New Biographical Evidence," 2–3.

15. Henry Fielding, *An Enquiry Into the Causes of the Late Increase in Robbers* (1751), 76.

16. M. Dorothy George, *London Life in the Eighteenth Century* (Academy Chicago Publishers, 1984), 173–174, 207, 399.

17. Ibid., 239.

18. Ibid., 54.

19. E. S. Turner, *All Heaven in a Rage* (Quality Book Club 1964), 51–53; George, *London Life,* 105.

20. George, *London Life,* 105–106.

21. Ibid., 78–86, 96, 96, 102.

22. Gretchen Holbrook Gerzina, *Black London* (Rutgers University Press, 1995), 5; Paul Edwards and James Walvin, *Black Personalities in the Era of the Slave Trade* (Louisiana State University Press, 1983), 17–18; William W. Wiecek, "Somerset: Lord Mansfield and the Legitimacy of Slavery in the Anglo-American World," *University of Chicago Law Review* 42, no. 86 (1974):95; George, *London Life,* 319; Samuel Estwick, *Considerations on the Negroe Cause, Commonly So-Called, Addressed to the Right Honorable Lord Mansfield, Lord Chief Justice of the Court of King's Bench* (J. Dodsley, 1772), 94.

23. Shyllon, *Black Slaves in Britain,* 9.

24. John Komlos, "On the Biological Standard of Living of Eighteenth-Century Americans: Taller, Richer, Healthier," *Research in Economic History* 20 (2001):233.

25. Burkhard Bilger, "The Height Gap," *New Yorker,* April 5, 2004, 38, 40.

26. Edwards and Walvin, *Black Personalities,* 24.

27. Gerzina, *Black London,* 19, 136; Edwards and Walvin, *Black Personalities,* 32; George, *London Life,* 140.

28. Hilary M. Beckles, *Natural Rebels, A Social History of Enslaved Black Women in Barbados* (University of Tennessee Press 1989), 35.

29. James Walvin, *Black Ivory: A History of British Slavery* (HarperCollins, 1992), 64, 76.

30. Hargrave, *Complete Collection of the State Trials,* 7.

31. Shyllon, *Black Slaves in Britain,* 78.

32. Prince Hoare, *Memoirs of Granville Sharp, Esq. Composed from His Own Manuscripts* (Henry Colburn, 1828), 1:105.

Chapter 2 Black Slaves in England

1. I owe my discussion of medieval English slavery primarily to David A. E. Pelteret, *Slavery in Early Mediaeval England from the Reign of Alfred Until the Twelfth Century* (The Boydell Press, 1995).

2. Karl Jacoby, "Slaves by Nature? Domestic Animals and Human Slaves," *Slavery and Abolition: A Journal of Slave and Post-Slave Studies* 89, 89–90, 94 (April 1994); David Brion Davis, *Slavery and Human Progress* (Oxford University Press, 1984), 15. See generally, Marjoire Spiegel, *The Dreaded Comparison: Human and Animal Slavery* (Mirror Books, 1996).

3. Yvon Garlon, *Slavery in Ancient Greece,* trans. Janet Lloyd (Cornell University Press, 1988), 40. The ox analogy was Aristotle's.

4. David Brion Davis, "At the Heart of Slavery," in *In the Image of God: Religion, Moral Values and Our Heritage of Slavery* (Yale University Press, 2001), 123, 127.

5. David Brion Davis, *Challenging the Boundaries of Slavery* (Harvard University Press, 2003), 12.

6. Davis, "At the Heart of Slavery," 123, 123–130; David Brion Davis, introduction to *A Historical Guide to World Slavery,* ed. Seymour Drescher and Stanley L. Engerman (Oxford University Press, 1998), ix, xi–xiv; Jacoby, "Slaves By Nature?," 90–92.

7. Davis, "At the Heart of Slavery," 123, 127.

8. William Godwin, *St. Leon: A Tale of the Sixteenth Century* (Arno Press, 1972) (1799); Gretchen Holbrook Gerzina, *Black London* (Rutgers University Press, 1995), 15.

9. Edward Long, *The History of Jamaica* (T. Lowndes, 1744), 1:178, quoting Hume. The quotation may be found in David Hume, *Essays: Moral, Political, and Literary,* ed. Thomas H. Green and Thomas H. Grose (Longmans, Green, and Co., 1875)(1754), 1:252.

10. Long, *History of Jamaica,* vol. 2, bk. 3, chap. 1; Richard Nisbet, *Slavery Not Forbidden by Scripture* (1773), in Roger Bruns, *Am I Not a Man and a Brother?: The Anti-*

slavery Crusade of Revolutionary America 1688–1788 (Chelsea House Publishers, 1977), 2:231–232.

11. Compare John Hamilton Baker, *The Common Law Tradition* (Hambledon Press, 2000), 325 ("the villein was not a slave in the Roman sense, nor was he owned by his lord") with William Holdsworth, *History of English Law* (Metheun & Co., 1938; Sweet and Maxwell, 1956), 3:491, 495 ("many of the Roman conceptions of property were applied to them. Their lord had absolute power over their bodies and their goods. He could sell them and treat them as he pleased for they were his chattels").

12. *Smith v. Brown and Cooper* may be found at 91 Eng. Rep. 566 (K.B. 1701).

13. *Bryan v. Walton,* 14 Ga. 185 (1853).

14. David Brion Davis, *The Problem of Slavery in Western Culture* (Cornell University Press, 1966), 38, 39; Holdsworth, *History of English Law,* 3:491, 495; see *Bryan v. Walton* ("where his lord was not concerned, a villein was a freeman in all his dealings with the world)."

15. *Pigg v. Caley,* Noy 27 (1618).

16. F. O. Shyllon, *Black Slaves in Britain* (Oxford University Press 1974), 2; James Walvin, *Black and White: The Negro and English Society 1555–1945* (Alan Lane/The Penguin Press, 1973), 1, 7.

17. Hugh Thomas, *The Slave Trade: The Story of the Atlantic Slave Trade 1440–1870* (Simon & Schuster 1997), 155–156; Shyllon, *Black Slaves in Britain,* 3.

18. Thomas, *The Slave Trade,* 156.

19. Ibid., 156; James Walvin, *Black and White: The Negro and English Society 1555–1945* (Alan Lane/The Penguin Press, 1973), 31, quoting Richard Hakluyt, *The Principal Navigations, Voiages, and Discoveries of the English Nation* (Historical Manuscripts Commission, 1904).

20. Thomas, *The Slave Trade,* 156–157.

21. Ibid., 198.

22. Ibid., 196–199. See also Walvin, *Black and White,* 36–37.

23. Walvin, *Black and White,* 39.

24. Ibid., 39.

25. Ibid.

26. Ibid., 107.

27. Gerzina, *Black London,* 3–4; Shyllon, *Black Slaves in Britain,* 2; Walvin, *Black and White,* 8.

28. William Shakespeare, *The Merchant of Venice,* act IV, scene I.

29. Gerzina, *Black London,* 22–23.

30. Paul Edwards and James Walvin, *Black Personalities in the Era of the Slave Trade* (Louisiana University Press, 1983), 20.

31. Walvin, *Black Ivory,* 11.

32. Gene Adams, "Dido Elizabeth Belle: A Black Girl at Kenwood," *Camden History Review* 10 (1984):12.

33. Gerzina, *Black London,* 10–11.

Chapter 3   Granville Sharp Meets Jonathan Strong

1. Granville Sharp, "An Account of the Occasion Which First Compelled G. S. to Study Law & Undertake the Defence of Negroe Slaves," *Abolition and Emancipation,* pt. 4, Granville Sharp Papers from Gloucestershire Record Office (reel 70) (Adam Matthew Publications Ltd., 1996), 17.

2. Unless otherwise noted, the facts of the Jonathan Strong matter are taken primarily from "An Account of the Occasion Which First Compelled G. S. to Study Law & Undertake the Defense of Negroe Slaves," Granville Sharp, *Abolition and Emancipation,* pt. 4, Granville Sharp Papers from Gloucestershire Record Office (reel 70) (Adam Matthew Publications Ltd., 1996), and from "Excerpts from Granville Sharp's Memorandum Book No. 1," ibid. (reel 79). See Thomas Clarkson, *History of the Rise, Progress, and Accomplishment of the Abolition of the Slave Trade by the British Parliament* (John W. Parker, 1839)(1808); Gretchen Holbrook Gerzina, *Black London: Life Before Emancipation* (Rutgers University Press, 1995); Prince Hoare, *Memoirs of Granville Sharp, Esq. Composed from His Own Manuscripts,* vol. 1 (Henry Colburn, 1828); E. C. P. Lascelles, *Granville Sharp and the Freedom of Slaves in England* (Oxford University Press, 1928); F. O. Shyllon, *Black Slaves in Britain* (Oxford University Press, 1974); James Walvin, *Black and White: The Negro and English Society 1555–1945* (Alan Lane/The Penguin Press, 1973).

3. Charles Sumner, *His Complete Works* (Lee and Sheppard, 1900), 4:298.

4. Hoare, *Memoirs of Granville Sharp, Esq.,* 1:53; Granville Sharp, *A Representation of the Injustice and Dangerous Tendency of Tolerating Slavery, or Even of Admitting the Least Claim to Private Property in the Persons of Men, in England* (Benjamin White and Robert Horsfield, 1769), 13 (making analogies to horses and dogs).

5. Walvin, *Black and White,* 118.

6. Paul Edwards and James Walvin, *Black Personalities in the Era of the Slave Trade* (Louisiana University Press, 1983), 30.

7. *Gelly v. Cleve,* quoted in *Judicial Cases Concerning American Slavery and the Negro,* ed. Helen Tunnileff Catterall (Carnegie Institute of Washington, 1926–1937), 1:3 n. 3.

8. Ruth Paley, *New Dictionary of National Biography* (Oxford University Press, forthcoming), 1.

9. Clarkson, *Abolition of the Slave Trade,* 94.

10. Olaudah Equiano, "The Life of Olaudah Equinano," in *The Classic Slave Narratives, ed.* Henry Louis Gates, Jr. (Mentor Books, 1987), 40, 47, 52, 65.

11. Ottobah Cugoano, *Thoughts and Sentiments on the Evil of Slavery* (n.s., 1787), iv.

12. See, for example, Thornton Stringfellow, "A Brief Examination of Scripture Testimony on the Institution of Slavery," in *The Ideology of Slavery: Proslavery Thought in the Antebellum South, 1830–1860,* ed. Drew Gilpin Faust (Louisiana University Press, 1981), 136–167.

13. David A. E. Pelteret, *Slavery in Early Mediaeval England from the Reign of Alfred Until the Twelfth Century* (The Boydell Press, 1995), 265.

14. David Brion Davis, *The Problem of Slavery in Western Culture* (Cornell University Press, 1966), 85–102.

15. "Cartright's Case," Rushworth (1569), 2:468, reprinted in Catterall, *Judicial Cases*, 1:9.

16. *Butts v. Penny*, 83 Eng. Rep. 518, 518 (K.B. 1677).

17. Gerzina, *Black London*, 76; Shyllon, *Black Slaves in Britain*, 10. The court ruled that Auker was "at liberty to serve any person until such time as the said Rich shall return from Barbadoes," ibid., 10 n. 5.

18. *Gelly v. Cleve*, 9.

19. The judges' decision is reported in two places: 91 Eng. Rep. 994 (K.B. 1697) and 90 Eng. Rep. 830 (K.B. 1697) as *Chamberlain v. Harvey*. The arguments of counsel are reported in *Chamberline v. Harvey*, 87 Eng. Rep. 598 (K.B. 1697). The quoted argument can be found at 601.

20. *Chamberline v. Harvey*, 87 Eng. Rep. 598, 599, 600 (K.B. 1697).

21. Ibid., 90 Eng. Rep. 830, 830 (K.B. 1697).

22. *Smith v. Brown and Cooper*, 91 Eng. Rep. 566 (K.B. 1701).

23. Holt noticed that the slave had been in Virginia when he was sold and that blacks could be sold as chattels there, "for the laws of England did not extend to Virginia," and suggested the plaintiff amend his complaint to reflect this. The Attorney-General corrected him: In Virginia, blacks weren't chattels, but real estate, and could be transferred only by deed, so "nothing was done," *Smith v. Brown and Cooper*, 91 Eng. Rep. 566, 566–567 (K.B. 1701).

24. *Smith v. Gould* is reported in two places: 91 Eng. Rep. 567, 567 (K.B. 1705) and 92 Eng. Rep. 338, 338 (K.B. 1706).

25. *Butts v. Penny*, 83 Eng. Rep. 518, 518 (K.B. 1677).

26. *Smith v. Gould*, 92 Eng. Rep. 338.

27. *Slavery, Abolition and Emancipation: Black Slaves and the British Empire*, ed. Michael Craton et al. (Longeman Group Ltd., 1976), 165; Prince Hoare, *Memoirs of Granville Sharp, Esq. Composed from His Own Manuscripts* (Henry Colburn, 1828), 1:7–8.

28. Hoare, *Memoirs of Granville Sharp, Esq.*, 1:174 (letter from Sharp to the Bishop of London in 1795).

Chapter 4   Granville Sharp, Abolitionist

1. Letter from William Wilberforce to Granville Sharp, April 17, 1792; Thomas Clarkson, *History of the Rise, Progress, and Accomplishment of the Abolition of the Slave Trade* (John W. Parker, 1839)(1808); F. O. Shyllon, *Black Slaves in Britain* (Oxford University Press, 1974), 137.

2. Charles Sumner, *His Complete Works* (Lee and Sheppard, 1900), 4:295.

3. Prince Hoare, *Memoirs of Granville Sharp, Esq., Composed from His Own Manuscripts* (Henry Colburn, 1828), 2:292.

4. Ibid., 199.

5. Ibid., 193.

6. E.C.P. Lascelles, *Granville Sharp and the Freedom of Slaves in England* (Oxford University Press, 1928), 95.

7. For example, 25 Geo. 2, c. 40 (1752); 23 Geo. 2, c. 31 (1750); 5 Geo. 2, c. 7 (1732).

8. Granville Sharp, *Abolition and Emancipation*, pt. 4, Granville Sharp Papers from Gloucestershire Record Office (reel 83) (Adam Matthew Publications Ltd., 1996) ("No Slavery in England," Anti-Slavery Society, July 1972, 3).

9. Hoare, *Memoirs of Granville Sharp, Esq.*, 1:55–56.

10. Roger Bruns, "Anthony Benezet's Assertion of Negro Equality," *Journal of Negro History* 56 (1971), 230, 232–233, and n. 11.

11. Ibid., 230, 232.

12. Roger Bruns, *Am I Not a Man and a Brother?: The Antislavery Crusade of Revolutionary America 1688–1788* (Chelsea House Publishers, 1977), 79.

13. Bernie Unti, "The Quality of Mercy: Organized Animal Protection in the United States 1866–1930" (Ph.D. diss., American University, 2002), 23.

14. Hoare, *Memoirs of Granville Sharp, Esq.*, 1:145.

15. Ibid., 62.

16. *Annual Register* 1767, 287 (sec. pagination).

17. John Holliday, *Life of William, Late Earl of Mansfield* (P. Elmsly, 1797), 90.

18. William Blackstone, *Commentaries on the Laws of England*, 1st ed. (Clarendon Press, 1765), 1:*61.

19. I take this discussion of Blackstone's *Commentaries* from Daniel J. Boorstin, *The Mysterious Science of the Law* (Beacon Press, 1958)(1941), 139–191.

20. Baron de Montesquieu, *The Spirit of the Laws*, trans. Thomas Nugent (Hafner Press, 1949)(1749), 236–238.

21. Ibid., 238–239. Irony can be misunderstood. The editor of this 1949 translation notes that Montesquieu's arguments "form a striking instance of the prejudice under which even a liberal mind can labor," ibid., 239 n. h.

22. Blackstone, *Commentaries*, 1st ed., 1:*123.

23. Ibid., *411–*412.

24. Thomas Day, *Dialogue Between a Justice of the Peace and a Farmer* (John Stockdale, 1785), 4.

25. Edward Christian in Blackstone, *Commentaries*, 17th ed. (E. Duyckinck, 1822), 1:*127n.

26. Blackstone, *Commentaries*, 2d ed. (Clarendon Press, 1766), 1:*425.

27. Ibid., *127.

28. Blackstone, *Commentaries*, 4th ed. (Clarendon Press, 1770), 1:*127.

29. Shyllon, *Black Slaves in Britain*, 61, 63.

30. Ibid., 72.

31. Ibid., 72–73.

32. Shyllon, *Black Slaves in Britain*, 63.

33. William Holdsworth, *History of English Law* (Metheun & Co., 1938; Sweet and Maxwell, 1956), 12:562, 563.

34. John Nicholls, *Recollections and Reflections Personal and Political as Connected with Public Affairs During the Reign of George III* (James Ridgway, 1820), 1:344.

35. Archer Polson, *Law and Lawyers, or, Sketches and Illustrations of Legal History and Biography* (Longman, Orme, Brown, Green, and Longmans, 1840), 1:185–186. Other descriptions harmonize with this one, P. D. Brown, *The Chathamites* (Macmillan, 1967), 240–241; Christopher Hibbert, *King Mob: The Story of Lord George Gordan and the London Riots of 1780* (World Publishing Co., 1958), 36.

36. Polson, *Law and Lawyers,* 1:186.

37. Ibid., 188–189.

38. Ibid., 186.

39. Ibid., 185–186.

40. James Oldham, *The Mansfield Manuscripts and the Growth of English Law in the Eighteenth Century* (University of North Carolina Press, 1992), 1:75; Polson, 1:187.

41. Shyllon, *Black Slaves in Britain,* 88; Henry Roscoe, *Lives of Eminent British Lawyers* (Fred B. Rothman & Co., 1830), 288.

42. "Life of the Author," in Blackstone, *Commentaries,* 18th ed. (Collina and Hannay; Collins and Co., N. and J. White; and Grigg and Elliot, 1832), 1:xviii.

43. Polson, *Law and Lawyers,* 2:68; "Life of the Author," in Blackstone, *Commentaries,* 18th ed., 1:xviii.

Chapter 5   John Hylas: The Test

1. Unless noted, the discussion of the Hylas case is drawn from Gretchen Holbrook Gerzina, *Black London: Life Before Emancipation* (Rutgers University Press, 1995); Prince Hoare, *Memoirs of Granville Sharp, Esq. Composed from His Own Manuscripts,* vol. 1 (Henry Colburn, 1828); E.C.P. Lascelles, *Granville Sharp and the Freedom of Slaves in England* (Oxford University Press, 1928); F. O. Shyllon, *Black Slaves in Britain* (Oxford University Press, 1974); James Walvin, *Black and White: The Negro and English Society 1555–1945* (Alan Lane/The Penguin Press, 1973).

2. Shyllon, *Black Slaves in Britain,* 41.

3. Details about Westminster Hall throughout this book were taken from John Hamilton Baker, *The Common Law Tradition* (Hambledon Press, 2000); Dorian Gerhold, *Westminster Hall: Nine Hundred Years of History* (James & James, 1999); James C. Oldham, *The Mansfield Manuscripts and the Growth of English Law in the Eighteenth Century* (University of North Carolina Press, 1992); Hilary St. George Saunders, *Westminster Hall* (Michael Joseph, 1951); Edward Foss, *Memories of Westminster Hall: A Collection of Interesting Incidents, Anecdotes and Historical Sketches, Relating to Westminster Hall, Its Famous Judges and Lawyers and Its Great Trials, with an Historical Introduction* (Estes & Lauriat, 1874).

4. Oldham, *The Mansfield Manuscripts,* 1:72–73.

5. Granville Sharp, *A Representation of the Injustice and Dangerous Tendency of Tolerating Slavery, or Even of Admitting the Least Claim to Private Property in the Persons of Men, in England* (Benjamin White and Robert Horsfield, 1769), 13.

6. Ibid., 5, 6, and n. *. The first case was *Gallway v. Caddee,* the second, *De Pinna v. Henriques.*

7. Sharp, *A Representation,* 13, 14, 15, 18 (making analogies to horses and dogs).

8. Ibid., 5.

9. *Pearne v. Lisle,* 27 Eng. Rep. 47 (Ch. 1749). Hardwicke's twentieth-century biographer thinks the *Pearne* opinion "hardly reaches the [usual] high standard and practical morality, and private justice [Hardwicke] exhibited. Philip Chesney Yorke, *The Life and Correspondence of Philip Yorke, Earl of Hardwicke, Lord High Chancellor of Great Britain* (Cambridge University Press 1913), 472.

10. *Shanley v. Harvey,* 2 Eden 125 (Ch. 1762)(Henley, J.). Sharp didn't try to distinguish *Gelly v. Cleve* or *Butts v. Penny,* though he must have known about them. He may have simply chosen to ignore them, which no lawyer would have done.

11. Shyllon, *Black Slaves in Britain,* 35.

12. Letter from William Blackstone to Granville Sharp, February 20, 1769, New York Historical Society.

13. Sharp, *A Representation,* 137–138 (making analogies to horses and dogs).

14. I take Sharp's entire discussion of villeinage from Sharp, *A Representation,* 107–136.

15. William Blackstone, *Commentaries on the Laws of England,* 18th ed. (Collina and Hanay; Collins and Co.; N. and J. White; and Grigg and Elliot, 1832), 2:*93.

16. Hoare, *Memoirs of Granville Sharp, Esq.,* 1:63–64, 64n. "The 1679 Habeas Corpus Act is an act for the better securing the Liberty of the subject, and for Prevention of Imprisonment beyond the Seas, 1 Car. II, c. 2 (1679)."

17. Unless otherwise noted, the sources for this discussion of the writ of habeas corpus are Chester James Antieau, *The Practice of Extraordinary Remedies: Habeas Corpus and the Other Common Law Writs* (Oceana Publications, 1987); William F. Duker, "The English Origins of the Writ of Habeas Corpus: A Peculiar Path to Fame," *New York University Law Review* 53 (1978):983; Neil Douglas McFeeley, "The Historical Development of Habeas Corpus," *Southwestern Law Journal* 30 (1976):585; William Holdsworth, *A History of English Law* (Metheun & Co., 1938; Sweet and Maxwell, 1956); Maxwell Cohen, "Habeas Corpus Cum Causa: The Emergence of the Modern Writ—II," *Canadian Bar Review* 18 (1940):172; Cohen, "Habeas Corpus Cum Causa," 10; Albert S. Glass, "Historical Aspects of Habeas Corpus," *St. John's Law Review* 9 (1934):55; Edward Jenks, "The Story of the Habeas Corpus," *The Law Quarterly* 69 (1902):64; William S. Church, *A Treatise on the Writ of Habeas Corpus Including Jurisdiction, False Imprisonment, Writ of Error, Extradition, Mandamus, Certiorari, Judgments, Etc.,* 2d ed., rev. and enlarg. (Bancroft-Whitney Co., 1893) 139–143, 155; Rollin C. Hurd, *A Treatise on the Right of Personal Liberty and on the Writ of Habeas Corpus,* 2d ed., rev. (Da Capo Press, 1972), 549–558; Blackstone, *Commentaries,* 18th ed., 3:*124–138.

18. Duker, "The English Origins," 983, 1002; Cohen, "Habeas Corpus Cum Causa," 10, 13.

19. Duker, "The English Origins," 983, 1035. See Chambers's Case, 79 Eng. Rep. 717 (K.B. 1629).

20. Bushell's Case, Vaughn 136 (K.B. 1670)(Vaughn, C.J.).

21. Neil Douglas McFeeley, "The Historical Development of Habeas Corpus," *Southwestern Law Journal* 30 (1976), 585, 589; Holdsworth, *History of English Law,* 9:119.

22. Holdsworth, *History of English Law,* 119, and n. 3; *Rex v. Gardner,* cited in Cohen, "Habeas Corpus Cum Causa," 10, 35, citing Tremaine, *Pleas of the Crown* (1723), 354. Blackstone, *Commentaries,* 1ˢᵗ ed. (Clarendon Press, 1765), 3:*129.

23. Oldham, *The Mansfield Manuscripts,* 1:78.

24. 56 Geo. III, c. 100 (1816).

25. Cohen, "Habeas Corpus Cum Causa," 172, 175; Blackstone, *Commentaries,* 1st ed., 1:*137.

26. Blackstone, *Commentaries,* 1ˢᵗ ed., 2:*258, *390–*395, *403.

27. Unless, like a pigeon, it had a habit of returning, Blackstone, *Commentaries,* 1st ed., 2:*392–*393.

28. Ibid., *393–*394, *335.

29. Erica Fudge, *Perceiving Animals: Humans and Beasts in Early Modern English Culture* (University of Illinois Press, 2000), 1, 13–14; Keith Thomas, *Man and the Natural World: A History of the Modern Sensibility* (Pantheon Books, 1983), 144, 159.

30. Douglas Chadwick, *The Fate of the Elephant* (Sierra Club Books, 1992), 225 (Henry Stanley estimated that each pound of ivory cost one African life).

31. Letter from William Blackstone to Granville Sharp, May 25, 1769, New York Historical Society.

32. Granville Sharp, *Abolition and Emancipation,* pt. 4, Granville Sharp Papers from Gloucestershire Record Office (reel 56) (Adam Matthew Publications Ltd., 1996).

Chapter 6   The Next Test: Thomas Lewis

1. Thomas Clarkson, *History of the Rise, Progress, and Accomplishment of the Abolition of the Slave Trade by the British Parliament* (John W. Parker, 1839)(1808), 75.

2. I thank Ruth Paley for this suggestion.

3. PRO KB 10/37, indictment 30. I thank Ruth Paley for obtaining this information at the Public Records Office. The facts of the *Lewis* trial are taken from a transcript, *The Case of Lewis, a Negro, v. Stapleton, His Master, 1771,* that may be found in the archives of the New York Historical Society.

4. Prince Hoare, *Memoirs of Granville Sharp, Esq. Composed from His Own Manuscripts* (Henry Colburn, 1828), 1:81.

5. William Blackstone, *Commentaries on the Laws of England,* 18th ed. (Collina and Hanay; Collins and Co.; N. and J. White; and Grigg and Elliot, 1832), 4:*219.

6. Ibid., 4:*218.

7. M. Dorothy George, *London Life in the Eighteenth Century* (Academy Chicago, 1984)(1925), 166–167.

8. John H. Langbein, *The Origins Of Adversary Criminal Trial* (Oxford University Press, 2003), 315 n. 306.

9. An anonymous attorney, *The Attorney's Compleat Guide to the Court of King's Bench, Containing the Whole Modern Practice of the Court* (printed by W. Strahan and M. Woodfall for P. Uriel, M. Folingsby, J. Williams, and G. Robinson, 1773), 169.

10. Ibid., 170.

11. Letter from Granville Sharp to Mrs. Banks, July 18, 1770, in Hoare, *Memoirs of Granville Sharp, Esq.,* 1:83.

12. Hoare, *Memoirs of Granville Sharp, Esq.,* 1:84.

13. Letter from Granville Sharp to Mrs. Banks, in Hoare, *Memoirs of Granville Sharp, Esq.,* 1:85–86.

14. Correspondence from Ruth Paley to Steven M. Wise, December 7, 2003; D. R. Bentley, *Select Cases from the Twelve Judges' Notebooks* (John Rees, 1997), 8.

15. James C. Oldham, *The Mansfield Manuscripts and the Growth of English Law in the Eighteenth Century* (University of North Carolina Press, 1992), 109.

16. Lord Campbell, *Lives of the Lord Chief Justices of England* (John Murray, 1849), 2:443.

17. Hoare, *Memoirs of Granville Sharp, Esq.,* 1:86.

18. Campbell, *Lives of the Lord Chief Justices,* 2:386–387.

19. David Lemmings, *Professors of the Law: Barristers and English Legal Culture in the Eighteenth Century* (Oxford University Press, 2000), 268.

20. Henry Roscoe, *Lives of Eminent British Lawyers* (Fred B. Rotherman & Co., 1830), 289.

21. Lemmings, *Professors of the Law,* 299–300.

22. Oldham, *The Mansfield Manuscripts,* 1:79; Lemmings, *Professors of the Law,* 59.

23. Archer Polson, *Law and Lawyers, Or, Sketches and Illustrations of Legal History and Biography* (Longman, Orme, Brown, Green, and Longmans, 1840), 1:184.

24. Gilbert Clark, *Life Sketches of Eminent Lawyers, American, Canadian, and English* (Lawyers' International Publishing Co., 1895), 124.

25. F. O. Shyllon, *Black Slaves in Britain* (Oxford University Press, 1974), 88, quoting William Grimmer, *Anecdotes of Bench and Bar* (1852), 68–69.

26. Roscoe, *Eminent British Lawyers,* 290–291.

Chapter 7 Lord Mansfield

1. Diary entry of Mrs. Prowse (Sharp's sister) for February 20, 1771, in E.C.P. Lascelles, *Granville Sharp and the Freedom of Slaves in England* (Oxford University Press, 1928), 28.

2. This document may be found in the records of the New York Historical Society.

3. John Locke, *The Second Treatise of Government, in Two Treatises of Government,* ed. Peter Laslett (Cambridge University Press, 1988), 287, sec. 27.

4. James C. Oldham, *The Mansfield Manuscripts and the Growth of English Law in the Eighteenth Century* (University of North Carolina Press, 1992), 101.

5. Archer Polson, *Law and Lawyers, or, Sketches and Illustrations of Legal History and Biography* (Longman, Orme, Brown, Green, and Longmans, 1840), 316.

6. *Millar v. Taylor*, 4 Burrow 2303, 2399, 98 Eng. Rep. 201, 253 (K.B. 1769); *Alderson v. Temple*, 4 Burrow 2239 (K.B. 1768).

7. There may have been other dissents recorded in cases that were either not reported or were reported in more obscure publications, Oldham, *The Mansfield Manuscripts*, 1:47.

8. Theodore C. Plucknett, *A Concise History of the Common Law* (Little, Brown and Co., 1956), 680.

9. Edward Heward, *Lord Mansfield: A Biography of William Murray 1st Earl of Mansfield 1705–1793, Lord Chief Justice for 32 Years* (Barry Rose, 1979), 129; Cecil Herbert Stuart Fifoot, *Lord Mansfield* (Oxford University Press, 1936), 183.

10. Letter from Thomas Jefferson to Philip Mazzei, November, 1785, in Thomas Jefferson, *Writings of Thomas Jefferson*, ed. Paul Leicester Ford (G. P. Putnam's Sons, 1894), 115.

11. *Jones v. Randall*, Lofft 383, 98 Eng. Rep. 98, 706, (K.B. 1774).

12. *Bauerman v. Radenius*, 7 T.R 668 (K.B. 1798).

13. Polson, *Law and Lawyers*, 317–318.

14. *Barwell v. Brooks*, 3 Doug. 371, 373, 99 Eng. Rep. 702, 703 (K.B. 1784).

15. Fifoot, *Lord Mansfield*, 201.

16. *Oxford English Dictionary*, 2d ed. (1989), 236, def. 2.

17. *Ingle v. Wordsworth*, 3 Burrow 1284, 1228, 1 W. Bl. 355, 356, 97 Eng. Rep. 834, 835 (K.B. 1762). See, for example, Fifoot, *Lord Mansfield*, 203–210.

18. William Holdsworth, *History of English Law* (Metheun & Co., 1938; Sweet and Maxwell 1956).

19. *Slater v. May*, 2 Raym. Ld. 1071, 1072 (K.B. 1704).

20. *Hassells v. Simpson*, 1 Douglas 89, 93 (K.B. 1781).

21. Alexander Pope, "Ode to Venus."

22. Lord Campbell, *Lives of the Lord Chief Justices of England* (John Murray, 1849), 2:220, 306.

23. Cicero, "De re publica," trans. Clinton Walker Keyes, (Loeb Classical Library, 1928), 211, sec. 3.22.33.

24. Cicero, "On Duties," in *Cicero: Selected Works*, trans. Michael Grant (Penguin Books, 1971), 163.

25. Ibid., 170.

26. Ibid., 200, 171.

27. John Holliday, *The Life of William, Late Earl of Mansfield* (P. Elmsly et al., 1797), 252–262. The case was *Chamberlain v. Evans*, reported in P. Furneaux, *Letters to the Honorable Mr. Justice Blackstone Concerning His Exposition of the Act of Toleration*, 2d ed. (T. Cadell, 1771), 251.

28. Humphrey W. Woolrych, *Lives of Eminent Serjeants-at-Law of the English Law* (Allen, 1869), 574.

29. William Blackstone, *Commentaries on the Laws of England*, 1st ed. (Clarendon Press, 1765), 1:*129. The third was the right of personal security.

30. Ibid., 1:*2.

31. Ibid., 1:*2–3.

32. Isaiah Berlin, "Two Concepts of Liberty," in *Four Essays on Liberty* (Oxford University Press 1969), 124.

33. Abraham Lincoln, *The Collected Works of Abraham Lincoln,* ed. Roy P. Basler (Rutgers University Press 1953–1955), 7:301–302 (emphasis in the original).

34. Campbell, *Lives* (John Murray, 1849), 2:261–262.

35. Charles Sumner, *His Complete Works* (Lee and Sheppard, 1900), 3:505.

36. H. Montgomerty Hyde, Judge Jeffreys 98 (Butterworth, 1948) see John H. Langbein, *The Origins of Adversary Criminal Trial* (Oxford University Press, 2003), 80n.69; *R. v. Barnardiston,* 9 Howell's State Trials 1333, 1355 (K.B. 1684).

37. The facts about Dido are drawn, unless otherwise noted, from Gene Adams, "Dido Elizabeth Belle: A Black Girl at Kenwood," *Camden History Review* 10 (1984).

38. James C. Oldham, "Eighteenth-Century Judges' Notes: How They Explain, Correct and Enhance the Reports," *American Journal of Legal History* 31 (1987):9, 27 n. 79.

39. *Money v. Leach,* 3 Burr. 1742 (K.B. 1765).

Chapter 8 Lewis v. Stapylton *Begins*

1. D. R. Bentley, *Select Cases from the Twelve Judges' Notebooks* (John Rees, 1997), 5–6.

2. Unless otherwise noted, the sources I rely upon for eighteenth-century criminal procedure and evidence are John H. Langbein, *The Origins of Adversary Criminal Trial* (Oxford University Press, 2003); Langbein, "Historical Foundations of the Law of Evidence: A View from the Ryder Sources," *Columbia Law Review* 96 (1996):1168; James C. Oldham, "Truth-Telling in the Eighteenth Century English Courtroom," *Law and History Review* 12 (Spring 1994):95; Oldham, *The Mansfield Manuscripts and the Growth of English Law in the Eighteenth Century* (University of North Carolina Press, 1992); John M. Beattie, "Scales of Justice: Defense Counsel and the English Criminal Trial in the Eighteenth and Nineteenth Centuries," *Law and History Review* 9 (1991):221; Stephan Landsman, "The Rise of the Contentious Spirit: Adversary Procedure in Eighteenth Century England," *Cornell Law Review* 75 (1990): 407; John H. Langbein, "Shaping the Eighteenth-Century Trial: A View from the Ryder Sources," *University of Chicago Law Review* 50 (1983):1; John Bodansky, "The Abolition of the Party-Witness Disqualification: An Historical Survey," *Kentucky Law Journal* 70 (1981–1982):91; John H. Langbein, "The Criminal Trial Before the Lawyers," *University of Chicago Law Review* 35 (1978): 263; Theodore F. T. Plucknett, *A Concise History of the Common Law* (Little, Brown and Co., 1956). See William Blackstone, *Commentaries on the Laws of England,* 1st ed. (Clarendon Press, 1765), 4:*355.

3. This rule had drawn severe criticism for more than a century; Blackstone thought it irrational. The usual, and plainly inadequate, reason given was that some misdemeanors were, at their core, civil or regulatory, such as failing to maintain a road.

Langbein, *Adversary Criminal Trial,* 36 and n. 132; John H. Langbein, "The Historical Origins of the Privilege Against Self-Incrimination at Common Law," *Michigan Law Review* 92 (1994):1047, 1049 n. 7.

4. Langbein, *Adversary Criminal Trial,* 175.

5. John M. Beattie, "Scales of Justice: Defense Counsel and the English Criminal Trial in the Eighteenth and Nineteenth Centuries," *Law and History Review* 9 (1991):221, 227.

6. Ibid., 221, 260 n. 20.

7. John M. Beattie, *Crime and the Courts in England 1660–1800* (Princeton University Press, 1986), 378.

8. Thomas Wontner, *Old Bailey Experience: Criminal Jurisprudence and the Actual Working of Our Penal Code of Laws* (J. Fraser, 1833), 59–60.

9. Compare Blackstone, *Commentaries,* 18th English ed., 1st American ed. (1832), 4:355 n. 22, with Langbein, *Adversary Criminal Trial,* 287–300; Langbein, "Historical Origins," 1047, 1069; Stephan Landsman, "The Rise of the Contentious Spirit: Adversary Procedure in Eighteenth Century England," *Cornell Law Review* 75 (1990):497, 540–541.

10. Unless otherwise noted, trial testimony is taken from *The Case of Lewis, A Negro, v. Stapleton, His Master,* 1771, in the archives of the New York Historical Society.

11. Nicholas Rogers, "Impressment and the Law in Eighteenth-Century Britain," in *Law, Crime, and English Society, 1660–1830,* ed. Norma Landau (Cambridge University Press, 2002), 71, 89.

12. William Seward, *Anecdotes of Some Distinguished Persons, Chiefly of the Present and Two Preceeding Centuries* (T. Cadell, Jr., and W. Davies, 1796), 4:495; Lord Campbell, Lives of the Lord Chief Justices of England (John Murray, 1858), 2:200.

13. N. A. M. Rodger, *The Wooden World: An Anatomy of the Georgian Navy* (Naval Institute Press, 1986), 173.

14. Unless otherwise noted, the notebook writings of Lord Mansfield and other eighteenth-century judges were taken from Oldham, *The Mansfield Manuscripts;* Oldham, "Eighteenth-Century Judges' Notes: How They Explain, Correct and Enhance the Reports," *American Journal of Legal History* 31 (1987):495; and Langbein, "Shaping the Eighteenth-Century Trial," 23.

15. J. H. Baker, *The Legal Profession and the Common Law: Historical Essays* (Hambleton Press, 1986), 317.

16. Barbara J. Shapiro, "'To a Moral Certainty': Theories of Knowledge and Anglo-American Juries 1600–1850," *Hastings Law Journal* 38 (1986):153, 162.

17. Jeremy Bentham, "Rationale of Judicial Evidence," in *A Bentham Reader,* vol. 2, book ix (Pegasus, 1969)(1827), 234; Oldham, "Truth-Telling," 110 n. 76.

18. Oldham, "Truth-Telling," 95, 111.

19. Langbein, "Historical Foundations," 1168, 1186.

20. At the beginning of the seventeenth century, Lord Coke believed that only Christians could swear the necessary oath, and William Hawkins, in his 1720s' *Trea-*

tise of the Pleas of the Crown had claimed it proper to disqualify an infidel "who believes neither the Old nor New Testaments to be the Word of God," William Hawkins, *A Treatise of the Pleas of the Crown* (E. and R. Nutt, 1724–1726), 2:434. In 1744, however, a Hindu was permitted to testify because he believed both in a God and an afterlife, *Omychund v. Barker*, 1, 21 Wils. 84, 84,95 Eng. Rep. 506, 506 (K.B. 1744). As late as 1786, one William Atkins was disqualified from testifying at the Old Bailey about the theft of a horse because he had never learned the catechism and was ignorant of an oath's obligations, of the next world, and of what happens to wicked people after they passed into it, *Rex v. White*, 4 T.R. 771, 100 Eng. Rep. 1293 (K.B. 1786).

21. John Fortescue, *De Laudibus Legum Anglaie*, S. B. Chrimes, trans. (Hyperion Press, 1979)(1942), 105.

22. A. Leon Higgenbotham, Jr., *In the Matter of Color—Race and the American Legal Process: The Colonial Experience* (Oxford University Press, 1978), 339.

23. Modern writers distinguish between an "assumption," which imposes the burden of persuasion on one party, and a "presumption," which imposes the burden of introducing evidence on some issue on the opponent of the party with the burden of persuasion. What Mansfield was prescribing was an assumption highly favorable to the prosecution. Harold A. Ashford and D. Michael Risinger, "Presumptions, Assumptions, and Due Process in Criminal Cases: A Theoretical Overview," *Yale Law Journal* 79 (1969), 165, 173.

24. *Chamberline v. Harvey*, 90 Eng. Rep. 830 (K.B. 1697); 91 Eng. Rep. 994 (K.B. 1697).

25. Oldham, *The Mansfield Manuscripts*, 1243.

26. Bentley, *Select Cases*, 21.

27. Sharp's reactions and observations can be found in a manuscript in the possession of the New York Historical Society titled "A Report of the Case of Lewis (a Negro) ag. Stapylton, with Remarks by G. Sharp."

28. *The King v. Edwards*, 7 T.R. 744, 745, 101 Eng. Rep. 1231, 1232 (K.B. 1798); *The King v. Reynolds*, 6 T.R. 496, 497–498, 101 Eng. Rep. 667, 668 (K.B. 1795).

29. Blackstone, *Commentaries*, 18th English, 1st American ed., 4:*424–*425.

30. *Rex v. D. S. Laval*, 3 Burr. 1434, 1436, 97 Eng. Rep. 913, 914 (K.B. 1763) ("The court is bound . . . to set the infants free from an improper restraint; but they are not bound to deliver the over to any body . . . ").

31. Oldham, *The Mansfield Manuscripts*, 110; *Rex v. Tubbs*, 2 Cowper 512, 98 Eng. Rep. 1215 (King's Bench 1776).

32. See, for example, *Clark v. Gautier*, 8 Fla. 361 (1959); *Shue v. Turk*, 56 Va. 81 (1859); *Thornton v. DeMoss*, 7 Miss. 229 (1856); *Peter v. Hargrave*, 46 Va. 12 (1848); *Foster v. Alston*, 6 How. 406 (Miss. 1842); *Ruddle's Exec. v. Ben*, 37 Va. 428 (1839); *De Lacy v. Antoine*, 34 Va. 686 (1836); *State v. Fraser*, 1 Ga. 373 (Super. Ct. 1831).

33. PRO KB 10/37, indictment 30. I thank Ruth Paley for going to the Public Records Office and confirming this fact.

Chapter 9   Sharp Fails, Again

1. There is no question today that Bryant Stapylton's hearsay statement would not be allowed. Forbidding juries from hearing "a story out of another man's mouth" has been said, next to the jury trial, to be Anglo-America's greatest contribution to the legal process, Gascoigne's Trial, *Howell State Trials* (1680), 7:959, 1019; Wigmore, Evidence, sec. 1354, 5:278 (Chadbourne rev. 1974). The rule appeared in the sixteenth century, but was not well-accepted and consistently applied until the turn of the nineteenth century. Eighteenth-century criminal judges might exclude it, and they might not. Some allowed hearsay when they saw no other way of obtaining important evidence or when it merely supplemented testimony already given under the oath that many continued to believe was indispensable to truth telling. This was the position of the 1773 *Compleat Guide:* "Mere hearsay evidence is not admissible, but may corroborate the testimony of a witness," Attorney of the Court, *Attorney's Compleat Guide to the Court of King's Bench, Containing the Whole Modern Practice of the Court 155* (printed by W. Strahan and M. Woodfall for P. Uriel, M. Folingsby, J. Williams, and G. Robinson, 1773). This was hearsay that Mansfield might or might not allow. With a party forbidden to testify, sometimes the only way her story could get into evidence was through someone relating what she had said. Mansfield allowed hearsay into evidence as late as 1785, *Rex v. Wilkinson*, see Mansfield's trial notes of the case in James C. Oldham, *The Mansfield Manuscripts and the Growth of English Law in the Eighteenth Century* (University of North Carolina Press, 1992), 2:1060, 1061. Other judges refused to allow hearsay because it had not been given under oath and, occasionally, because it deprived the opposing party of the ability to cross-examine the declarant. Hearsay was "no evidence," they would tell the jury, immaterial, and they were not to give it much weight in their deliberations. Other judges excluded it altogether and told the jury to ignore it.

2. Judge and jury vaguely believed it was better to acquit the guilty, than convict the innocent. "[I]t is better that ten guilty persons escape, rather than one innocent suffer," Blackstone had said, William Blackstone, *Commentaries on the Laws of England,* 1st ed. (Clarendon Press, 1765), 4:*358.

Mansfield didn't require the jury to demand that Lewis prove Stapylton guilty "beyond a reasonable doubt," either. That standard had been explicitly invoked for the first time in the Boston Massacre Trials of 1770. But Mansfield was still not using it in 1781, when he instructed the jury in the trial of Lord George Gordon, charged with treason for inciting the anti-Catholic riots in which Mansfield's house and library were incinerated, the judge himself barely escaping the rope the mob brought with them: "If the scale should hang doubtful, and you are not fully satisfied that he is guilty, you ought to lean on the favorable side and acquit him," *Trial of Lord George Gordon for High Treason,* Howells State Trials 21:485, 647 (K.B. 1781). Barbara J. Shapiro argues that the "beyond a reasonable doubt" standard was consistent with the "fully satisfied standard," Barbara J. Shapiro, "'To a Moral Certainty': Theories of Knowledge and Anglo-American Juries 1600–1850," *Hastings Law Journal* 38 (1986):153, 171.

Eighteenth-century judges possessed a nearly unrestricted ability to prod jurors into returning a desired verdict. Mansfield's immediate predecessor, Dudley Ryder, related a case in which one drunk had prosecuted his equally inebriated companion for robbery: "I told the jury I thought there was no ground to find [the defendant] guilty on this single evidence, and the jury found him Not Guilty," John H. Langbein, "Shaping the Eighteenth-Century Trial: A View from the Ryder Sources," *University of Chicago Law Review* 50 (1983):1, 23. When Mansfield desired an outcome, he usually got it. After an Irish priest was sentenced by a judge in the 1767 Surrey assizes to life imprisonment for saying the prohibited Catholic Mass, Mansfield led the Twelve Judges in subverting the religiously intolerant statutes by interpreting them into worthlessness. To convict a defendant of saying Mass, the prosecution would have to prove the man was in fact a priest and that the service he was conducting was in fact a Mass. No prosecutor ever succeeded in doing that again. The following year, he gave a jury a reminder: "[I]f you bring him in guilty, the punishment is very severe, a dreadful punishment indeed! Nothing less than a perpetual punishment! So that if you have the least doubt, you ought by no means to bring him in guilty," Edward Heward, *Lord Mansfield: A Biography of William Murray 1st Earl of Mansfield 1705–1793, Lord Chief Justice for 32 Years* (Barry Rose, 1979), 153 (the case was *Rex. v. Webb*). They did not.

3. John M. Beattie, *Crime and the Courts in England 1660–1800* (Princeton University Press, 1986), 341.

4. James Boswell, *Private Papers of James Boswell from Malahide Castle,* ed. Geoffrey Scott and Frederick H. Pottle (W. E. Rudge, 1928–1934), 7:109.

5. Bushell's Case, 124 Eng. Rep. 1006 (K.B. 1670).

6. One jury had twice voted to acquit a defendant on a charge of attempted rape. But the judge refused to accept either verdict and each time told them to reconsider. The third time they delivered the conviction the judge believed the evidence demanded, John H. Langbein, "The Criminal Trial Before the Lawyers," *University of Chicago Law Review* 35 (1978): 263, 291–293 (the Arrowsmith case).

7. Charles Cottu, *On the Administration of Criminal Justice in England* (R. Stevens, 1822), 99.

8. In the 1764 perjury trial of Philip Webb, Solicitor to the Treasury, Mansfield grew so impatient with the protracted length of discussion that he directed a court officer to tell the jurors to hurry up and decide. The jury found Webb not guilty after seventy minutes of deliberation, Oldham, *The Mansfield Manuscripts,* 1097.

9. Ephesians 6:5; 1 Corinthians 7:20–21; Philemon 16.

10. Letter from Granville Sharp to Mrs. Banks, February 22, 1771, in Prince Hoare, *Memoirs of Granville Sharp, Esq. Composed from His Own Manuscripts* (Henry Colburn, 1828), 1:87–88.

11. Communication from Ruth Paley to Steven Wise, December 12, 2003.

12. Unless otherwise noted, trial testimony is taken from the case of *Lewis, A Negro, v. Stapylton, His Master,* New York Historical Society, 1771.

13. Letter from Joseph Banks to Granville Sharp, New York Historical Society, February 16, 1772.

Chapter 10   The Struggle for the Body of James Somerset

1. 648 F. 2d 135, 171 (3rd Cir. 1981).

2. C. Hurd Rollin, *A Treatise on the Right of Personal Liberty and on the Writ of Habeas Corpus*, 2d ed. rev. (Da Capo Press, 1972), 222–223.

3. Ruth Paley, "After Somerset: Mansfield, Slavery and the Law in England 1772–1830," *Law, Crime, and English Society, 1660–1830*, ed. Norma Landau (Cambridge University Press, 2002), 165, 178–181.

4. Ibid., 165, 175.

5. The writ of habeas corpus usually didn't even apply to pressed men, N.A.M. Rodger, *The Wooden World: An Anatomy of the Georgian Navy* (Naval Institute Press 1986), 187.

6. William S. Church, *A Treatise on the Writ of Habeas Corpus Including Jurisdiction, False Imprisonment, Writ of Error, Extradition, Mandamus, Certiorari, Judgments, Etc.*, 2d ed., rev. and enlarg. (Bancroft-Whitney Co. 1893), 228–231, 249; Hurd Rollin, *A Treatise*, 86.

7. F. O. Shyllon, *Black Slaves in Britain* (Oxford University Press, 1974), 77.

8. Ruth Paley, *New Dictionary of National Biography* (Oxford University Press, forthcoming 2004).

9. Shyllon, *Black Slaves in Britain*, 86.

10. Ibid.

11. David Lemmings, *Professors of the Law: Barristers and English Legal Culture in the Eighteenth Century* (Oxford University Press, 2000), 28.

12. Humphrey W. Woolrych, *Lives of Eminent Serjeants-at-Law of the English Law* (Allen, 1869), 630.

13. Edmund Heward, *Lord Mansfield* (Barry Rose Publishers, Ltd., 1979), 62.

14. Woolrych, *Lives*, 626.

15. Ibid., 614.

16. Shyllon, *Black Slaves in Britain*, 128.

17. Woolrych, *Lives*, 617n.

18. Charles Sumner, *His Complete Works* (Lee and Sheppard, 1900), 3:502–504 (emphasis in the original).

19. Shyllon, *Black Slaves in Britain* (Oxford University Press 1974), 136, quoting James Stephen, *Essays in Ecclesiastical Biography* (Longman, Brown, Green, and Longmans, 1849), 540.

20. Jonathan Swift, *Gulliver's Travels* (Harmondsworth, 1994), 273.

21. Lemmings, *Professors of the Law*, 76.

22. Shyllon, *Black Slaves in Britain*, 130.

23. See Lemmings, *Professors of the Law*, 347.

24. Adam Smith, *An Inquiry into the Causes of the Wealth of Nations*, ed. E. Cannan (1904) (1776), 2:118.

25. Lemmings, *Professors of the Law*, 275–279 (8,535 pounds in 1771).

26. Shyllon, *Black Slaves in Britain*, 131.

27. Granville Sharp, *Memorandum Concerning the Case of James Somerset,* New York Historical Society.

28. Shyllon, *Black Slaves in Britain,* 114.

29. Ibid. See PRO KB/21/40, "Friday next after the octave of St. Hilary, 12th George III," and "Saturday after the morrow of Holy Trinity 12th George III." I thank Ruth Paley for obtaining this information at the Public Record Office. See Attorney of the Court, *Attorney's Compleat Guide to the Court of King's Bench, Containing the Whole Modern Practice of the Court* (printed by W. Strahan and M. Woodfall for P. Uriel, M. Folingsby, J. Williams, and G. Robinson, 1773), 234–244.

30. In *Rex v. Clarke,* Mansfield initially issued a habeas corpus writ ordering Mr. Clarke, who ran a private mad-house, to produce Mrs. Ann Hunt, an inmate, *Rex. c. Clark,* 3 Burr. 1362, 97 Eng. Rep. 875 (K.B. 1762). In *Rex v. DeLaval,* Sir Francis was directed to produce the body of a young female apprentice, *Rex v. DeLaval,* 3 Burr. 1434, 97 Eng. Rep. 913 (K.B. 1763). That case referred to "Francis Howland's Case" *(Rex v. Mary Johnson),* in which Johnson was ordered to bring up Howland, who was a ten-year-old girl, Francis Howland's Case *(Rex v. Mary Johnson),* 2 Ld. Raym. 1333, 92 Eng. Rep. 370 (K.B. n.d.). In *The King v. Reynolds,* a naval commander, Captain Reynolds, was ordered to produce John West, a pressed apprentice, *The King v. Reynolds,* 6 T.R. 496, 101 Eng. Rep. 667 (K.B. 1795). Perhaps this is why the modern historian J. H. Baker refers to Somerset's case as *R. v. Knowles, ex parte Sommersett.* J. H. Baker, *An Introduction to English Legal History,* 2d ed. (Butterworths, 1979), 127 n. 34.

31. Dorothy M. George, *London Life in the Eighteenth Century* (Academy Chicago, 1984)(1925), 166–170.

32. Correspondence from Ruth Paley to Steven M. Wise, January 15, 2004.

33. Shyllon, *Black Slaves in Britain,* 125.

34. Prince Hoare, *Memoirs of Granville Sharp, Esq. Composed from His Own Manuscripts* (Henry Colburn, 1828), 1:106.

35. Letter from Granville Sharp to Anthony Benezet, August 21, 1772, reprinted in Roger Bruns, *Am I Not a Man and a Brother?: The Antislavery Crusade of Revolutionary America 1688–1788* (Chelsea House Publishers, 1977), 197.

36. Shyllon, Black Slaves in Britain, 82, 83–84.

37. Ibid., 106–107.

38. See ibid., 82.

39. Letter from Francis Hargrave to Granville Sharp, January 25, 1772, in "Copies of Letters & Papers Entirely in the Hand Writing of the Celebrated Granville Sharp Relating to the Slave Trade," New York Historical Society.

40. Shyllon, *Black Slaves in Britain,* 85; Archer Polson, *Law and Lawyers, or, Sketches and Illustrations of Legal History and Biography* (Longman, Orme, Brown, Green, and Longmans, 1840), 2:109–111; *A Catalogue of Manuscripts Formerly in the Possession of Francis Hargrave, Esq.* (W. Clarke and Sons and Joseph Butterworth and Son, 1818).

41. Opinion of Mr. Attorney General De Grey, "Copies of Letters & Papers," New York Historical Society.

42. Letter from Granville Sharp to Francis Hargrave, January 26, 1772, in Hoare, *Memoirs of Granville Sharp, Esq.,* 1:108–111.

43. Letter from Francis Hargrave to Granville Sharp, January 31, 1772, in "Copies of Letters & Papers," New York Historical Society.

44. *Dred Scott v. Sandford,* 60 U.S. 393, 535 (MacLean, J., dissenting).

45. Hoare, *Memoirs of Granville Sharp, Esq.,* 1:121–122.

46. Ibid., 122; Letter from Granville Sharp to Anthony Benezet, August 21, 1772, reprinted in Bruns, *Am I Not a Man and a Brother?,* 197.

47. Gretchen Holbrook Gerzina, *Black London: Life Before Emancipation* (Rutgers University Press, 1995), 104–105.

48. Letter from Granville Sharp to Francis Hargrave, February 6, 1772, in Hoare, *Memoirs of Granville Sharp, Esq.,* 1:108–111.

Chapter 11   Lord Mansfield Is Deceived

1. *The Biographical Dictionary of the Common Law* gives Ashurst's role in the *Somerset* case as one of the half-dozen reasons he appears. Neither Aston nor Willes appears. Ashurst admired Mansfield greatly and, in 1798, dissented when Lord Kenyon, Mansfield's pompous successor, overruled his predecessor on an issue decided "when that noble lord presided in the court whose abilities all the world confessed." *Jordaine v. Lashbrooke,* 7 T.R. 601, 101 Eng. Rep. 1154 (K.B. 1798).

2. Edward Foss, *The Judges of England* (Longman, Brown, Green and Longmans, 1848–1864), 8:403.

3. Cecil Herbert Stuart Fifoot, *Lord Mansfield* (Oxford University Press, 1936), 49; J. C. Jeaffreson, *A Book About Lawyers* (Hurst and Blackett 1867), 2:233, 234.

4. William Holdsworth, *History of English Law* (Metheun & Co., 1938; Sweet and Maxwell, 1956), 12:486.

5. F. O. Shyllon, *Black Slaves in Britain* (Oxford University Press 1974), 90–91, quoting the *London Evening Post,* February 8, 1772.

6. All references to Henry Marchant's diary are taken from Henry Marchant, *Journall of Voyage from Newport in the Colony of Rhode Island to London,* February 7, 1772 (microfilm, Rhode Island Historical Society).

7. Shyllon, *Black Slaves in Britain,* 83.

8. Thomas T. Morris, *Southern Slavery and the Law 1619–1860* (University of North Carolina Press, 1996), 66–71; Adele Hast, "The Legal Status of the Negro in Virginia, 1705–1765," *Journal of Negro History* (July 1969) 54:217.

9. George Sheldon, *A History of Deerfield, Massachusetts* (Deerfield, 1895), 1:905 ("As slavery came into [Massachusetts] and was accepted under the English common law without legislation, so it was abolished by force of public opinion without statute law.")

10. Bernard Bailyn, *The Ordeal of Thomas Hutchinson* (Harvard University Press, 1974), 378 n. 5.

11. The questions and answers may be found in the Collections of the Massachusetts Historical Society for the Year M, DCC, XCV (Samuel Hall, 1795).

12. For report of the *Slew* case, see George H. Moore, *Notes on the History of Slavery in Massachusetts* (Greenwood Publishing Group, 1966)(1866), 113–114.

13. L. Kinvin Wroth and Hiller B. Zobel, *Legal Papers of John Adams* (Harvard University Press, 1965), 2:54.

14. Ibid., 58–59.

15. Robert M. Spector, "The Quock Walker Cases (1782–1783): Slavery, Its Abolition, and Negro Citizenship in Early Massachusetts," *Journal of Negro History* (1968) 53:12, 24; *Caleb Dodge v. Z.* (Essex Inferior Ct. of Commons 1774), in G. W. Williams, *History of the Negro Race in America from 1619 to 1880* (Arno Press and the New York Times, 1968), 231.

16. *An Argument in the Case of James Somerset, a Negro* (E. Russell, 1774).

17. John Adams to Dr. Jeremy Belknap, March 21, 1795, *Massachusetts Historical Society Collection*, 3:401 (5th series).

18. Ibid.

19. Wroth and Zobel, *Legal Papers*, 2:48, 50.

20. Ibid., 56, 57, and n13; Baron de Montesquieu, *The Spirit of the Laws*, trans. Thomas Nugent (Hafner Press, 1949), 238.

21. Wroth and Zobel, *Legal Papers*, 2:51, 61–62.

22. Emory Washburn, "Somerset's Case, and the Extinction of Villeinage and Slavery in England," *Proceedings of the Massachusetts Historical Society for 1863–1864* (February 1864):307, 324.

Chapter 12   Upon What Principle Is It That a Man Can Become a Dog for Another Man?

1. *Harvard College v. Canada (Commissioner of Patents)*, 4S.C. 445, 2002 SCC (Supreme Court of Canada, 2002), 76, para #54, *Somerset* citation omitted.

2. Serjeant Davy's argument can be found in a manuscript in the records of the New York Historical Society that reports the first day's proceedings in the *Somerset* case.

3. Theodore F. T. Plucknett, *A Concise History of the Common Law* (Little, Brown and Co. 1956), 267.

4. Henry Marchant, *Journal of Voyage from Newport in the Colony of Rhode Island to London*, February 7, 1772 (microfilm, Rhode Island Historical Society).

5. John Nicholls, *Recollections and Reflections Personal and Political as Connected with Public Affairs During the Reign of George III* (James Ridgway, 1820), 1:342.

6. David Lemmings, *Professors of the Law: Barristers and English Legal Culture in the Eighteenth Century* (Oxford University Press, 2000), 216–217; F. O. Shyllon, *Black Slaves in Britain* (Oxford University Press, 1974), 88.

7. James C. Oldham, *The Mansfield Manuscripts and the Growth of English Law in the Eighteenth Century* (University of North Carolina Press, 1992), 2:1093.

8. *Leach v. Money*, 19 Howells State Trials 1002 (1765); Humphrey W. Woolrych, *Lives of Eminent Serjeants-at-Law of the English Law* (Allen, 1869), 580–581.

9. Shyllon, *Black Slaves in Britain*, 88.

10. Oldham, *The Mansfield Manuscripts,* 803 n. 100.

11. Ibid., 790.

12. Emphasis added.

Chapter 13 Flourishing Away on the Side of Liberty

1. F. O. Shyllon, *Black Slaves in Britain* (Oxford University Press, 1974), 134–135, quoting the *Gazetter* for February 14, 17, and 20, 1772.

2. "Forestalling" was "the buying or bargaining for any corn, cattle, or other merchandize, by the way as they come to the market to be sold before they are brought, to the intent to sell the same again at an advanced price, or buying and selling again in the same market"; "engrossing" was "the getting into one's possession, or buying up, large quantities of corn, or other dead victuals, with an intent to sell them again," James C. Oldham, *The Mansfield Manuscripts and the Growth of English Law in the Eighteenth Century* (University of North Carolina Press, 1992), 2:932.

3. Shyllon, *Black Slaves in Britain,* 94, quoting the *Gazetter* and *New Daily Advertiser* (May 13, 1772).

4. Ibid., 93–95; Prince Hoare, *Memoirs of Granville Sharp, Esq. Composed from His Own Manuscripts* (Henry Colburn, 1828), 1:125–126 .

5. John Baker, *The Diary of John Baker,* ed. Philip C. Yorke (Hutchinson & Co., Ltd., 1931), 233–234.

6. Shyllon, *Black Slaves in Britain,* 93–95; Hoare, *Memoirs of Granville Sharp, Esq.,* 1:135.

7. Ibid.

8. Ibid., 134.

9. Samuel A. M. Estwick, *Considerations of the Negroe Cause Commonly So Called, Addressed to the Right Honourable Lord Mansfield, Lord Chief Justice of the Court Of King's Bench,* 2d ed. (J. Dodsley, 1773), 22n.

10. *The Case of* James Sommersett, *a Negro, on a Habeas Corpus, King's Bench, 1771 and 1772,* in Francis Hargrave, *Collection of the State Trials* (1776), 11:340, Appendix no. 7.

11. *Somerset v. Stewart,* 1 Lofft 499 (K.B. 1772).

12. *Howells State Trials* (1772), 20:1, 24–25.

13. Shyllon, *Black Slaves in Britain,* 135; Hoare, *Memoirs of Granville Sharp, Esq.,* 1:125–126.

14. Ibid., 134–135, quoting the *Morning Chronicle,* May 15, 1772.

15. Letter from Charles Stewart to James Murray, June 15, 1772, *Proceedings of the Massachusetts Historical Society* (October 1909–June 1910) 43:451.

Chapter 14 The Death of the Joint Opinion

1. William Holdsworth, *History of English Law* (Metheun & Co., 1938; Sweet and Maxwell, 1956), 12:560.

2. F. O. Shyllon, *Black Slaves in Britain* (Oxford University Press 1974), 108.

3. Emory Washburn, "Somerset's Case, and the Extinction of Villeinage and Slavery in England," *Proceedings of the Massachusetts Historical Society* (February 1864):307, 324.

4. Archer Polson, *Law and Lawyers, or, Sketches and Illustrations of Legal History and Biography* (Longman, Orme, Brown, Green, and Longmans, 1840), 1:188.

5. Capel Lofft's account of Wallace's argument seems too abbreviated in light of other versions. But his argument is taken from Lofft's account unless otherwise noted.

6. Shyllon, *Black Slaves in Britain*, 101.

7. *Scot's Magazine* (1772) 34:297.

8. *Gazetter* (May 15, 1772).

9. *Pearne v. Lisle*, 27 Eng. Rep. 47 (Ch. 1749).

10. Philip C. Yorke, *The Life and Correspondence of Philip Yorke, Earl of Hardwicke, Lord High Chancellor of Great Britain* (Harvard University Press, 1913), 2:513.

11. Ibid., 530.

12. Letter from Alleyne to Sharp, May 18, 1772, New York Historical Society.

13. See Joseph Story, *Commentaries on the Conflicts of Laws*, ed. Melvin M. Bigelow, 8th ed. (Hilliard, Grey and Co., 1883)(1834), 104–105, sec. 13.

14. *State v. Bell*, 66 Tenn. 9, 11 (1872).

15. David Brion Davis, *The Problem of Slavery in the Age of Revolution 1770–1823* (Cornell University Press, 1975), 471.

16. *State v. Mann* 13 N.C. 168, 170–171 (1829).

17. Prince Hoare, *Memoirs of Granville Sharp, Esq. Composed from His Own Manuscripts* (Henry Colburn, 1828), 1:131.

18. Ibid., 132.

19. Shyllon, *Black Slaves in Britain*, 143, quoting the *Gazetter*, May 18, 1772.

20. Letter from Charles Stewart to James Murray, June 15, 1772, *Proceedings of the Massachusetts Historical Society* (October 1909–June 1910) 43:451.

21. *Parliamentary History* 29 (1792), Column 1349.

22. Jean Barbot, *Barbot on Guineau: The Writings of Jean Barbot on West Africa, 1678–1712*, ed. P.E.H. Hair, Adam Jones, and Robin Law (Hakluyt Society, 1992), 2:550.

23. Howard Jones, *Mutiny on the Amistad*, rev. ed. (Oxford University Press, 1987), 24.

24. Frederick Douglass, *Narrative of the Life of Frederick Douglass, an American Slave, Written by Himself* (New American Library, 1968)(1845), 57.

Chapter 15   All We Can Do Is Declare the Law

1. James C. Oldham, *The Mansfield Manuscripts and the Growth of English Law in the Eighteenth Century* (University of North Carolina Press, 1992), 1:80. This exchange is not found in the transcript of the hearing found at the New-York Historical Society.

2. The *Gazetter*.

3. The *Gazetter.*

4. The *Gazetter.*

5. Lofft.

6. The *Gazetter.*

7. Lofft.

8. The *Gazetter.*

9. Lofft.

10. Ibid.

11. The reversal had come on the highly technical point that, in an outlawry prosecution, the name of the county was required and this had been omitted. However, Mansfield's first biographer, who knew the Chief Justice, reported that he told friends, "I am decidedly against the prosecution. His [Wilkes's] consequence will die away if you will let him alone; but by public notice of him you will increase his consequence; the very thing he covets, and has in full view," John Holliday, *The Life of William Late Earl of Mansfield* (P. Elmsly, 1797), 184. Mansfield sentenced Wilkes to prison for ten months and twelve months on the two counts of seditious libel.

12. The *Gazetter.*

13. David Brion Davis, *The Problem of Slavery in the Age of Revolution 1770–1823* (Cornell University Press, 1975), 482 n. 21. Davis gives no citation for this claim and cannot now recall its source, communication from David Brion Davis to Steven M. Wise, February 13, 2004. I have been unable independently to verify it.

14. Thomas R. R. Cobb, *An Inquiry into the Law of Negro Slavery in the United States of America* (Negro Universities Press, 1968)(1858), 278–282.

15. Mark Weiner, "New Biographical Evidence on Somerset's Case," *Slavery and Abolition* 23, no. 1 (April 2002):121.

16. Oldham, *The Mansfield Manuscripts,* 2:1162 and n. 2.

17. Samuel A. M. Estwick, *Considerations of the Negroe Cause Commonly So Called, Addressed to the Right Honourable Lord Mansfield, Lord Chief Justice of the Court of King's Bench,* 2d ed. (J. Dodsley, 1773), v.

18. Ibid.

19. *Gentleman's Magazine,* pt. 1, 334 (1789), in F. O. Shyllon, *Black Slaves in Britain* (Oxford University Press, 1974), 14 n. 2 (emphasis in the original).

20. Estwick, *Considerations of the Negroe Cause,* 4–15, 27–32, 34–40.

21. Ibid., 45.

Chapter 16   The Mansfield Judgment

1. Letter from Charles Stuart to James Murray, June 15, 1772, *Proceedings of the Massachusetts Historical Society* 43 (October 1909–June 1910): 450, 451.

2. Ibid., 451.

3. F. O. Shyllon, *Black Slaves in Britain* (Oxford University Press, 1974), 50.

4. Charles Dickens, *Barnaby Rudge* (Macmillan & Co., 1955)(1841), 483.

5. James C. Oldham, "New light on Mansfield and Slavery," 27 *Journal of British Studies* 27 (1988):45, 55.

6. Capel Lofft, *Reporter of Cases Adjudged in the Court of Kings Bench from Easter Term 12 George 3 to Michaelmas 14 George 3* (both inclusive) (1776), xvi. See William M. Wiecek, "Somerset: Lord Mansfield and the Legitimacy of Slavery in the Anglo-American World," *University of Chicago Law Review* 42 (1974), 86, 144.

7. William R. Cotter, "The Somerset Case and the Abolition of Slavery in England," *History* 79 (1994):31, 56, quoting a letter from Granville Sharp to Dr. Findlay, August 14, 1772.

8. J. J. Hecht, *Continental and Colonial Servants in 18th Century England* (Smith College, 1954), 41.

9. Letter from the Archivist of Scone Palace to Steven M. Wise, Esq., April 28, 2003.

10. Jerome Nadelhoft, "The Somersett Case and Slavery: Myth, Reality, and Reprecussions," *Journal of Negro History* 51 (1966):193, 201; James Walvin, *Black and White: The Negro and English Society 1555–1945* (Allen Lane, Penguin Press, 1973), 127.

11. *The Case of* James Sommersett, *a Negro, on a* Habeas Corpus, King's Bench, 1771 and 1772, in Francis Hargrave, *Collection of the State Trials* (1776), 11:339, Appendix no.7.

Chapter 17   Versions of the Mansfield Judgment

1. *Who's Who in History: England 1714–1789,* vol. 4 (Basil Blackwell, 1964).

2. *Scots Magazine* (June 1772) 34:297. See F. O. Shyllon, *Black Slaves in Britain* (Oxford University Press, 1974), 108–110 and 110 n. 1.

3. Granville Sharp, *The Just Limitation of Slavery, in the Laws of God, Compared with the Unbounded Claims of the African Traders and British American Slaveholders* (1776), Appendix 8.

4. James Oldham, "New Light on Mansfield and Slavery," *Journal of British Studies* 27 (1988):45, 58–60. See J. H. Baker, *English Legal Manuscripts* (Zug, 1975), 2:281.

5. Oldham, "New Light," 45, 58.

6. Ibid., 45, 56–58.

7. *Gentleman's Magazine* (June 1772) 42:293–294. See Oldham, "New Light," 45, 55.

8. Ibid., 45, 55–60.

9. Lord Campbell, *The Lives of the Chief Justices of England* (John Murray, 1858), 3:317–318.

10. James C. Oldham, *The Mansfield Manuscripts and the Growth of English Law in the Eighteenth Century* (University of North Carolina Press, 1992), 1:5; William Holdsworth, *History of English Law* (Metheun & Co., 1938; Sweet and Maxwell, 1956), 12:464.

11. Shyllon, *Black Slaves in Britain,* 166.

12. William M. Wiecek, "*Somerset:* Lord Mansfield and the Legitimacy of Slavery in the Anglo-American World," *University of Chicago Law Review* (1974) 42:86, 145.

13. T.R.R. Cobb, *An Inquiry into the Law of Negro Slavery in the United States of America* (Negro Universities Press, 1868)(1858).

14. Ibid., 169 n. 1.

15. *Scott v. Emerson,* 16 Mo. 387, 394 (1852).

16. William Snyder, *A Collection of Important Judicial Opinions by Eminent Judges* (Baker, Voorhis & Co., 1883), 112.

17. Bernard Shientag, "Lord Mansfield Revisited: A Modern Assessment," *Fordham Law Review* (1941) 10:345, 259.

18. *City Press,* July 20, 1972, 9.

19. *The New Encyclopedia Britannica,* 15th ed. (1998), 10:704.

20. Shyllon, *Black Slaves in Britain,* 110; James Walvin, *Black and White: The Negro and English Society 1555–1945* (Allen Lane/Penguin Press, 1973), 124.

21. Shyllon, *Black Slaves in Britain,* 165.

22. Oldham, *The Mansfield Manuscripts,* 1:7; Shyllon, *Black Slaves in Britain,* 166.

23. *Blackstone's Commentaries on the Laws of England,* 18th ed. (Collins and Hanway, 1832), 1:334 n. 3.

Chapter 18   Ripples of Liberty

1. 3 B. & C. 448, 470, 107 Eng. Rep. 450, 458–459 (K.B. 1824)(Best, J.).

2. Thomas Thompson, *The African Trade for Negro Slaves Consistent with Humanity and Revealed Religion* (Simmons & Kirkby, 1772), 9.

3. Edward Long (A planter), *Candid Reflections Upon the Judgment Lately Awarded by the Court of King's Bench in Westminster Hall on What Is Commonly Called the Negroe Cause* (T. Lowndes, 1772).

4. Ibid., iii.

5. Ibid., 2, 74.

6. Ibid., 48–49.

7. Letter from Francis Hargrave to Granville Sharp, January 12, 1773, New York Historical Society.

8. Ibid.,

9. Samuel A. M. Estwick, *Considerations of the Negroe Cause Commonly So Called, Addressed to the Right Honourable Lord Mansfield, Lord Chief Justice of the Court of King's Bench,* 2d ed. (J. Dodsley, 1773), vi, vii, 20–22, note a, and 45–46.

10. Ibid., 71, 74.

11. Ibid., 74–82.

12. Ibid., 74. See Winthrop D. Jordan, *White Over Black: American Attitudes Toward the Negro* (Penguin Books, 1971)(1968), 216–263, 482–511; Arthur O. Lovejoy, *The Great Chain of Being: A Study of the History of an Idea* (Harper & Row, 1960).

13. A copy of the two-page decision in the case may be found in the records of the New York Historical Society.

14. Ruth Paley, "After Somerset: Mansfield, Slavery and the Law in England 1772–1830," in *Law, Crime, and English Society,* ed. Norma Landau (Cambridge University Press, 2002), 165, 180.

15. The facts of, and arguments in, Joseph Knight, *A Negro v. John Wedderburn* are taken from *Howell's State Trials*, 20:1–21; F. O. Shyllon, *Black Slaves in Britain* (Oxford University Press, 1974), 177–183; James Boswell, *Life of Samuel Johnson*, ed. Ernest Rhys, 2d ed. (Clarendon Press, 1950)(1791), 86, 88, 95, 101, 127, 129, 200, 202–203, 212–214.

16. Lord Kenyon's Court of King's Bench refused to investigate their validity in the cases of John Hamlet and the Truro harbor sailors.

17. Ruth Paley speculates it may have been because "as transients, they fell outside the provisions of the 1679 (Habeas Corpus) act," Ruth Paley, "After Somerset," 165, 180.

18. 3 Bos. & Pul. 69, 127 Eng. Rep. 39 (C.P. 1802). See William R. Cotter, "The Somerset Case and the Abolition of Slavery in England," History 79 (1994):31, 54.

19. Cotter, "The Somerset Case," 31, 55; Ruth Paley says there were six blacks, Ruth Paley, "After Somerset," 165, 180; although William R. Cotter says there were nine, Cotter, "The Somerset Case," 47–48.

20. William Wetmore, *Life and Letters of Joseph Story*, ed. W. W. Story (Little, Brown, 1851), 1:552 (letter from Lord Stowell to Josep Story, January 9, 1828).

21. 2 Hagg. 94, 118, 130, 166 Eng. Rep. 179,187, 191 (Adm. 1827) (Lord Stowall).

22. Patricia Bradley, "Slavery in Colonial Newspapers: The Somerset Case," *Journalism History* 12 (1985):2, 5, quoting *New-York Journal*, August 27, 1772.

23. An argument in the *Case of James Sommersett a Negro Determined by the Court of King's Bench; Wherein It Is Attempted to Demonstrate the Present Unlawfulness of Domestic Slavery in England* . . . (E. Russell, 1774); Jeremy Belknap, Massachusetts Historical Society, Collections (1st ser) (1795–1835), 4:201.

24. Shyllon, *Black Slaves in Britain*, 110, quoting the *London Packet* (June 26–29, 1772).

25. Philip D. Morgan, *Slave-Counterpoint: Black Culture in the Eighteenth-Century Chesapeake and Lowcountry* (University of North Carolina Press, 1998), 461.

26. *Williamsburg Virginia Gazette* (June 30, 1774), quoted in Ira Berlin, *Slaves Without Masters: The Free Negro in the Antebellum South* (The New Press, 1974), 11–12.

27. David Waldstreicher, *The Struggle Against Slavery: A History in Documents* (Oxford University Press, 2001), 41–43.

28. Lawrence M. Friedman, *A History of American Law* (Simon and Schuster, 1973), 94–98; *Commonwealth v. Aves*, 36 Mass. 193, 209 (1836); *Dred Scott v. Sandford*, 60, U.S. 343, 529, 535 (1856) (MacLean, J., dissenting).

29. *Dred Scott v. Sandford*, 534.

30. Thomas T. Morris, *Southern Slavery and the Law 1619–1860* (University of North Carolina Press, 1996), 61–80; George Stroud, *A Sketch of the Laws Relating to Slavery in the Several States of the United States of America* (Negro Universities Press, 1968), 11 (1827).

31. *Jarman v. Patterson*, 23 Ky. 644. (1822).

32. *Mahoney v. Ashton*, 4 H. and McH. 295, 299 (Md. 1799).

33. *Denison v. Tucker, Transactions of the Supreme Court of Michigan 1805–1814*, ed. William Blume (Univeristy of Michigan Press, 1835), 1:385 (treaty applies); *Pattison v.*

Whittaker, Transactions of the Supreme Court of Michigan 1805–1814, 1:414 (treaty didn't apply).

34. Cotter, "The Somerset Case," 31, 32. See Jonathan Elliot, *Debates on the Federal Constitution*, 2d ed. (J. B. Lippincott 1836), 1:453 ("At present, if any slave elopes to any of those states where slaves are free, he becomes emancipated by their laws").

35. Article 4, sec. 2(1) of the Constitution of the Confederate States of America.

36. See the concurring opinions of Justices Nelson, Grier, Daniel, and Campbell, and the dissents of Justices Maclean and Curtis.

37. See the excellent discussion in Don E. Fehrenbacher, *The Dred Scott Case: Its Significance in American Law and Politics* (Oxford University Press, 1978), 50–61.

38. *Commonwealth v. Aves*, 35 Mass. 193 (1836); Leonard Levy, *The Law of the Commonwealth and Chief Justice Shaw* (Harper Torchbooks, 1967), 64 n. 18.

39. *Jackson v. Bulloch*, 12 Conn. 38 (1837).

40. *Lemmon v. The People*, 20 NY 562 (1860). See ibid. at 643 (J. Clerke, dissenting).

41. *Scott v. Emerson*, 15 Mo. 576, 582 (1852).

42. William Wiecek, "Somerset: Lord Mansfield and the Legitimacy of Slavery in the Anglo-American World," *University of Chicago Law Review* 42 (1974) 86, 133.

Chapter 19   Second Thoughts?

1. "Lord Mansfield Revisited: A Modern Assessment," *Fordham Law Review* 10:387–388 (1941):345, 387–388.

2. Unless otherwise noted, I take the facts of the *Zong* case from F. O. Shyllon, *Black Slaves in Britain* (Oxford University Press, 1974), 184–199; Prince Hoare, *Memoirs of Granville Sharp, Esq. Composed from His Own Manuscripts* (Henry Colburn, 1828), 1:352–367; and *Gregson v. Gilbert*, 3 Doug. 233, 99 Eng. Rep. 629 (K.B. 1783).

3. Hoare, *Memoirs of Granville Sharp, Esq.*, 1:359.

4. Letter from Granville Sharp to William Dillyn (a few days before May 28, 1783), in Roger Bruns, *Am I Not a Man and a Brother?: The Antislavery Crusade of Revolutionary America 1688–1788* (Chelsea House Publishers, 1977), 486.

5. James Walvin, *Black and White: The Negro and English Society 1555–1945* (Allen Lane, Penguin Press, 1973), 144; Prince Hoare, *Memoirs of Granville Sharp, Esq.*, 2:4.

6. Ruth Paley, "After Somerset: Mansfield, Slavery and the Law in England 1772–1830," *Law, Crime, and English Society, 1660–1830*, ed. Norma Landau (Cambridge University Press, 2002), 165, 183.

7. James C. Oldham, *The Mansfield Manuscripts and the Growth of English Law in the Eighteenth Century* (University of North Carolina Press, 1992), 2:1237–1238.

8. *Jones v. Schmoll*, 1 T.R. 130n, 99 Eng. Rep. 1012n (K.B. 1785). See Oldham, *The Mansfield Manuscripts*, 2:1237; Shyllon, *Black Slaves in Britain*, 203–204.

9. Oldham, *The Mansfield Manuscripts*, 2:1243.

10. Unless otherwise noted, I take the facts of the two princes of Calabar case from Randy J. Sparks, *The Two Princes of Calabar: An Eighteenth-Century Atlantic Odyssey* (Harvard University Press, 2004); Paley, "After Somerset," 165. *The Diaries and Letters*

of His Excellency Thomas Hutchinson, Esq., ed. Peter Orlando Hutchinson (Houghton, Mifflin, & Co., 1886), 274–277 (entry for August 29, 1779).

11. Letter from Ephraim Robin John to Charles Wesley, August 17, 1774, in Sparks, *The Two Princes of Calabar*, 94.

12. Sparks, *The Two Princes of Calabar*, 99. The owner of the ship was Henry Lippincott and the habeas corpus case was named *King v. Lippincott*.

13. Walvin, *Black and White*, 128, quoting *A Letter to Philo-Africanus* (1788), 39.

14. *Rex v. Inhabitants of Thomas Ditton*, 4 Doug, 300, 99 Eng. Rep. 891 (K.B. 1785).

15. *Decisions of the Court of King's Bench, Upon the Laws Relating to the Poor*, ed. Edmund Bott, 3rd ed. (Whieldon and Butterworth, 1793).

16. Dorothy M. George, *London Life in the Eighteenth Century* (Academy Chicago, 1984)(1925), 116, 130, 131, 214, 215, 221–224, 237, 309–310, 352 n. 44.

17. "The Sixth Joint Debate at Quincy, October 13, 1858," in *The Lincoln-Douglas Debates*, ed. Harold Holzer (HarperCollins 1993), 285.

18. David Zarefsky, *Lincoln, Douglas and Slavery: In the Crucible of Public Debate* (University of Chicago Press, 1990), 134–35, 60–61, 193–194; Garry Wills, *Lincoln at Gettysburg: The Words That Remade America* (Simon & Schuster 1992), 97.

19. Letter from Granville Sharp to Anthony Benezet, August 21, 1772, in Roger Bruns, *Am I Not a Man and a Brother?: The Antislavery Crusade of Revolutionary America 1688–1788* (Chelsea House Publishers, 1977), 196, 197.

20. *Journal of the House of Commons* 33 (November 13, 1770–November 17, 1772):789.

21. Letter from Granville Sharp to Dr. Fothergill, October 27, 1772, in Hoare, *Memoirs of Granville Sharp, Esq.*, 1:157.

22. Samuel A. M. Estwick, *Considerations of the Negroe Cause Commonly So Called, Addressed to the Right Honourable Lord Mansfield, Lord Chief Justice of the Court of King's Bench*, 2d ed. (J. Dodsley, 1773), 71–79; Edward Long, *The History of Jamaica: Or, General Survey of the Antient and Modern State of that Island* (T. Lowndes 1773), 2:475–484.

23. "Minutes from the Abolition Convention," quoted in Winthrop D. Jordan, *White Over Black: American Attitudes Toward the Negro 1550–1812* (Penguin Books, 1971)(1968), 505.

24. Thomas Jefferson, *Notes on the State of Virginia*, ed. William Peden (University of North Carolina Press, 1955), 53–54.

25. Charles White, *An Account of the Regular Gradation in Man, and in Different Animals and Vegetables: And from the Former to the Latter* (C. Dilly, 1799); Josiah C. Nott, *Two Lectures on the Natural History of the Caucasian and Negro Races* (Dale & Thompson, 1844); Louis Agassiz, "The Diversity of Origin of the Human Races," *Christian Examiner* 49 (1850):110; Samuel G. Morton, "Observations on the Size of the Brain in Various Races and Families of Man," *Proceedings of the Academy of Natural Sciences Philadelphia* 4 (1849):221; William Stanton, *The Leopard's Spots: Scientific Attitudes Towards Race in America 1815–1859* (University of Chicago Press, 1960), 144

(*New York Tribune* quote); Estwick, *Considerations of the Negroe Cause,* 77–78, note p. Hume revised his essays continuously, and I have been unable to locate this phrase exactly as Estwick quoted it.

26. Owen O. Lovejoy, *The Great Chain of Being: A Study of the History of an Idea* (Harper & Row 1960), viii (1936) (emphasis in the original).

27. Agnes Marie Sibley, *Alexander Pope's Prestige in America* (King's Crown Press, 1949), 23. See Edward Heward, *Lord Mansfield: A Biography of William Murray 1st Earl of Mansfield 1705–1793, Lord Chief Justice for 32 Years* (Barry Rose, 1979), 13–16, 25–28.

28. Alexander Pope, Essay on Man, Epistle 1 (N. Möeller and Son, 1798) (1733–1734), 20, lines 246–249.

29. Ruth Marcus, "Powell Regrets Backing Sodomy Law," *Washington Post,* October 26, 1990. The case was *Bowers v. Hardwick,* 478 U.S. 186 (1986) overruled, *Lawrence v. Texas,* 123, S. CT. 2472 (2003).

30. Leo Pfeffer, *This Honorable Court: A History of the United States Supreme Court* (Octagon, 1978) (1965). Compare Roberts's vote in *West Coast Hotel v. Parrish,* 300 U.S. 379 (1937) with his vote in *Morehead v. New York ex rel. Tipaldo,* 298 U.S. 587 (1936). President Roosevelt had been threatening to seek to expand the number of Supreme Court justices in order to give him enough appointments to ensure his New Deal legislation would withstand constitutional challenge.

31. James M. McPherson, *Battle Cry of Freedom: The Civil War Era* (Oxford University Press, 1988), 294–295.

32. Michael Klarman, *From Jim Crow to Civil Rights* (Oxford University Press, 2004) 294–295, 300, 302–303, 309–310; Richard Kluger, *Simple Justice: The History of Brown v. Board of Education and Black America's Struggle for Equality* (Alfred A. Knopf, 1976), 595, 596, 655, 680, 691, 692, 694, 698.

33. Oldham, *The Mansfield Manuscripts,* 1:1x.

Chapter 20   *The Beginning of the End of Human Slavery*

1. 672 N.Y.S. 2d 1007, 1009 (Supr. Ct. Suffolk Cty. 1998).

2. Sir James Stephens, *Essays in Ecclesiastical Biography* (Longman, Brown, Green, and Longmans, 1849), 540.

3. Ibid.

4. Prince Hoare, *Memoirs of Granville Sharp, Esq. Composed from His Own Manuscripts* (Henry Colburn, 1828), 2:245, 308; ibid., 1:370.

5. For the story of the Sierra Leone colony, see Gretchen Holbrook Gerzina, *Black London: Life Before Emancipation* (Rutgers University Press, 1995), 139–173; David Brion Davis, *The Problem of Slavery in the Age of Revolution* (Cornell University Press, 1975), 1770–1823 382–383 n. 50; James Walvin, *Black and White: The Negro and English Society 1555–1945* (Alan Lane, Penguin Press, 1973), 144–158; E.C.P. Lascelles, *Granville Sharp and the Freedom of Slaves in England* (Oxford University Press, 1928), 81–87.

6. Hoare, *Memoirs of Granville Sharp, Esq.*, 2:234, 235.

7. Ibid., 235.

8. Lascelles, *Granville Sharp*, 134.

9. Davis, *The Problem of Slavery*, 397, 401.

10. Hoare, *Memoirs of Granville Sharp, Esq.*, 2:328.

11. Ibid., 1:210, 341–354.

12. Ibid., 189 (letter from James Sharp to Granville Sharp, October 6, 1775).

13. William R. Cotter, "The Somerset Case and the Abolition of Slavery in England," *History* 79 (1994):31, 56, quoting Granville Sharp, *Just Limitation of Slavery and the Laws of God, Compared with the Unbounded Claims of the African Traders and British-American Slaveholders* (1776), Appendix 9.

14. Hoare, *Memoirs of Granville Sharp, Esq.*, 1:xxxviii, xxxix.

15. Henry Roscoe, *Lives of Eminent British Lawyers* (Fred B. Rotherman & Co., 1830), 292.

16. Ibid., 301.

17. Letter from J. Alleyne to Granville Sharp, January 13, 1773, New York Historical Society.

18. Letter from Francis Hargrave to Granville Sharp, January 12, 1773, New York Historical Society.

19. James C. Oldham, "New Light on Mansfield and Slavery," *Journal of British Studies* 28 (1988):65–66.

20. John T. Noonan, Jr., *Persons & Masks of the Law: Cardozo, Holmes, Jefferson, and Wythe as Makers of the Masks* (Farrar, Straus and Giroux, 1976), 10.

21. Slavery Convention, 60 LNTS 253, signed September 25, 1926, entered into force on March 9, 1927.

22. 82 UNTS 279 (August 8, 1945) (Nuremburg Charter); U.N. Documnet A/811 (December 10, 1948) (Universal Declaration of Human Rights, Article 4). See *Siderman de Blake v. Republic of Argentina*, 965 F. 2d 699, 715 (9th Cir. 1992), cert. den., 113 S. Ct. 1812 (1993) (the rights of human beings identified at Nuremberg are "universal and fundamental").

23. Supplementary Convention on the Abolition of Slavery, the Slave Trade, and Institutions and Practices Similar to Slavery, 360 UNTS 117, signed September 7, 1956, entered into force on April 30, 1957.

24. The European Convention on Human Rights, 87 UNTS 103, signed November 4, 1950, entered into force on September 3, 1953 (Articles 4(1) and 15(2)).

25. American Convention on Human Rights, signed November 22, 1969, entered into force on July 18, 1978 (Article 6 (1)).

26. African Charter on Human and Peoples' Rights, 1520 UNTS No 26, signed on June 27, 1981, entered into force on October 21, 1986 (Article 5).

BIBLIOGRAPHY

A Catalogue of Manuscripts Formerly in the Possession of Francis Hargrave, Esq. W. Clarke and Sons and Joseph Butterworth and Son, 1818.

Adams, Gene. "Dido Elizabeth Belle: A Black Girl at Kenwood." *Camden History Review* (1984).

Agassiz, Louis. "The Diversity of Origin of the Human Races." *Christian Examiner* 49 (1850):110.

Antieau, Chester James. *The Practice of Extraordinary Remedies: Habeas Corpus and the Other Common Law Writs.* Oceana Publications, 1987.

Ashford, Harold A., and Michael D. Risinger. "Presumptions, Assumptions, and Due Process in Criminal Cases: A Theoretical Overview." *Yale Law Journal* 79 (1969):165.

Attorney of the Court. *The Attorney's Compleat Guide to the Court of King's Bench, Containing the Whole Modern Practice of the Court.* Printed by W. Strahan and M. Woodfall, for P. Uriel, M. Folingsby, and J. Williams, and G. Robinson, 1773.

Bailyn, Bernard. *The Ordeal of Thomas Hutchinson.* Harvard University Press, 1974.

Baker, J. H. *An Introduction to English Legal History.* 4th ed. Butterworths Lexis/Nexis, 2002.

_____. *The Common Law Tradition.* Hambledon Press, 2000.

_____. *The Legal Profession and the Common Law: Historical Essays.* Hambledon Press, 1986.

_____. *An Introduction to English Legal History.* 2d ed. Butterworths, 1979.

_____. *A History of English Judges' Robes* (reprinted from *Costume,* no. 12, 1978).

_____. *English Legal Manuscripts.* Zug 1975.

_____. *The Diary of John Baker.* Edited by Philip C. Yorke. Hutchinson & Co., Ltd., 1931.

Barbot, Jean. *Barbot on Guineau: The Writings of Jean Barbot on West Africa, 1678–1712.* Edited by P.E.H. Hair, Adam Jones, and Robin Law. Hakluyt Society, 1992.

Beattie, John M. "Scales of Justice: Defense Counsel and the English Criminal Trial in the Eighteenth and Nineteenth Centuries." *Law and History Review* 9 (1991):221.

_____. *Crime and the Courts in England 166–1800.* Princeton University Press, 1986.

Beckles, Hilary M. *Natural Rebels, A Social History of Enslaved Black Women in Barbados.* University of Tennessee Press, 1989.

Bentley, D. R. *Select Cases from the Twelve Judges' Notebooks.* John Rees, 1997.

Berlin, Ira. *Slaves Without Masters: The Free Negro in the E Antebellum South.* The New Press, 1974.

Berlin, Isaiah. "Two Concepts of Liberty," in *Four Essays on Liberty.* Princeton University Press, 1969.

Birks, Michael. *Gentlemen of the Law.* Stevens & Sons Limited, 1960.

Blackham, Robert J. *Wig and Gown: The Story of the Temple—Gray's and Lincoln's Inn.* Sampson Low, Marston & Co., Ltd., n.d.

Blackstone, William. *Commentaries on the Laws of England.* Clarendon Press, 1765.

_____. *Commentaries on the Laws of England.* 2d ed. Clarendon Press, 1766.

_____. *Commentaries on the Laws of England.* 3rd ed. Clarendon Press, 1768.

_____. *Commentaries on the Laws of England.* 4th ed. Clarendon Press, 1770.

_____. *Commentaries on the Laws of England.* 17th ed. E. Duyckinck, 1822.

_____. *Commentaries on the Laws of England.* 18th English, 1st American ed. Collina and Hannay; Collins and Co., N. and J. White; and Grigg and Elliot, 1832.

Bodansky, John. "The Abolition of the Party-Witness Disqualification: An Historical Survey." *Kentucky Law Journal* 70 (1981–1982):91.

Boorstin, Daniel J. *The Mysterious Science of the Law.* Beacon Press 1958 (1941).

Boswell, James, *Life of Samuel Johnson.* Edited by Ernest Rhys. Clarendon Press, 1950 (1791).

_____. *Private Papers of James Boswell from Malahide Castle.* Edited by Geoffrey Scott and Frederick H. Pottle. W. E. Rudge, 1928–1934.

Bott, Edmund, ed. *Decisions of the Court of Kings Bench, Upon the Laws Relating to the Poor.* 3rd ed. Whieldon and Butterworth, 1793.

Bradley, K. B., *Slaves and Masters in the Roman Empire: A Study in Control.* Oxford University Press, 1987.

Bradley, Patricia. "Slavery in Colonial Newspapers: The Somerset Case." *Journalism History* 12 (1985):2.

Brown, Marshall, *Wit and Humor of Bench and Bar.* T. H. Flood & Co., 1899.

Brown, P. D. *The Chathamites.* MacMillan, 1967.

Bruns, Roger. *Am I Not a Man and a Brother?: The Antislavery Crusade of Revolutionary America 1688–1788.* Chelsea House Publishers, 1977.

_____. "Anthony Benezet's Assertion of Negro Equality." *Journal of Negro History* 65 (1971):230.

Campbell, Lord. *Lives of the Lord Chief Justices of England.* John Murray, 1858.

Carretta, Vincent. "Olaudah Equiano or Gustavus Vassa? New Light on an Eighteenth Century Question of Identity." Slavery and Abolition 20 (December, 1999):96.

Catterall, Helen. *Judicial Cases Concerning American Slavery and the Negro.* Carnegie Institution of Washington, 1926–1937.

Church, William S. *A Treatise on the Writ of Habeas Corpus Including Jurisdiction, False Imprisonment, Writ of Error, Extradition, Mandamus, Certiorari, Judgments, Etc.* 2d ed., rev. and enlarg. Bancroft-Whitney Co., 1893.

Cicero. *Cicero: Selected Works.* Translated by Michael Grant. Penguin Books, 1971.

_____. *Basic Works of Cicero.* Edited by Moses Hadas. The Modern Library/Random House, 1951.

Clark, David, and Gerard McCoy. *The Most Fundamental Legal Right: Habeas Corpus in the Commonwealth.* Oxford University Press, 2000.

Clark, Gilbert. *Life Sketches of Eminent Lawyers, American, Canadian, and English.* Lawyers' International Publishing Co., 1895.

Clarkson, Thomas. *The History of the Rise, Progress, and Accomplishment of the Abolition of the African Slave Trade by the British Parliament.* John W. Parker, 1839 (1808).

Cobb, Thomas R. R. *An Inquiry into the Law of Negro Slavery in the United States of America.* Negro Universities Press, 1968 (1858).

Cohen, Maxwell. "Habeas Corpus Cum Causa: The Emergence of the Modern Writ—I." *Canadian Bar Review* 18 (1940):10.

_____. *Habeas Corpus Cum Causa: The Emergence of the Modern Writ—I." Canadian Bar Review* 18 (1940):172.

Colonial Society of Massachusetts. *Law in Colonial Massachusetts* 1630–1800. University of Virginia Press, 1984.

Commager, Henry Steele. *Documents of American History.* 3rd ed. Columbia University Press, 1943.

"Considerations on a Late Determination in the Court of King's Bench on the Negroe Cause." *Gentleman's Magazine* 42(1772):307–308.

Cook, M. "J. J. Rousseau and the Negro." *Journal of Negro History* 21 (1936):298.

Coquillette, Daniel R., *The Anglo-American Heritage.* Carolina Academic Press, 1999.

Cotter, William R. "The Somerset Case and the Abolition of Slavery in England." *History* 79 (1994):31.

Cottu, Charles. *On the Administration of Criminal Justice in England.* R. Stevens, 1822.

Cover, Robert. *Justice Accused: Antislavery and the Judicial Process.* Yale University Press, 175.

Cushing, John D. "The Cushing Court and the Abolition of Slavery in Massachusetts: More Notes on the 'Quock Walker Case.'" *American Journal of Legal History* 5 (1961):118.

Darnton, Robert. *George Washington's False Teeth: An Unconventional Guide to the Eighteenth Century.* W. W. Norton & Co., 2003.

Davis, David Brion. *Challenging the Boundaries of Slavery.* Harvard University Press, 2003.

_____. Introduction to *A Historical Guide to World Slavery.* Edited by Seymour Drescher and Stanley L. Engerman. Oxford University Press, 1998.

_____. "At the Heart of Slavery." In *In the Image of God: Religion, Moral Values and Our Heritage of Slavery.* Yale University Press, 2001.

_____. *The Problem of Slavery in Western Culture.* Cornell University Press, 1966.

_____. *The Problem of Slavery in the Age of Revolution* 1770–1823. Cornell University Press, 1975.

_____. *Slavery and Human Progress.* Oxford University Press, 1984.

Day, Thomas. *Dialogue Between a Justice of the Peace and a Farmer.* John Stockdale, 1785.

Donald, David Herbert. *Lincoln.* Simon & Schuster, 1995.

Douglass, Frederick. *Narrative of the Life of Frederick Douglass, an American Slave, Written by Himself.* New American Library, 1968 (1845).

Duker, William F. "The English Origins of the Writ of Habeas Corpus: A Peculiar Path to Fame." *New York University Law Review* 53 (1978):983.

Edwards, Paul, and James Walvin. *Black Personalities in the Era of the Slave Trade.* Louisiana State University Press, 1983.

Ellenborough, Lord Edward. *Collection of Rules and Orders of the Court of King's Bench.* W. Reed, 1811.

Elliot, Jonathan. *Debates on the Federal Constitution.* 2d ed. J. B. Lippincott, 1836.

Engerman, Stanley, Seymour Drescher, and Robert Paquette, eds. *Slavery.* Oxford University Press, 2001.

Equiano, Olaudah. "The Life of Olaudah Equiano." In *The Classic Slave Narratives,* edited by Henry Louis Gates, Jr. Mentor Book, 1987.

Estwick, Samuel A. M. *Considerations of the Negroe Cause Commonly So Called, Addressed to the Right Honourable Lord Mansfield, Lord Chief Justice of the Court of King's Bench.* 2d ed. J. Dodsley, 1773.

_____. A West Indian (now known to be Samuel Estwick), *Considerations of the Negroe Cause Commonly So Called, Addressed to the Right Honourable Lord Mansfield, Lord Chief Justice of the Court of King's Bench.* J. Dodsley, 1772.

Fehrenbacher, Don E, *The Dred Scott Case: Its Significance in American Law and Politics.* Oxford University Press, 1978.

Fiddes, Edward. Lord Mansfield and the Somersett Case." *The Law Quarterly Review.* Stevens and Sons, 1934.

Fifoot, C.H.S. *Lord Mansfield.* Oxford University Press, 1936.

Finkelman, Paul. *Slavery and the Founders: Race and Liberty in the Age of Jefferson.* 2d ed. M. E Sharpe, Inc., 2001.

Fisher, Ruth Anna. "Granville Sharp and Lord Mansfield." *Journal of Negro History* 28 (1943):381.

Fletcher, F. T. "Montesquieu's Influence on Anti-Slavery Opinion in England." *Journal of Negro History* 18 (1933):417.

Fortescue, John. *De Laudibus Legum Anglaie.* Translated by S. B. Chrimes. Hyperion Press, 1979 (1942).

Foss, Edward. *Memories of Westminster Hall: A Collection of Interesting Incidents, Anecdotes and Historical Sketches, Relating to Westminster Hall, Its Famous Judges and Lawyers and Its Great Trials, with an Historical Introduction.* Estes & Lauriat, 1874.

_____. *The Judges of England.* John Murray, 1848–1864.

Friedman, Lawrence M. *A History of American Law.* Simon and Schuster, 1973.

Fudge, Erica. *Perceiving Animals: Humans and Beasts in Early Modern English Culture.* University of Illinois Press, 2000.

Garlon, Yvon. *Slavery in Ancient Greece.* Translated by Janet Lloyd. Cornell University Press, 1988.

Gentleman's Magazine, London.

Gerhold, Dorian. *Westminster Hall: Nine Hundred Years of History.* James & James, 1999.

Gerzina, Gretchen Holbrook. *Black London: Life Before Emancipation.* Rutgers University Press, 1995.

George, Dorothy M. *London Life in the Eighteenth Century.* Academy Chicago, 1984 (1925).

Glass, Albert S. "Historical Aspects of Habeas Corpus." *St. John's Law Review* 9 (1934):55.

Green, Thomas Andrews. *Verdict According to Conscience—Perspectives on the English Criminal Jury Trial 1200–1800.* University of Chicago Press, 1985.

Hargrave, Francis. *A Complete Collection of the State Trials,* #548. "The Case of James Somersett, a Negro, on a Habeus Corpus, King's Bench": 12 George III. A.D. 1771–1772 (1776).

Hast, Adele. "The Legal Status of the Negro in Virginia, 1705–1765." *Journal of Negro History* 54 (July 1969):217.

Hawkins, William. *A Treatise of the Pleas of the Crown.* E. and R. Nutt, 1724–1726.

Hecht, Jean J. *Continental and Colonial Servants in 18th Century England.* Smith College, 1954.

Heward, Edward. *Lord Mansfield: A Biography of William Murray 1st Earl of Mansfield 1705–1793, Lord Chief Justice for 32 Years.* Barry Rose, 1979.

_____. "Lord Manfield's Note Books." *Law Quarterly Review* 92 (1976):438.

Hibbert, Christopher. *King Mob: The Story of Lord George Gordon and the London Riots of 1789.* World Publishing Co., 1958.

Higgenbotham, A. Leon, Jr. *In the Matter of Color: Race and the American Legal Process—The Colonial Experience.* Oxford University Press, 1978.

Hoare, Prince. *Memoirs of Granville Sharp, Esq. Composed from His Own Manuscripts.* 2 vols. Henry Colburn, 1828.

Holdsworth, William. *History of English Law.* 2 vols. Metheun & Co.; Sweet and Maxwell, 1956 (1938).

Holliday, John. *The Life of William, Late Earl of Mansfield.* P. Elmsly, 1797.

Hume, David. *Essays: Moral, Political, and Literary.* Edited by Thomas H. Green and Thomas H. Grose. Longmans, Green, and Co., 1875 (1754).

Hurd, John Codman. *The Law of Freedom and Bondage in the United States.* Negro Universities Press, 1968 (1858).

Hurd, Rollin C. *A Treatise on the Right of Personal Liberty and on the Writ of Habeas Corpus.* 2d. ed. rev. Da Capo Press, 1972 (1876).

Hyde, H. Montgomery. *Judge Jeffreys.* Butterworth, 1948.

Jacoby, Karl. "Slaves by Nature? Domestic Animals and Human Slaves." *Slavery and Abolition: A Journal of Slave and Post-Slave Studies* (April 1994).

Jefferson, Thomas. *Writings of Thomas Jefferson.* Edited by Paul Leicester Ford. Putnam's Sons, 1894.

_____. *Notes on the State of Virginia.* Edited by William Peden. University of North Carolina Press, 1955 (1785).

Jenks, Edward. "The Story of the Habeas Corpus." *The Law Quarterly* 69 (1902):64.

Jones, Howard. *Mutiny on the Amistad.* Rev. ed. Oxford University Press, 1987.

Jordan, Winthrop D. *White over Black: American Attitudes Toward the Negro 1550–1812.* Penguin Books, 1971 (1968).

King, Peter. *Crime, Justice, and Discretion in England: 1740–1820.* Oxford University Press, 2000.

Klarman, Michael. *From Jim Crow to Civil Rights.* Oxford University Press, 2004.

Kluger, Richard. *Simple Justice: The History of* Brown v. Board of Education *and Black America's Struggle for Equality.* Alfred A. Knopf, 1976.

Komlos, John. "On the Biological Standard of Living of Eighteenth Century Americans: Taller, Richer, Healthier." *Research in Economic History* 20 (2001):233.

Landsman, Stephan. "The Rise of the Contentious Spirit: Adversary Procedure in Eighteenth Century England." 75 *Cornell Law Review* 75 (1990):497.

Langbein, John H. *The Origins of Adversary Criminal Trial.* Oxford University Press, 2003.

———. "Historical Foundations of the Law of Evidence: A View from the Ryder Sources." *Columbia Law Review* 96 (1996): 1168.

———. "The Historical Origins of the Privilege Against Self-Incrimination at Common Law." *Michigan Law Review* 92 (1994): 1047.

———. "Shaping the Eighteenth-Century Trial: A View from the Ryder Sources." *University of Chicago Law Review* 50 (1983):1.

———. "The Criminal Trial Before the Lawyers," *University of Chicago Law Review* 35 (1978):263.

———. "The Origins of Public Prosecution at Common Law." *The American Journal of Legal History* 17 (1973): 313.

Lascelles, E.C.P. *Granville Sharp and the Freedom of Slaves in England.* Oxford University Press, 1928.

Lemmings, David. *Professors of the Law: Barristers and English Legal Culture in the Eighteenth Century.* Oxford University Press, 2000.

Levy, Leonard. *The Law of the Commonwealth and Chief Justice Shaw.* Harper Torchbooks, 1967.

Lincoln, Abraham. *The Collected Works of Abraham Lincoln.* Edited by Roy P. Basler. Rutgers University Press, 1953–1955.

Locke, John. *Two Treatises of Government.* Edited by Peter Laslett. Cambridge University Press, 1988.

Lofft, Capel. *Reporter of Cases Adjudged in the Court of Kings Bench from Easter Term 12 George 3 to Michaelmas 14 George 3* (both inclusive) (1776).

Long, Edward. *The History of Jamaica: Or, General Survey of the Antient and Modern State of That Island.* T. Lowndes, 1774.

———. *Candid Reflections Upon the Judgment Lately Awarded by the Court of King's Bench in Westminster Hall on What Is Commonly Called the Negroe Cause.* T. Lowndes, 1772.

Lovejoy, Owen O. *The Great Chain of Being: A Study of the History of an Idea.* Harper & Row, 1960. (1936).

Marchant, Henry. *Journall of Voyage from Newport in the Colony of Rhode Island to London, February 7, 1772.* Rhode Island Historical Society (microfilm).

Massachusetts Historical Society for the Year M, DCC, XCV. Collections, 1795.

McFeeley, Neil Douglas. "The Historical Development of Habeas Corpus." *Southwestern Law Journal* 30 (1976): 585.

McPherson, James M. *Battle Cry of Freedom: The Civil War Era.* Oxford University Press, 1988.

Mian, Badshah K. *English Habeas Corpus: Law, History, and Politics.* Cosmos of Humanists Press, 1984.

Michaels, Teresa. "'That Sole and Despotic Dominion,' Slaves, Wives and Game in Blackstone's Commentaries." *Eighteenth-Century Studies.* (Winter 1993–1994):27.

Miller, John Chester. *The Wolf by the Ears: Thomas Jefferson and Slavery.* University of Virginia Press, 1991.

Miller, William Lee. *Arguing About Slavery: The Great Battle in the United States Congress.* Alfred A. Knopf, 1996.

Montesque, Baron de. *The Spirit of the Laws.* Translated by Thomas Nugent. Hafner Press, 1949.

Moore, George H. *Notes on the History of Slavery in Massachusetts.* Greenwood Publishing Group, 1966 (1866).

Moran, C. G. *The Heralds of the Law.* Stevens & Sons Ltd., 1948.

Morano, Anthony. "A Reexamination of the Development of the Reasonable Doubt Rule." *Boston University Law Review* 55 (1975):516.

Morgan, Philip D. *Slave-Counterpoint: Black Culture in the Eighteenth-Century Chesapeake and Lowcountry.* University of North Carolina Press, 1998.

Morris, Thomas T. *Southern Slavery and the Law 1619–1860.* University of North Carolina Press, 1996.

Morton, Samuel G. "Observations on the Size of the Brain in Various Races and Families of Man." *Proceedings of the Academy of Natural Sciences Philadelphia* 4 (1849): 221.

New Encyclopedia Britannica. 15th ed. 1998.

Nicholls, John. *Recollections and Reflections Personal and Political as Connected with the Public Affairs During the Reign of George III.* James Ridgway, 1829.

Noonan, John T. Jr., *Persons & Masks of the Law: Cardozo, Holmes, Jefferson, and Wythe as Makers of the Masks.* Farrar, Straus and Giroux, 1976.

Nott, Josiah C. *Two Lectures on the Natural History of the Caucasian and Negro Races.* Dale & Thompson, 1844.

Ogude, S. E. "Facts into Fiction: Equiano's Narrative Reconsidered." *Research in African Literature* 13 (Spring 1982):31.

Oldham, James C., "New Light on Mansfield and Slavery." *Journal of British Studies* 27 (January 1988):45.

_____. *The Mansfield Manuscripts and the Growth of English Law in the Eighteenth Century.* University of North Carolina Press, 1992.

_____. "Truth-Telling in the Eighteenth Century English Courtroom." *Law and History Review* 12 (Spring 1994):95.

_____. "Eighteenth-Century Judges' Notes: How They Explain, Correct and Enhance the Reports." 31 *American Journal of Legal History* 31 (1987):9.

Paley, Ruth. *New Dictionary of National Biography*. Oxford University Press, forthcoming.

_____. "After Somerset: Mansfield, Slavery and the Law in England 1772–1830." *In Law, Crime, and English Society, 1660–1830,* edited by Norma Landau. Cambridge University Press, 2002.

Patterson, James. *The Liberty of the Press, Speech, and Public Worship Being Commentaries on the Liberty of the Subject and the Laws of England*. MacMillian and Co., 1880.

Paulson, Pauleson. *Hogarth: His Life, Art, and Times*. Yale University Press, 1971.

Pelteret, David A. E. *Slavery in Early Mediaeval England from the Reign of Alfred Until the Twelfth Century*. The Boydell Press, 1995.

Plucknett, T. F. T. *Studies in English Legal History*. The Hambledon Press, 1983.

_____. *A Concise History of the Common Law*. Little, Brown and Co., 1956.

Polson, Archer. *Law and Lawyers, Or, Sketches and Illustrations of Legal History and Biography*. 2 vols. Longman, Orme, Brown, Green, and Longmans, 1840.

Pope, Alexander. *Essay on Man,* Epistle 1 (N. Möeller and Son, 1798)(1733–1734).

Proceedings of the Massachusetts Historical Society 43 (October 1909–June 1910).

Rodger, N.A.M. *The Wooden World: An Anatomy of the Georgian Navy*. Naval Institute Press, 1986.

Rogers, Nicholas. "Impressment and the Law in Eighteenth-Century Britain." In *Law, Crime, and English Society, 1660–1830,* edited by Norma Landau. Cambridge University Press, 2002.

Roscoe, Henry. *Lives of Eminent British Lawyers*. Fred B. Rotherman & Co., 1830.

Seward, William. *Anecdotes of Some Distinguished Persons, Chiefly of the Present and Two Preceding Centuries*. T. Cadell, Jr., and W. Advise, 1796.

Shapiro, Barbara J. "'To a Moral Certainty': Theories of Knowledge and Anglo-American Juries 1600–1850." *Hastings Law Journal* 38 (1986):153.

Sharp, Granville. Manuscripts, New York Historical Society. Unpublished.

_____. *Abolition and Emancipation*. Part 4. Granville Sharp Papers from Gloucestershire Record Office (reels 54–83). Adam Matthew Publications Ltd., 1996.

_____. *An Appendix to the Representation of the Injustice and Dangerous Tendency of Tolerating Slavery, or Even of Admitting the Least Claim of Private Property in the Persons of Men, in England*. Benjamin White and Robert Horsefield, 1772.

_____. *A Representation of the Injustice and Dangerous Tendency of Tolerating Slavery, or Even of Admitting the Least Claim of Private Property in the Persons of Men, in England*. Benjamin White and Robert Horsfield, 1769.

Shaw, Robert B. *A Legal History of Slavery in the United States*. Northern Press, 1991.

Sheldon, George. *A History of Deerfield, Massachusetts*. Deerfield, 1895.

Shientag, Bernard L. "Lord Mansfield Revisited: A Modern Assessment." *Fordham Law Review* 10 (November 1941):345.

Shyllon, F. O. *Black Slaves in Britain*. Oxford University Press, 1974.

Sibley, Agnes Marie. *Alexander Pope's Prestige in America*. King's Crown Press, 1949.

Simpson, A. W. *Leading Cases in the Common Law*. Oxford University Press, 1995.

Smith, Adam. *An Inquiry into the Causes of the Wealth of Nations.* Edited by E. Cannan. 1904.

Snyder, William L. *A Collection of Important Judicial Opinions by Eminent Judges.* Baker, Voorhis & Co., 1883.

Sparks, Randy. *The Two Princes of Calabar: An Eighteenth Century Atlantic.* Harvard University Press, 2004.

Spector, Robert M. "The Quock Walker Cases (1781–1783): Slavery, Its Abolition, and Negro Citizenship in Early Massachusetts." *Journal of Negro History* 3 (1968):12.

Spiegel, Marjorie, *The Dreaded Comparison: Human and Animal Slavery.* Mirror Books, 1996.

St. George Saunders, Hilary. *Westminster Hall.* Michael Joseph 1951.

Stanton, William. *The Leopard's Spots: Scientific Attitudes Towards Race in America 1815–1859.* University of Chicago Press, 1960.

Stephen, James. *Essays in Ecclesiastical Biography.* Longman, Brown, Green, and Longmans, 1849.

Stephen, James Fitzjames. *A History of the Criminal Law of England.* MacMillan and Co., 1883.

Steuart, A. F. "Letters from Virginia 1774–1781. *The Magazine of History* (March 1906) (April 1906).

Stone, George Winchester, Jr., and George M. Kahrl. *David Garrick: A Critical Biography.* Southern Illinois University Press, 1979.

Story, Joseph. *Commentaries on the Conflicts of Laws.* Edited by Melvin M. Bigelow. 8th ed. Little, Brown, and Co., 1883 (1846).

Story, William Wetmore. *Life and Letters of Joseph Story.* Edited by W. W. Story. Little, Brown, 1851.

Stoughton, John. *William Wilberforce.* A. C. Armstrong & Son, 1880.

Stringfellow, Thornton. "A brief examination of scripture testimony on the institution of slavery." In *The Ideology of Slavery—Proslavery Thought in the Antebellum South, 1830–1860.* Edited by Drew Gilpin Faust. Louisiana State University Press, 1981.

Stroud, George. *A Sketch of the Laws Relating to Slavery in the Several States of the United States of America.* Negro Universities Press, 1968 (1827).

Stuart, Charles. *A Memoir of Granville Sharp.* American Anti-Slavery Society, 1836.

Sturtz, Linda. *Within Her Power: Propertied Women in Colonial Virginia.* Routledge, 2002.

Sumner, Charles. *His Complete Works.* Lee and Sheppard, 1900.

Thomas, Hugh. *The Slave Trade: The Story of the Atlantic Slave Trade 1440–1870.* Simon & Schuster, 1997.

Thomas, Keith. *Man and the Natural World: A History of the Modern Sensibility.* Pantheon Books, 1983.

Thompson, Thomas. *The African Trade for Negro Slaves Consistent with Humanity and Revealed Religion.* Simmons & Kirkby, 1772.

Transactions of the Supreme Court of Michigan 1805–1814. Edited by William Blume. University of Michigan Press, 1835.

Turner, E. S. *All Heaven in a Rage.* St. Martin's Press, 1965.

Unti, Bernie. *The Quality of Mercy: Organized Animal Protection in the United States 1866–1930.* 2002.

Waldstreicher, David. *The Struggle Against Slavery—A History in Documents.* Oxford University Press, 2001.

Walvin, James. *Black Ivory: A History of British Slavery.* HarperCollins, 1992.

_____. *Black and White: The Negro and English Society 1555–1945.* Alan Lane/The Penguin Press, 1973.

Washburn, Emory. *Proceedings of the Massachusetts Historical Society for 1863–1864* (1864):307.

Weiner, Mark. "New Biographical Evidence on Somerset's Case." *Slavery and Abolition* (April 2002)23:121.

_____. *Black Trials: Citizenship from the Beginnings of Slavery to the End of Caste.* Knopf, 2004.

White, Charles. *An Account of the Regular Gradation in Man, and in Different Animals and Vegetables: and from the Former to the Latter.* C. Dilly, 1799.

Wiecek, William, "The Origins of the Law of Slavery in British North America." *Cardozo Law Review* 17 (1996):1711.

_____. "Somerset: Lord Mansfield and the Legitimacy of Slavery in the Anglo-American World." *University of Chicago Law Review* 42 (1974):86.

Wiencek, Henry. *An Imperfect God: George Washington, His Slaves, and the Creation of America.* Farrar, Straus & Giroux, 2003.

Williams, G. W. *History of the Negro Race in America from 1619 to 1880.* Arno Press and the *New York Times,* 1968.

Williams, Gomer. *History of the Liverpool Privateers and Letters of Marque with an Account of the Liverpool Slave Trade.* William Heinemann, Edward Howell, 1897.

Wills, Garry. *Lincoln at Gettysburg: The Words that Remade America.* Simon & Schuster, 1992.

Wontner, Thomas. *Old Bailey Experience: Criminal Jurisprudence and the Actual Working of Our Penal Code of Laws.* J. Fraser, 1833.

Woods, John A. "The Correspondence of Benjamin Rush and Granville Sharp, 1773–1809." *Journal of American Studies* 1 (1967).

Woolrych, Humphrey W. *Lives of Eminent Serjeants-at-Law of the English Law.* Allen, 1869.

Wroth, L. Kinvin, and Hiller B. Zobel. *Legal Papers of John Adams.* Harvard University Press, 1965.

Yorke, Philip Chesney. *The Life and Correspondence of Philip Yorke, Earl of Hardwicke, Lord High Chancellor of Great Britain.* Cambridge University Press, 1913.

Zarefsky, David. *Lincoln, Douglas and Slavery—In the Crucible of Public Debate.* University of Chicago Press, 1990.

INDEX